Crisis in the Global Mediasphere

Crisis in the Global Mediasphere

Desire, Displeasure and Cultural Transformation

Jeff Lewis

First published 2011 by
PALGRAVE MACMILLAN

Palgrave Macmillan in the UK is an imprint of Macmillan Publishers Limited, registered in England, company number 785998, of Houndmills, Basingstoke, Hampshire RG21 6XS.

Palgrave Macmillan in the US is a division of St Martin's Press LLC, 175 Fifth Avenue, New York, NY 10010.

Palgrave Macmillan is the global academic imprint of the above companies and has companies and representatives throughout the world.

Palgrave® and Macmillan® are registered trademarks in the United States, the United Kingdom, Europe and other countries.

ISBN 978–0–230–24742–0 hardback

This book is printed on paper suitable for recycling and made from fully managed and sustained forest sources. Logging, pulping and manufacturing processes are expected to conform to the environmental regulations of the country of origin.

A catalogue record for this book is available from the British Library.

Library of Congress Cataloging-in-Publication Data
Lewis, Jeff.
  Crisis in the global mediasphere : desire, displeasure and cultural transformation / Jeff Lewis.
    p.   cm.
  Includes bibliographical references.
  ISBN 978–0–230–24742–0 (alk. paper)
  1. Mass media—Political aspects.   2. Mass media—Social aspects.
  3. Mass media and culture.   I. Title.
  P95.8.L49 2011
  302.23—dc22   2010033962

10   9   8   7   6   5   4   3   2   1
20   19   18   17   16   15   14   13   12   11

Printed and bound in Great Britain by
CPI Antony Rowe, Chippenham and Eastbourne

To Jack Clancy: *friend, mentor, humanist*

Contents

List of Tables, Figures and Plates

Tables

Figures

Plates

Acknowledgements

My deepest gratitude to Belinda Lewis for her conversation, support, friendship and brilliant editing. Thanks also to Sian Lewis and Jay Lewis who helped me clarify the underlying thesis of this book, and whose support and encouragement has once again been immeasurable. Thanks to Jay for research support, especially for Chapters 2 and 3; thanks to Sian for support on Chapters 4 and 5.

I am indebted to my colleagues in the Human Security Program at RMIT—especially Paul James, John Handmer and Damian Grenfell. Thanks to Lauren Murray, Alan Cumming, Tony Dalton and Kim Humphery. Thanks to colleagues in the School of Media and Communication—especially Chris Hudson and Sharenjeev Johal whose scholarly interests and good humour are an inspiration. I am also grateful for the financial support provided by the School of Media and Communication under Lauren Murray and RMIT University more generally. Thanks to other colleagues for their support and interest— I Nyoman Darma Putra, Chris Rojek and Mila Steele. Many thanks to my graduate students, particularly Dr Diana Bossio, Dr Kristen Sharp and Prayudi Ahmed. Special thanks to Stephen Gaunson who has made an invaluable contribution to this book.

Thankyou to Christabel Scaife and Catherine Mitchell at Palgrave Macmillan.

Thankyou for the use of photographs—Belinda Lewis (Plates 3.1 and 6.1), George Paterson (Plate 1.1) and Simon Richards (Plates 4.1 and 6.2).

Many thanks to Terry Batt for the use of his extraordinary painting 'Business as Usual' on the cover of this book.

Acknowledgements

Introduction

For he has judged the great prostitute, who corrupted the earth with her sexual immorality, and he has avenged the blood of his servants at her hand.' A second said, 'Hallelujah! Her smoke goes up forever and ever.'

'Revelations', *The Bible*

What's going to happen is, very soon, we're going to run out of petroleum, and everything depends on petroleum. And there go the school buses. There go the fire engines. The food trucks will come to a halt. This is the end of the world.

Kurt Vonnegut, *Rolling Stone*, 2006

There apparently is a great deal of interest in celestial bodies, and their locations and trajectories at the end of the calendar year 2012. Now, I for one love a good book or movie as much as the next guy. But the stuff flying around through cyberspace, TV and the movies is not based on science. There is even a fake NASA news release out there....

Don Yeomans, NASA senior research scientist, 2010

Revelations

There are two primary drivers in the force of human culture—one towards a generative order, creativity and pleasure, and the other towards violence, destruction and displeasure. Through the rise of modern humans and their cultures, these dispositions have worked in contingent ways, sometimes in clear opposition, other times in conjunctive and almost indistinguishable convocation. This book reconsiders these dispositions in terms of a contemporary cultural setting, a globalizing world that is dominated by crisis, social complexity and multiplying

1

knowledge systems. These knowledge systems and their respective concordia of meanings are themselves shaped and amplified through a media-dominated culture—a mediasphere which articulates human consciousness and the ways in which the world appears to us as 'real'.

In this sense, the mediasphere is that collective space in which our individual consciousness engages with a pre-existing and always evolving dynamic of knowing that assembles through language, power, history and the labyrinthal processes of meaning-making. The media, therefore, is to be understood as an open-bordered space in which text producers and consumers become exchangeable identities within a vaporous and contingent interaction of human imagining. In a contemporary global context, therefore, it is not possible to speak of a world that exists outside the mediasphere; nor is it possible to speak of media or media representations that are not infused by the conditions of everyday experience and the social processes that comprise culture(s) (Lewis, 2008).

To put this simply, human consciousness is both a cause and an effect of the contemporary media. In the study of crisis, thereby, this book is not concerned with glib questions about whether the media propagates crisis, or whether contemporary crisis is real or imagined. Nor indeed, does this book focus specifically on the micro-matters of national communications policy and its regulatory framework. While these issues may arise, particularly in terms of power relationships that emerge through media representation and meaning-making, this book is focused more directly on the formation of crisis and crisis consciousness within a global mediasphere. The media, in this sense, is to be understood as more than a set of industries or definable communications processes; rather, the media is the kernel of contemporary cultural consciousness and our multiplying knowledge systems. To this end, the media refers both to corporate entertainment and information institutions, as well as the vast array of communications practices, texts, agencies and knowledge systems that form the web of contemporary culture. The rise of computer- and digital-based systems of text-production and telecommunications has blurred the boundaries of media making and consumption, facilitating a radical expansion in the corpus of media, media-based activities and mediating agents. Thus, any definition of media should include those major and minor organizations that generate news and entertainment across the globe; it should also include the vast network of individuals, communities and organizations that are connected through computers and other telephonic systems.

These networks constitute the material framework of the mediasphere and its astonishing concordia of cultural contiguities. In this sense, the mediasphere is comprised as much by banks, social networkers, garage bands, traders, governments, bloggers, students and criminals, as it is the province of Hollywood, the BBC or the *New York Times*. As we will discuss in detail in Chapter 1, the processes of mediation and the formation of complex knowledge systems are entirely infused within the survival and economic patterns of contemporary culture, such that our entire fabric of being is now a contingency of the global mediasphere. Contemporary crisis conditions and an evolving crisis consciousness, thereby, are intrinsic to this sense of being and its formation in the global mediasphere.

Apocalypse now?

It is generally agreed that we are living through an accelerating phase of mass species extinction. From the beginning of the Holocene geological phase, around 11,000 years ago, these extinctions have become increasingly associated with human activities. Particularly over the past hundred years, humans have destroyed, polluted and over-exploited natural life systems, leading to the extinction of up to two million animal species (Elewa, 2008). And indeed, if we are to take seriously the apocalyptic prescience of former US Vice-President and now environmental crusader, Al Gore, then we might soon add one further species to the list—ourselves. Along with numerous other global warming campaigners, Gore argues that

> Our over-scheduled, over-populated, hyper-stimulated existence is designed to monopolize our attention, to sell us things, to speed us from one place to another. Nature, by contrast, is slow-moving, undemanding, maybe underwhelming for many people. But if you never put yourself in the midst of nature—to understand that its essence is our essence—then you're inclined to treat it as trivial. You become willing to abuse and destroy it through carelessness, not recognizing that to do so is wrong. We've come to accept that if nature can yield something of value to the lucrative engines of commerce, then we should grab it and rip it out, never thinking twice about the wounds left behind. According to this way of thinking, if exploitation results in injury to the environment, so be it: nature will always heal itself. But the magnitude of environmental destruction is now on a scale few ever foresaw; the wounds no longer simply heal themselves. We have to act affirmatively to stop the harm.
>
> (Gore, 2006: 61)

This assault on nature, propitiated through population growth and extravagant, greenhouse gas producing lifestyles, Gore argues, is the most pressing crisis facing all humanity. This view accords with the Fifth Assessment Report (2010) of the Intergovernmental Panel on Climate Change. According to the IPCC assessment reports, the production of greenhouse gases (GHG) like carbon dioxide and methane, along with the destruction of global carbon sinks like forests, is creating a radical disruption to planetary life systems. Human or 'anthropogenic' activity is generating significant negative impacts on the planetary systems' key vulnerabilities. Gore notes that these vulnerabilities are associated with many climate-sensitive systems, including 'food supply, infrastructure, health, water resources, coastal systems, ecosystems, global biochemical cycles, ice sheets and modes of oceanic and atmospheric circulation' (2006: 42). The manifestation of these biospheric changes are evident in severe and prolonged drought in regions like North Africa and Australia, increased incidence and intensity of storms like Katrina (2005) and the Fourth of July Storms (2009) in the USA, and rising summer temperatures across the globe. The spectacle of the 2009 Australian bushfires—the deadliest and most destructive on record—seemed somehow to emblazon the climate change message in mediated images of fireballs that reached hundreds of feet in the air and destroyed everything in their path.

Certainly, extreme weather events and changing climatic patterns are being identified in public and media discussions as part of an aggregating climate change crisis. And yet less than a decade before, the world news was dominated by another crisis event: the militant attacks on the New York World Trade Center and subsequent 9/11 wars. In language that is also apocalyptic, journalist and novelist, Norman Mailer, declared

> [T]he best explanation for 9/11 is that the Devil won a great battle that day. Yes, Satan as the pilot who guided those planes into that ungodly denouement.... Yes, as if part of the Devil's aesthetic acumen was to bring it off, exactly as if we were watching the same action movie we had been looking at for years. That may be at the core of the immense impact 9/11 had on America. Our movies came off the screen and chased us down the canyons of the city.
>
> (Mailer, 2003: 110–111)

The Biblical force of Mailer's description fortified much of the Presidential rhetoric, which contrasted the innocence and divine purity of the victim—America—against the Satanic inhumanity of the perpetrators—al-Qa'ida. Mailer's reference to 'the movies' invokes the powerful tradition of apocalyptic anxiety that abounds in fictional and religious narrative. Images of the twin towers' incendiary that were beamed across the world recalled the prescience of *The Towering Inferno* (Guillermin and Allen, 1974), as well as the farrago of Hollywood war movies in which the enemy strikes at the heart of American cultural and spiritual ascendancy.

Fear of defeat, of course, is a familiar motif in war-bound cultures like America. Yet the force of apocalypse and notions of an end to humanity reach beyond international conflict. In *The Day after Tomorrow* (Emmerich, 2004) the end of the world is presaged through extreme weather events and climate change. During the Cold War, the threat of nuclear Armageddon was invoked through films like Stanley Kubrik's *Dr Strangelove* (1964), and songs like Bob Dylan's *A Hard Rain* and P. F. Sloan's *Eve of Destruction* (recorded by Barry McGuire). Reaching even further back in history, predictions of human species doom were replete in major civilizational catastrophes, wars and disease epidemics. During the periods of Bubonic Plague, for example, there were innumerable accounts of the end of humankind and a vision of cosmological vengeance. The Plague, which appears to have emerged in Asia after a series of earthquakes, floods and famines, spread to Europe and provoked a Biblical revivalism that was rooted in Old Testament prophecy. According to John Kelly's (2005) account of the first great Plague around 1348, the rodents that spread the disease to humans were accidental travellers on trading vessels. Thus, while public officials and theologians imagined a cosmological retribution in the disease, the vector of illness might be more acutely recognized as a complement of Europe's rising global economy and the modernizing impact of transportation and trade.

In either case, it is clear that Medieval Europe had fallen victim to its own economic success and rising power. The invocation of Biblical anxieties about human mortality and divine justice darkened the shadows of this success. Like the modern crises of disease, violence and ecological destruction, the Medieval crises were replete with visionary despair. According to John Acocella (2005): 'The Black Death, the pandemic of bubonic plague that hit Europe in the mid-fourteenth century, is like a disaster movie: a menace stalks the land; cries go up in the streets; millions of people die.' Clearly, similar visions have accompanied the rise of modern diseases and blights, including HIV-AIDS. The emergence of AIDS in the 1980s and 1990s was accompanied by a complex discursive and social rupture which conflated sex, death, religion and community morality. Within this vortex of uncertainty and apocalyptic dread, numerous religious and political organizations—including governments—invoked the wrath of nature, god and divine justice against gays, injecting drug users and social liberals, who had brought upon the land this terrible retribution. Impacting upon the most personal of human interactions, the disease accumulated an extraordinary and often disjunctive armada of meanings and constituted values.

Then, of course, there was the Millennium Bug, Bird Flu and Swine Flu. Through dire warnings of civilizational collapse and darkness, governments and other Messianic agents offered us a deliverance from evil diseases and communications inertia. And yet we still cannot rest easy. Former US President, George W. Bush, invested millions of dollars of public money in programmes that were designed to promote teenage chastity, Creationism in schools and the virtues of marriage. The 2012 End of the World scenario was fostered across the Internet and a range of subterranean knowledge systems. Based on prophecies of the Sumerians and Central American Maya civilization, the end of humankind was to occur in a cataclysmic event, imagined through planetary impact, ecological disaster and eruptions of human violence. The clues were too obvious to ignore—9/11 warfare, global inequality, racial hatred, economic collapse and the accelerating impact of climate change. Like the horrors of Sodom and Gomorrah, the dissolution of the contemporary world is to be avenged by nature, if not by god.

Bizarre as these apocalypse cults may seem, their invocation of narrative mythology and ecological science is not entirely dissimilar to the informational and fictional narratives that dominate our media and more mainstream knowledge systems. Even science has looked at the 2012 prophecy and the possibility of human extinction through celestial impact. Applying the scientific frame of knowledge established through the Enlightenment lineage, NASA (2010) and other astronomical organizations have looked seriously at the possibility of an asteroidal or planetary collision as predicted by the Maya and the Sumerian apocalypse. Thus, while films like *2012* (Emmerich, 2009) present a spectacle of human calamity, astronomers have more rationally eliminated the prospects of the asteroid 433 Eros striking the Earth.

Yet, even the great knowledge systems of science have their own apocalyptic vision inscribed in the knowing of the great unknowns—dying of the sun, magnetic reversals, resource exhaustion, planetary collisions like the impact that destroyed the dinosaurs. Science tells us that it must all end—planets, stars, solar systems, galaxies, the universe. But like our own personal mortal occlusion, the timing is never certain. This same message appeared in a 2009 NASA report entitled *Extreme Space Weather* (2009). The report outlines the ways in which intense solar flare activity would effect the Earth's magnetic fields, leading ultimately to the destruction of energy grids, communications and navigation systems as the polar fields radically invert. The recovery period of up to 10 years and cost of 2+ trillion dollars parallels the almost incomprehensible figures that have been attached to the Global Financial Crisis (GFC) (2008–2010) and the massive public investment in recovery. Again, the spectre of complete collapse emerged throughout the expert systems, as well as the financial and popular media. At its peak, the GFC was expected to cause irrecoverable damage to the world economy and to the underlying fabric of global capitalism, particularly in its incarnation as neo-liberal, market triumphalism.

Yet, in the context of a looming, global food crisis that is likely to threaten the viability of over a billion humans across the planet, the salvation of the first world elite might seem somewhat disproportionate. At least inasmuch as the neo-liberal ideology orders the world in terms of a powerfully rendered hierarchy, the GFC might simply be understood as a manifestation of solipsistic first world insecurity—a fear and trembling that links cultural consciousness to a historical spectre of apocalypse and civilizational collapse. In the course of the GFC, that is, the corporate entertainment and information media became mesmerized by the threat of first world economic recession and the modulation of the ideology and its privileged hierarchy; if we were to believe the mainstream media and public officials, this recession would constitute a major human catastrophe. It is within this context that the media presentation of extreme poverty merely backgrounds the economic knowledge systems and modes of cultural consciousness that support the foreground of this hierarchy and its ideological privilege. Thus, while the global economic recession had its greatest impact on the world's poor, the narratives that comprised the GFC were largely fostered around the interests of wealthy nations and citizens. Indeed, for much of the corporate, global media the financial crisis confirmed the need for a US-dominated global system, along with its military, cultural and economic primacy.

Through all of these apocalyptic renderings and their representation in various narrative forms, there exists a profound sense of anxiety, a crisis consciousness that seems to exceed the conditions by which our cultural order and pleasures are formed. Indeed, we might usefully trace these anxieties through a deep cultural genealogy to, for example, the black ecstasy of Biblical parables—Daniel, Sodom and Gomorrah, Babel and of course the starkly epiphanal Eros of Revelations. But in any case, it is clear that the ubiquity of this crisis consciousness and fear of the end invokes the cultural dispositions we identified at the beginning of this discussion—that is, towards pleasure and displeasure. These dispositions, which infuse insecurity with a broader and more historically connected apocalypse, are amplified through popular imaginings across the contemporary mediasphere. Thus, the willingness of radio audiences in 1938 to conceive as truth the apocalyptic narrative of George Orwell's *War of the Worlds* is symptomatic of these deep anxieties. Orson Welles' famous radio adaptation of the novel, which panicked American audiences into believing they were being invaded by extra-terrestrials, represents the convocation of a deep epistemological and cultural history of crisis that was simply amplified through the power of the emerging mediasphere.

Crisis consciousness and the global grid

This book focuses on a crisis consciousness that has evolved over a long period of human history, but which has become more radically proportioned within contemporary culture and the global mediasphere. The emergence of this crisis consciousness might seem especially surprising for economically developed societies which are clearly the most affluent, militarily powerful, democratic and seemingly secure social organizations that have ever appeared on Earth. With astonishingly rigorous systems of law and social management, sanitation, water and food supply, community infrastructure, health, social welfare, emergency protection and the longest life expectancy of any social group in history, the people who live in the developed world might be considered the acme of all humankind. At no other time in human history has such a vast social group been so safe, disease-free and able to determine and exercise their pleasures, choice and sense of life destiny.

And yet, if we are to believe the news and entertainment narratives that occupy the central place of our consciousness and modes of interaction, this same social group is besieged by threat, insecurity and crisis. The first world citizens' experience of life, it would seem, is perpetually compromised by social and psychological fragility, and a desperate need to secure themselves perpetually against the spectre of personal and collective doom. In this sense, modern life for many people is dominated by mental and emotional agitation, depression, insomnia, credit stress, the need for psychological counselling or medication, eating disorders, shopping therapy, illicit drugs, sexual dysfunction and alcohol. While people of the developing world may be starving, many citizens of the first world are indulging themselves into states of psychological and physiological catastrophe. Relationships are frequently under stress and many individuals are reporting a vague but cloying sense of social and personal disconnectedness. And even by the comfort of hermetically sealed offices and homes, the extravagant delights of shopping malls, designer shoes, surround sound, home cinema, iPhones and the Internet—even through all of this, the spectre of our fears continues to savage our desires and the culturally propagated fantasy of infinite pleasure.

Within this context, this book contends that this contemporary crisis consciousness has evolved through the volition of historically formed crisis conditions and a complex association of mediation and knowledge systems. These crisis conditions are themselves embedded in a set of economic practices, discourses and systems, including the phenomenon I am calling the 'economy of pleasure'. This new kind of economy has evolved through the conflux of surplus-based economic processes and various forms of symbolic exchange, particularly their most recent incarnation within the global mediasphere.

Chapter 1 provides a more detailed theoretical outline for the empirical studies that follow; however, I want to acknowledge at the outset that this book deviates somewhat from a sociological paradigm that defines contemporary human societies in terms of a primary historical divide: modern and pre-modern (see Giddens, 1990, 1999; Beck, 1992; Bauman, 2000; Taylor, 2007). While clearly this distinction is valuable, my own study of contemporary human crisis suggests that a much more significant historical division occurs at the interface of the Pleistocene and Holocene geological periods (about 11,000 years Before Present). Indeed, a problem I have found with many studies of human cultural transformation is their tendency to focus almost exclusively on European or western civilization and the sense in which history is the narrative of social progress. This imagining of cultural evolution and social progress sets the present in a privileged hierarchical relationship with the past—that is, from a perspective that is entirely embedded in the idea that the present is the apex of all history. More broadly, this vision of history grounds itself in a modernist and largely European-western imagining of global conditions and cultural values. Indeed, even when such texts see fault in the current conditions, this is usually in terms of what Jurgen Habermas calls the 'incomplete project' of modernity. Thus, the sociological paradigm which centres on the modern/pre-modern dualism is inevitably centred upon the completion of the project of European modernism, often to the neglect of more broad-reaching historical associations and explanations.

Alternative histories

More recent scholarship, influenced by postcolonial and cultural studies, has sought to deconstruct this Euro-centric framework. My own studies are situated within this alternative paradigm, particularly as they seek to re-render our understandings across historical and cultural spaces. This approach, however, is not designed to override or erase the significant contribution of the western-based knowledge systems, but rather to situate this contribution against a range of other social groupings, knowledge systems and cultural formations. Even so, this alternative approach introduces a number of conceptual difficulties. In particular, my application in this book of the term 'civilization' refers to those larger social congregations that have formed since the rise of agriculture; these congregations are characterized by significant levels of economic, technological, military, urban and governmental organization. To this end, I am applying the term as a description of these large organizational social systems without assumptions of cultural superiority or consummate historical value.

Similarly, the use in this book of the concept of 'evolution' is designed to be value-neutral, at least inasmuch as I am referring simply to a process of transformation that is captured by conditions of cultural and historical volition. In this sense, my use of the term 'evolution' parallels Michel Foucault's term 'genealogy' which defines the intricate processes of historical connection and change.

Even more difficult are the descriptors that distinguish the relative global conditions of wealth and poverty, particularly within a contemporary setting. With few conceptual options, in fact, I am forced to use common terms that distinguish various human groups according to national characteristics and performance descriptors—per capita gross domestic product, aggregate education levels, technology applications, modes of governance, military power and so on. Through these indices, the collective of nations can be divided between the wealthy first, advanced, or developed world (OECD nations); the emerging economies (India, Brazil, China); and the third, developing, underdeveloped world. All of these terms are limited both by their inscribed ideologies and values, as well as their inability to acknowledge the actual complexity of global and local hierarchical systems. However, for practical and pragmatic purposes, the current study will deploy terms like 'advanced', 'first' and 'developing' world with a parenthetical acknowledgement of their intrinsic deficiencies.

Understanding globalization

In many respects, these conceptual complexities are evident in the application of the key concept of 'globalization'. There are now innumerable definitions of this concept with many scholars debating the breadth of its historical application (see Lewis, 2008: 288–300). In the context of the current study, the concept of globalization is applied in terms of a general process of human mobility and cultural transformation. We can thus identify four broad categories of globalization, each beginning at a particular historical moment and evolving through changing cultural conditions.

1. *Hunter-gatherer migrations.* The early migratory patterns of hunter-gatherer communities can be regarded as an establishment globalization. While debates about the early migration patterns of *Homo erectus* and *Homo sapiens* continue, it's clear that modern humans were migrating across most of the planet between 60 and 100,000 years ago. What is also clear is that these human groups were attracted into new territories for reasons that are still present—population pressure, resource exhaustion, ecological damage, competition, curiosity and hope for a better life. During the hunter-gatherer phases of migration, modern humans moved into areas that were already settled (perhaps by more primitive human groups like Neanderthals), as well as occupied previously uninhabited terrain. Many highly durable, indigenous cultures were established by these early migrants, including the Australian Aborigines whose culture survived with relatively few changes for around 60,000 years.
2. *Early agricultural civilizations and empires.* The second category of globalization emerged during the Holocene geological period as human groups began to develop agriculture and congregate in increasingly dense and large urban settlements. Initially, these settlements surrounded the agricultural lands they relied upon, traded through and protected. This urban concentration enabled the creation of powerful armies which further facilitated the civilization's expansion and capacity to trade with, invade and colonize other lands and peoples. These agricultural empires included the Mediterranean city states, the Indian Mogul empire, the great Chinese dynasties and

the American Incas, Aztecs and Maya civilizations. The expansionary model developed by these civilizations, along with their cultural and geo-political cartographies, continue into the present. Moreover, the knowledge systems that were established by many of these civilizations—technology, art, philosophy and science—have provided a cultural template for many modern knowledge systems, Moreover, texts like the Bible, the Qu'ran and the Upanishads, along with their complex renderings of parable, faith and ritual, retain an extraordinary cultural force in contemporary belief systems across the globe.

3. *Westernism and industrial globalization.* This form of globalization emerged with the European Enlightenment and constitutes a specific kind of civilizational expansion. Like the earlier forms of agricultural globalization, western expansionism was constituted around militarism, trade and advanced knowledge systems and technologies. However, unlike the earlier forms, western expansionism was forged through a distinctive set of organizational, commercial, communicational and technological innovations. Of course, particular genealogical lines can be drawn from the western systems of science and technology, particularly through Greek and Eurasian cultural cartographies; however, the rise of westernism is accompanied by a rapid and self-perpetuating commitment to rationality and innovation which clearly accelerated Europe's economic, industrial and military advantages.

   The normative framework of westernism, conveyed through the spread of 'the state' and new communications networks, has undergone numerous micro shifts in power and emphasis; however, it remains a forceful hegemony in the political and symbolic ordering of the world. Powerful states and imperial state systems like America, the EEC and Japan remain at the centre of this westernist mode of globalization.

4. *Advanced mediational globalization—the mediasphere.* This fourth globalization vector extends and accelerates the communicational framework that has supported each of the other three categories of globalization. While the development of language was essential to hunter-gatherer migration, and writing was essential to the formation of civilizational expansion, mass printing was the framework upon which the state and accelerated industrialism were developed by western states. The emergence of the electrical, electronic and digital media has enabled the establishment of new, or at least newly proliferating, trans-national flows constituted around the trade and

exchange of images, information, finance and representational texts. Thus, while westernism remains a normative model of contemporary globalization and seeks perpetually to replicate itself through this advanced communicational mode of globalization, the amplitude that is produced through mediation nevertheless enables the outward and inward flow of other, alternative knowledge systems. That is, the acceleration and expansion of cultural interactions and contiguities releases many new modes of knowing, imaginings and voices into the global mediasphere. Thus, the solidity of western global domination is being shadowed by alternative knowledge systems and modes of being. While this book investigates these alternatives in considerable detail, a simple example of the amplification of these alternative modes may be seen in the spread of anti-western ideologies and language wars associated with *jihadism*, anti-consumerist movements and Radical Environmentalism.

This book applies this approach to crisis and globalization across a range of themes and cultural localities. While Chapter 1 provides a broad theoretical framework for the study, the subsequent chapters are focused on those areas of crisis that have become mainstays of the modern corporate media and broader zones of public discussion—economy and the Global Financial Crisis; new modes of sexuality and human relationships; global inequality and poverty; ecology, sustainability and global warming; and globally constituted modes of terrorism and political violence.

1
Imagining the End: Crisis Culture and the Pleasure Economy

...no man can ever identify himself aright unless his eyes be closed: as if darkness were indeed the proper element of our essence, though light be more congenial to our clayerer part.

Ishmael, *Moby Dick* (p. 57)

What are you, figure of the die I turn over in your encounter with my fortune? Nothing, if not that presence of death which makes of human life a reprieve obtained from morning to morning in the name of meanings whose sign is your crook.

Jacques Lacan, 'Seminar on *The Purloined Letter*', 1956

The world will eat more food over the next fifty years than has been consumed over the whole of human history.

Dr Megan Clark, CEO, CSIRO, 2009

The end

Homo sapiens sapiens[1] might have been created in a crucible of fear and desire. These primal dispositions are not simply the 'fight or flight' instincts of other higher species; rather, they represent a precarious detente that connects our essential animality to a more complex rendering of culture, economy and social organization. Through nearly 200,000 years of genetic, ecological and cultural history, this remarkably vulnerable and adaptive species has conjured from its immanent conditions a consciousness that has transformed the planetary life systems into an image of itself.

Enlightenment philosophy often describes the fear-desire nexus in terms of a divided human nature—aggression against compassion, self-interest against compassion. However, it is perhaps more productive to consider this nexus as a conduit of human complexity, a conduit that engages the expansiveness of human animality through its ultimate expression in culture. In this sense, there is no 'baser nature' that condemns us to the liberatory constraint of civilization and moral order; there is simply an expressive detente that acknowledges our necessarily complicated dispositions by which the being in ourselves is conveyed within a cultural form. Desire and fear, in other words, are not simply intrinsic to some primal condition of animality, but are the expressive core of our outer being, our being-in-the-world, as Heidegger calls it.

To put this more directly, humans are complicated and precarious creatures who are formed in a contingent and sometimes contradictory relationship with their own animality, consciousness, other humans, history and their current ecological and material conditions. We are not determined by others and the otherness of the world: like all other species, we have simply evolved through the dialogue of all that is within and around us. Our consciousness, in this sense, is the blessing and burden of our being, the source of all that may be wonderful, possible and pleasurable, as well as the dim shadow that condemns us with dread. Our survival as a species has been clearly fostered through the evolution of self-awareness and the multiplying range of our reasoning and imagination; but it has also been challenged through the recognition of our fears and the spectre of injury, disease, loss and death which perpetually haunts the prospects of our joy. In this sense, our *anthropos* is to be understood in terms of evolving systems that are created as much in the deep past as in the ever-unfolding conditions of the now.

Thus, a vision of 'the end'—the end of pleasure or its prospect—is inscribed in the conditions of our beginning as much as in the desire that mobilizes our individual and collective being. Out of that desire, inevitably, the shadow of the end must fall. This is clearly the contingent fallibility of our consciousness, the knowing that is the spawn and horrifying 'other' of our presence and prospect of pleasure. As the historical footnote of all human consciousness, we are perhaps the only species that truly dies, because we are the only species that knows we die. Equally, we may be the only species that truly experiences pleasure, as we are the only species that can name it, consider it and distinguish it from its loss.

It is precisely this precariousness, this detente of being, that is the source of human crisis and crisis consciousness. As a beginning point, therefore, this book argues that the study of 'the human' and human crisis must necessarily proceed through the study of the desire for pleasure and the crisis that is enshrined in the prospects of its loss. Thus, if we accept the assumption that pleasure can be formed around a range of human experiences—libidinal, material, familial, communal, aesthetic—then we can acknowledge that its pursuit and loss are critical to the human experience. Through the emergence of language and other symbolic systems from around 60–100,000 years Before Present (BP), the anthropological evidence for this proposition becomes increasingly strong. Human societies express their cosmological and ecological presence in natural life systems through a multitude of narrative and pictorial forms. Australian Aboriginal and European (Magdalenian) Palaeolithic rock art, for example, very forcefully demonstrates the presence and pleasure of being human. Through this aestheticization of the human experience, these drawings and paintings were created by hunter-gatherer communities some time between 10 and 30,000 years BP. Among these images are ochre stencils of human hands, and pictures of animals that were central to the social group's economy and cultural self-conception. The animals, in particular, were not only hunted for food, clothing and tools, they were totemic symbols that marked the ancestral lineage of particular clans and familial systems. That is, they were symbols that brought life and death, desire and loss, together in a narrative of precarious but compelling celebration. The animal symbology represented a profound intimacy between humans, their natural life systems and the cosmological essence by which their knowledge systems ordered their tribal life and personal death (Flood, 2004; Heyd and Clegg, 2005; Curtis, 2006). In a very real sense, these images represent a miraculous harmony of contending dispositions—our consciousness, animality and culture.

Language and the big chill

As intimated in the Introduction to this book, the hunter-gatherer communities who created the world's rock art were forced to confront a significant, global-wide ecological crisis that was to change the entire species and the ways in which consciousness and culture articulated the desire-fear nexus. Of course, crisis exists within and across various gradients of social duress and social change: in this sense, crisis is a relative concept. Having said this, however, the convergence of ecological and cultural crises that occurred at the end of the last major glacial phase, around 11,000 years ago, marks one of the most significant rupture for *Homo sapiens* and the mechanisms of human survival. From the perspective of this book, the rupture has precipitated a broad range of ongoing and escalating crisis conditions evolving through the rise of agricultural economy and culture into the present.

According to recent evolutionary theories of assimilation, modern humans migrated in continuous waves across much of the planetary land mass during the last glacial phase, 75–11,000 years BP (Williams, 2003; Smitha et al., 2005). During this major migratory phase—the original globalization—these human groups developed sophisticated language systems, clearly a prerequisite for travel and the complex organizational strategies required for survival and adaptation (see Nobel and Davidson, 1996). The development of language represents a critical evolutionary moment for these (anatomically) modern humans and human cultures. It may be assumed that the slow period of glaciation affected the ways in which humans conducted their economies and cultural practices, and that the innovation of language may have developed in relation to specific ecological conditions. However, these adaptations and changes, including the innovation of language, were not so much determined by ecological conditions; rather culture, population pressure, economy and ecology worked together to create particular kinds of adaptation and transformation.

The migratory waves and intricate processes of assimilation and adaptation were clearly generated through a protracted period of push and pull factors. Humans' own evolving consciousness, language, imagination and knowledge systems stimulated and facilitated the extraordinary attraction of migration, exploration and territorial occupation. The power to represent the world through various language forms—orality, narrative, dance, song, painting—was clearly critical for the capacity of human groups to confront and adapt to the slowly developing environmental conditions associated with glaciation. Language was also important for social organization, economic innovation and the capacity to settle disputes and interact with other human groups.

Equally, however, and as Thomas Malthus (2008, orig. 1823) first established, there were push factors which compelled human groups to seek other territories for settlement and survival. Malthus and other demographers argue that human population growth necessarily propels human groups into competition for territory and natural resources. This resource imperative may seem less relevant for hunter-gatherer tribal groups than for the more densely populated urban societies that emerged during the progress of the Holocene. The Malthus principle, however, defines demographic pressure in terms of population over resources; ecological and climatic changes in Africa and other parts of the world might certainly have played a part in driving migration waves as the hunter-gatherer communities increased in numbers and resources could no longer be easily exploited using the economic strategies, technologies and knowledge systems that were embedded in their cultural practices.

Even so, archaeologists disagree about the degree to which the push and pull factors operated for hunter-gatherer migrations, and the mechanisms by which occupations were consolidated. It needs to be remembered, of course, that these communities existed by certain kinds of relatively exclusive nomadic zones and resource management. Relying on the presence of particular animals, fish and floral systems, hunter-gatherers were generally careful to avoid resource exhaustion through over-hunting, over-population and excess harvesting. Plants and animals needed to have the capacity to reproduce and recover from human interventions. To ensure recovery periods, the communities continually moved across their totemically defined territorial zones and created elaborate laws and inter-tribal rituals to maximize survival prospects and minimize inter-tribal and inter-clan conflict.

In this context, hunter-gatherers evolved through relatively peaceful cultural arrangements. Of course violence and conflict were always possible within and outside the social groups; there is evidence to suggest that hunter-gatherer communities recognized that their survival was precarious and that systems of peaceable resolution to potential conflict were preferable to violence and warfare. To cite two examples— first, there is increasing evidence that primitive humans, Neanderthals, co-existed and perhaps interbred with more modern humans in Europe between 40 and 32,000 BP (Currat and Excoffier, 2004). While there is considerable debate about the character and tone of this cohabitation, and indeed about the degree of interbreeding, the archaeological evidence suggests a relatively peaceful co-existence and certainly no hint that the more modern and technologically advanced human groups sought deliberately to inflict a genocidal elimination of their resource rivals. Geneticists are currently investigating the levels of inter-breeding, which, even if it is minimal, suggests a more complicated image of human aggression and processes of peace-making in the hunter-gatherer lifestyle.

A second and more detailed image of highly ritualized systems of peace and inter-tribal management is evident in the Australian Aboriginal cultures. At the time of the European invasion of the Australian land mass (1788–), the indigenous people were living a remarkably peaceful and highly sophisticated hunter-gatherer lifestyle. Craniological studies indicate that there were at least three types of humans occupying the land mass during the 60,000+ year pre-history period: a more primitive, robust type, a more modern gracile type and a third, 'in-between' type which was dominant at the time of European incursion. This craniological history demonstrates a strong level of inter-breeding between the various migratory waves into Australia (Flood, 2004). The anthropological evidence also indicates that Australian Aborigines were a very settled and peaceful people who had developed sophisticated mechanisms for inter-tribal (inter-national) trade, dispute resolution, sport, ceremonial exchange and inter-marriage. As Josephine Flood (2004) has demonstrated, these mechanisms for inter-tribal corroboree functioned like a parliament of nations: they connected family groups through inter-marriage, song sharing and the exchange of resources that helped prevent violent seizure and warfare.

The point here is not to deny the significance of economic and ecological crisis as a precipitant of human mobility and migration for hunter-gatherers; nor is it to suggest that hunter-gatherer lifestyles were not vulnerable to violence and competitive pressures. It is rather to elucidate these crises in terms of a broader state of 'being human'. Thus, the push factors which drove the first waves of Pleistocene expansionism are demonstrably linked to some other condition that mobilizes human actions and which remains cogent within the current phase of human planetary expansionism—those processes and practices we are popularly referring to as globalization. In considering the ways in which the agonistic contingency of desire-fear has evolved through human animality, consciousness and culture, we necessarily encounter the vectoral energy which draws and drives these complicated patterns into action.

Thawing of the ice: one great human crisis

The geological transition from the Pleistocene to the Holocene, around 11,000 BP, is marked by a quite rapid and radical rise in global temperature. Whereas glaciation occurred over a relatively long period, the thawing of the ice and increase in temperature was markedly swift, bringing forward significant pressures on species adaptation. By the time of the transition, much of the planetary land mass had been occupied by *Homo sapiens sapiens*. And while the groups were obviously quite nuanced, they had all developed language, similar economic practices and forms of ritualized law. Of course, these societies were not equally secure and affluent, and there were ongoing challenges for social and economic maintenance, as well as intra- and extra-tribal tensions that could occasionally lead to outbreaks of intra- and extra-tribal violence. Moreover, the challenges of resource management and population growth were common to most of these groups as they continued to work though the difficulties of being-in-the-world and negotiating their physical and conscious engagement with perpetually changing natural and social environments (see Panter-Brick et al., 2001).

In places like Australia, in which hunter-gatherer cultures survived until the invasion of Europeans in 1788, the lifestyle of most of the Aboriginal groups was affluent and stable with very few changes to economic practices and the economic toolkit over a period of between 40–70,000 years (Flood, 2004; David et al., 2006). During this period, many distinctive languages had evolved across the continent and there was an abundance of ritualized art, cultural practices, and complex social mores and lores which were critical to the survival and coherence of the social group. Intrinsic to these lores, of course, was the constituency of the group and the ways in which culture identified those human individuals who were inside and those who were outside. Significant also to these ritualized social functions, as Claude Levi-Strauss demonstrated some time ago, was the concept of a cosmological beginning (creation myths) which connected humans to their animality and life sources against the fear of the end. In the animistic religions that dominated the hunter-gatherer lifestyles, humans saw themselves as the physical incarnation of a spirit world that stretched across all time and which united the spirit to all other animate and inanimate phenomena (Ong, 2002). Within the condition of all-time, animals and the cosmos were frequently regarded by hunter-gatherer communities as the ancestral relatives of humans: as noted above, a miraculous harmony of living and existing in death. For Aboriginal Australians this convergent zone was (and is) called 'the Dreaming'.

The creation myths that connect humans to their animate and inanimate ancestry are a central dimension of tribal systems of knowledge (epistemology) and notions of the self. Through a highly detailed symbolic and 'totemic' system, hunter-gatherer communities often identified themselves and their kin through an intimate and cosmological relationship with nature and their own animality. While hunter-gatherer communities certainly impacted on their ecological systems, tribal lore made it very clear that excessive impact would endanger individuals and community life. That is to say, hunter-gatherer communities recognized that the excessive impact would endanger the survival of the whole group and so controls were exercised through careful environmental management, systems of territorial mobility, and the endowment of nature and natural objects with cultural and totemic value. Most hunter-gatherer communities, therefore, imagined themselves to be direct descendants of the surrounding flora and fauna—the ecosystem upon which all life depends.

These controls on excess, however, were imperfect, and as humans continued to proliferate across the globe, their impact became increasingly evident. By the end of the Pleistocene and the relatively rapid glacial retreat, the increases in human population and the excessive hunting of particular species of mammals (especially marsupials) were contributing to the formation of a major human crisis. While there is some debate about the respective impact of climate change and over-hunting, it is nevertheless clear that human activities had a major impact on the extinction of many of the larger mammals in Europe, the Americas and Australasia towards the end of the Pleistocene. The slow moving and largely defenceless megafauna in Australia, for example, were certainly the victims of excess and poor environmental management. With the rising seas, broadening of the deserts and shrinking of the watered and coastal regions of the Australian continent, the economic impact of these extinctions was acutely felt. In particular, the shrinking of the more verdant and watered areas of the land mass forced tribal groups into greater concentration and contiguity, creating new competitive pressures. Even so, the indigenous people of Australia were able to maintain their hunter-gatherer lifestyle through a range of cultural, economic and technological adaptation, including the refinement of the toolkit and new forms of semi-settlement and food management. Human constructions like tidal fish-traps, eel-chanels and stone dwellings were observed by many of the early European settlers, particularly in the southern areas of the continent (see Flood, 2004).

Agriculture and the fertile crescent

For human groups living in drier parts of the planet, however, the ecological pressures were greater and the adaptations more innovative and substantial. While there is considerable scholarly debate about the emergence of agriculture, it is nevertheless quite clear that the human groups living in the areas around present-day Turkey and other parts of West Asia were among the first people to cultivate crops and establish significant, stable urban settlements. This adaptation was undoubtedly linked to the evolution and availability of particular kinds of grain and other botanical species (Kennett et al., 2009), as well as the pressures of rapid global warming (Bellwood, 2004; Wright, 2004). But it is also due to the ingenuity and creative adaptations that had characterized the cultural and economic practices of humans, especially from the emergence of language. These adaptations contributed to various forms of social, ritual and technological experimentations, including methods of food sharing and grain cultivation (Bellwood, 2004: 23–27). Indeed, and as I have suggested above, the radical move to settlement and animal husbandry and crop cultivation was engendered through push and pull factors—significant modifications to the environment, continued population pressure and the human capacity for imagining and innovation.

With the contraction of food sources, the nomadic groups in areas like the Fertile Crescent began to experiment with new forms of economy which led ultimately to a system of agrarianism, urbanization and systems of trade. Of course, many other peoples had developed various mechanisms for cultivating and supporting food sources, but these were the first significant human groups to embrace a method of plant cultivation and animal husbandry that substantially replaced the alternative economy of nomadic hunting and gathering.

Rupturing the creation-death harmony

Not surprisingly, these new settlement and economic systems were associated with radical changes in religion and cosmology, concepts of self and systems of social organization and knowledge. Thus, while the new economic and cultural adaptations that formed around the Fertile Crescent and Mediterranean Basin were designed to secure the survival of human groups, they brought with them a radical amplification of vulnerability, fear and new forms of anxiety. Indeed, while many historians have identified the change to agriculture as a major marker of human progress, the evidence is far from unambiguous, particularly in terms of those indicators of human security that are associated with health, aggression control, modes of social governance, economic stability and resources (Bellwood, 2004; Wright, 2004).

Husbandry, crop cultivation and fixed zones of settlement necessarily involved the surrender of hunter-gatherer advantages of small scale economy, mobility and flexibility. Through the surrender of this ecological mobility in favour of greater human control, the settled communities became increasingly vulnerable to the vicissitudes of climate, disease and the aggressive interests of other human groups. Not only were crops and domesticated animals subject to disease, the increasing agglomeration of humans introduced new problems of hygiene, sanitation and contagion. Because they were fixed in space and constituted around increasing densities and numbers of people, human settlements became vulnerable to drought, flood, fire, crime, disease and warfare. These new vulnerabilities demanded a radical realignment of the relationship between the human and non-human (nature), and a complete reappraisal of humans' relationship with the cosmos.

In order to overcome, or at least limit, these vulnerabilities, the pre-industrial agricultural societies developed several significant strategies. These can be summarized in the following terms.

1. The development of surplus value

The core of the economy was agriculture and the exploitation of primary resources (stone, metals, timber and so on). While much of the world's agriculture was originally 'subsistence', the systematic production of surplus crop enabled the production of a more expansive and exchangeable symbolic surplus 'value'. This surplus value enabled the communities to save product for later consumption or for the trade of other products and needs. The most significant 'value' over and above the crop itself was the land upon which people live and in which crops were grown. As well as providing food, this form of surplus value laid the foundation for a capitalist economy in which value expands and becomes more systematically symbolized. While the most obvious form of symbolic value exchange was through currency (gold, money, finance), symbolic value became integrated into other value products such as gemstones, textiles, spices, art, architecture and exotic animals. Both product and symbolic value were integrated into an evolving system of social hierarchy based on value and property. This hierarchy based on control of surplus value became the dominant organizational framework by which agricultural societies were ordered.

2. Population growth and labour specialization

Unlike hunter-gatherer communities who sought to control carefully their population size in order to ensure ecological equilibrium, agricultural communities released their reproductive capacity in order to generate greater economic security, particularly through the deployment of agricultural labour and military power. Larger families, communities and urban settlements provided a stronger labour base for increasing agricultural expansion and hence management of particular kinds of vulnerability. The increasing population would also aid community resilience in the face of natural disasters.

Increased population size also enabled greater diversification and specialization of labour. These forms of specialization were valuable for innovation, skill development and the production of value products. Surplus labour also contributed to the establishment and expansion of social hierarchies and the emergence of power nodes. Surplus labour is cheap, enabling wealthier and more powerful groups to use their control of property and other value products to control weaker groups. Surplus labour could be deployed in security and military forces both to protect the property of the primary group, as well as assault and steal from others.

As agricultural societies became industrialized, larger populations were also valuable as production and trade drivers, providing demand for value-based products.

3. Militarism and militaristic governance

As noted, the increasing agglomeration of humans in urban settlements increased the need for centralizing systems of social control and management. Over the 11,000 years of Holocene history, social groupings have established various governmental and management systems ranging from dynastical autocracy to more inclusive models of democracy. All of these systems, however, have several common themes: they are all based around hierarchy where leaders control or seek to control the social group; they are all fortified by violence and the exertion of military force both within and outside the social group and its territory; they have a structured symbolic system (ideology) which seeks to legitimate the power, hierarchical system and decisions of the central leaders; sovereigns, dictators and democratic governments have all created as sense of collective identity and hierarchy which distinguishes the whole social group from outsiders. In a very real sense, the new economic and cultural systems associated with agriculturalism invented a new type of human violence, a violence that has frequently affiliated itself with a vision of the end—such as genocide, holocaust, nuclear Armageddon.

4. Technological innovation

Through the confluence of vulnerability and extraordinary imagining, these new agricultural societies were set on a path of constant adaptation and innovation. While the tendency of modern commentary is to locate innovation within industrial society and the Enlightenment, there are clear examples of peaks and troughs in these processes of change and innovation, and in the civilizational mass which supported them. Long before industrial Europe had invented the printing press or ballistics, for example, these and many other technological innovations had been developed in China. The point is simply that the extreme vulnerability of agricultural societies bound them to a restless trajectory of innovation: any slip in the volition would risk being overrun by famine, disease or the violence of others.

5. Language and representation

The increasing complexity of settled communities and the need for centralized systems of control and governance contributed to a range of technological adaptations around language. As Walter Ong (2002) explains, oral societies were small, highly mobile and resisted the encumbrance of excess property which they would otherwise need to carry across their totemic terrains. Memory was also ephemeral, and was bound to elders, who had lived for the longest time and bore the greatest memory of things known. The innovation of surplus value and the resonance of increasing urban complexity required more substantial memory and information systems. Writing, print and electrical media are all adaptations that facilitated the expansion and greater complexity of social organizations and the management of human populations.

These responses to increased vulnerability are not simply reactive, but are part of the human creative psyche and capacity for cultural adaptation and the pursuit of pleasure. Indeed, through all of these economic, technological and governmental transformations, the agricultural societies also embarked on a ceaseless process of cultural innovation, particularly in terms of communicational practice, belief systems and religion. In considering the intensification of the desire-fear nexus and increasing social vulnerability of Holocene cultures, we might expect there to be a radical shift in the ways in which humans conceive of themselves and their relationship to nature—that is, their cosmology.

Indeed and as already noted, many hunter-gatherer communities aestheticized their relationship with nature through a pictorial and narrative harmonization of creation and death. The nexus is delicately poised through the totemic rendering of hunted animals that are both the life source of the community, as well as the ancestral compendium of their spirit world. In the imaginings of these communities and their mythic representations, creation and the perpetuity of the tribal group is maintained through an intimate relationships with nature: in this sense, the tribe can never be 'uncreated' or destroyed; the tribe and nature necessarily transcend the calamity of an individual's death.

Agricultural communities, however, shatter these intricate renderings, as nature becomes both a servant and powerful enemy of their desires and pleasures. The mystery and embedded identification of the human with their own animality and nature is subsumed within a powerful social hierarchy. Through a major historical and cultural rupture, nature becomes enslaved by cultivation and husbandry; yet the powerful forces of nature can wreak havoc through floods, droughts, disease and violence, threatening the viability of the whole social group.

Thus, the emergence of civilizational religious and mythical narratives gives us a critical insight into the ways in which the cultural imaginary and knowledge systems of agricultural societies have been formed, and continue into the present. Emerging in the early agrarian civilizations of the Mediterranean, India, China and the Americas, these religions share a range of common threads and themes. The most spectacular of these themes is a propensity for apocalyptic cosmological violence by which the harmony of human and nature is shattered by crisis. Of course these religions and their constituent narratives are many things, including mechanisms for social management, law and validations of hierarchical systems and dynastical hierarchy; however, many of the religions share an imagery of vengeful and violent deities who control the cosmos and who impose their will over subjects and nature. Whether by cyclical renewal or eternal transformations in bliss or damnation, these major agricultural religions present a vision of 'the end' which frequently warns humankind against the excesses of carnality or unrestrained pleasure. In the Abrahamic religions (Judaism, Christianity and Islam), specifically, the vision of a cataclysmic social death forms the basis of moral teaching and the ideological power of the spirit deity (Cook, 2003). Constituted around eternal reward for obedience, these religions create a framework for social conformity that condemns miscreants to eternal misery in personal or collective damnation. This apocalypse is not simply personal, but functions for the abjuration of all humanity in the revelation of some great occlusion. The nexus of life and death, therefore, is suspended in a violent and cruel imagining of being-in-the-world, an imagining that forestalls the pursuit of pleasure beyond the hierarchy of power that controls it.

Moreover, while the cyclical religions of Ancient Greece or Vedic India might seek to console their worshippers with the lure of reincarnation and renewal, irreverent or excessive behaviour is nevertheless punishable by various forms of degenerative rebirth. Social catastrophe and a vision of world annihilation are inscribed into the myths of these cyclical religions: in Vedic culture the world is trapped between its Creation by Brahma and the total annihilation by Shiva; in Ancient Greece the Ages of Man myth tells of the apocalypse events that had already destroyed mortal society many times and which were likely to be continued as the gods, including Zeus, inflict their wrath or neglect over humankind.

This cosmological imposition of power and fear is almost impossible to find in the older mythic visions of hunter-gatherer communities. Thus, while the cosmological emphasis of hunter-gatherers was on

Creation over death, the value production, desires and vulnerabilities of the agricultural religions and cultures seem more forcefully focused on fear and a deeply coded anxiety of loss and apocalypse. Of course, hunter-gatherer mythologies convey their cosmological warnings, but they are generally free of monstrous, human-like deities who so often exercise their power in ways that are so vicious and disproportionate to the mortal beings they control.

Even through the Enlightenment and into the present, these apocalyptic religions retain a remarkable degree of cultural, social and political significance. With the rise of secularism and scientific knowledge systems, it might be expected that these old modes of religious faith (superstition) would have fallen away. And while many reasons have been offered for the continuation of agricultural religions beyond the Age of Reason and into the Information Age, it is certainly feasible to suggest that these religions—like agriculture itself—are grounded in the evolution of our crisis consciousness: that is, in our deep anxieties about ourselves, nature, pleasure and loss. For John Micklethwait and Adrian Wooldridge (2009) the current 'revival' of these agricultural religions across the world is, among other things, a manifestation of the continuity of these anxieties, even as they are conjured and expressed through the evolving circumstances of the present. While modernity and science might seem to suppress agricultural faith-based knowledge systems, the survival and flourishing of these knowledge systems is associated with the ways in which science is itself implicated in the calamity and violence that persist into the present.

Indeed, and as noted in the Introduction, even science has its particular modes of apocalyptic anxiety, particularly as it is fostered around material finitude, as well as the vast array of violent and destructive technologies it has helped to create. Science, like the religions through which its knowledge systems emerged, has clearly contributed to an end vision that condemns the world to schism, divisiveness and warfare. When science and religion become inter-fused through various forms of social imagining and narrative knowledge systems the force of the apocalypse is even more potent. Consider, for example, the evangelical language of the Cold War, the 9/11 wars and the threat of Iranian nuclear armament.

The power of these 'end of the world' motifs and narratives is also resonant in contemporary popular culture and aesthetics. While apocalypse is frequently invoked through religious allusion, even secular texts are inscribed with a forceful anxiety about social or even species occlusion. We cited a number of examples of these apocalyptic popular texts in the Introduction, particularly around the prospects of nuclear annihilation; however, a vision of the end is common to many contemporary narratives, especially in fantasy and science fiction genres which imagine 'the world' as a vulnerable and mortal entity. We need to only consider the writings of Jules Verne, George Orwell, Aldous Huxley, as well as visual narratives such as *Star Wars* (George Lucas, 1977–), *Doctor Who* (BBC, ongoing) and *The Day after Tomorrow* (Roland Emmerich, 2004). The fantasy experience, in fact, has become a mainstay of the video games industry where players frequently assume a Messianic responsibility for saving the world.

Mel Gibson's film *Apocalypto* (2006) exposes this end of the world sensibility through a compression of civilizational transformation in Central America. Gibson's narrative presents a vision of history that epitomizes the Holocene economic and cultural volition; the agrarianist apocalyptic vision is marshalled through the destruction of hunter-gatherer cultures and the means by which a crisis consciousness has evolved through agrarianism to the modern imaginary. While the film presents a familiar motif of Hollywood heroics, it nevertheless explores the ways in which civilizations brutalize one another from the privilege of their power. Gibson takes up this theme through his somewhat atavistic account of the Maya and the shadow of its own ritualized modes of violence. In its literal sense, 'modern' means most recent, and so the Maya regarded themselves as a modern civilization that had the right, indeed, the cosmological duty, to govern ruthlessly. The Maya's civil mass and reliance on agriculture rendered them vulnerable to the vicissitudes of climatic, human and natural disasters. In order to appease cosmological forces and wrathful gods, the Maya performed various forms of fertility rites, including human sacrifice. While the historical accuracy of these rites has been questioned, it is nevertheless clear that Gibson narrative identifies these practices with a fundamental human brutality that is itself borne from fear and profound anxieties about human vulnerability. In this sense, this human brutality merely mimics the cosmological forces or 'gods' that so indifferently preside over the precariousness of human existence (Plate 1.1).

Expressing his own (and the public's) anxiety about present social and cultural conditions, Gibson tells the story of a hunter-gatherer tribe in the Mesoamerican forest who are enslaved by the Maya and presented for ritual sacrifice. The film self-consciously contrasts the complex and formidable social structures of the Maya with the more earthy and 'natural' lifestyle of the forest people, particularly their more spontaneous and joyful fertility and sexual pleasures. This dissonance of pleasure and

Plate 1.1   Inca ruins in the Andes Mountains. Like the Maya, the Incas were a powerful civilization which engaged in ritual human sacrifice as a way of appeasing their gods.
Photograph by George Paterson.

displeasure, a common motif in apocalypse narratives, is represented by the beauty and fertility of the hero's wife. Trapped in the earth, she evades defilement by the Maya dragoons, but her deliverance is only possible through the Messianic return of her captured husband.

Gibson's elegy to the passing of the forest people becomes more explicitly allegorical when, towards the end of the film, the heroic survivors of the civilizational sacrifice confront a new danger in the image of a Spanish galleon. The title and tenor of the film are clearly designed as prescience to a more horrific epoch of violence and destruction: European modernity. As in *The Passion of the Christ* (Gibson, 2004), Gibson is intrigued by the brutality and doom that is inscribed in human civilization, and the ways in which 'goodness' and purity (the Mesoamericans, Christ) are brutalized by civilizational desire. While there is a certain Romantic primitivism or naturalism inscribed in the film's noble savage motif, *Apocalypto* nevertheless conveys for us a sense of a fear-desire contingency and the ways in which this interdependent tension has been conveyed through the representational mediums developed through agrarian cultures. The eschatological vision of the film betrays a deep anxiety that is not a parenthesis of modern cultures, but which indicates a profound yearning, a doubt, that is integrated into our contemporary culture and state of being.

Westernism, media and the emergence of the economy of pleasure

My argument here is that the end of the last glacial period contributed to a protracted phase of crisis and transformation—including changes in the way humans think and conceive of themselves and their world. I have so far argued that an historical volition was established through the rise of agriculture, surplus-based economies and a particular kind of crisis consciousness that has its roots in a range of knowledge systems, including the apocalyptic religions. These eschatological religions and the related crisis-based knowledge systems are replicated through innumerable narratives: indeed, the power and ubiquity of this apocalyptic vision establishes a template for the narrative structures that predominate agrarian history, particularly through the evolution of Europe and cultural westernism. Our task in this section is to understand the ways in which the cultural and economic volition of the Holocene evolved through the emergence of westernism and a mediated economy of desire/pleasure.

The emergence of industrial modernism and the global predominance of westernism extended the economic and cultural volition that was established through the Holocene transformation and the adoption of agriculture. In its expanded form, 'westernism' does not simply apply to those countries of Western Europe in which this form of civilizational culture evolved; it also refers to those other global terrains which have adopted the cultural characteristics, practices and economic frameworks that have emerged as a global paradigm.

While many scholars might propose the term 'modern' as the defining characteristic of this paradigm, there is a sense in which this concept is somewhat deceptive. As noted in the Introduction, the term 'modern', like 'progress', assumes an historical privilege whereby the present is the self-determining apex of this civilizational volition. From the perspective of this book, these transformations are positive and negative, drawing together both pleasures and displeasures for different human groups and modes of social experience. Indeed, as the characteristics of the agricultural transformations are extended into the present, this dual disposition towards desire-fear and pleasure-displeasure becomes increasingly intensified through amplitude of mediation and the dynamic multiplication of our knowledge systems—that is, through the conditions of what I have elsewhere called language wars.

These language wars represent the marshalling of the knowledge systems through the generation of discourses (language) that concentrate around a cultural politics of inclusion and exclusion. These concentrated discourses or ideologies are propagated by social groups who struggle within the hierarchical system for control of surplus and symbolic value. Both pre-industrial and industrial agricultural societies propagated a self-validating knowledge system and ideology that commonly defined outsiders (others) as inferior, uncivilized, barbarians, evil agents or even non-human animals. This radical disavowal of others enabled the civilized group to murder, enslave and steal from less powerful social groups, including of course hunter-gatherers. In many respects, this ordering of outsiders reflected the civilization's internal ordering whereby human individuals and groups were situated on a gradient of social value: like property and other units in the economic system, human bodies, their labour and sexual-reproductive capacities were marked as tradable objects. Dominant individuals and groups fortified own privilege and pleasures through the propagation of ideologies that proclaimed their divine lineage and special relationship with god. In this sense, leadership is granted its special value through the manipulation of Messianic imagery: deliverance from the apocalypse could only be assured by obedience to a divinely appointed ruler.

Modern, industrialized societies maintained and enhanced many of these practices and hierarchical frameworks, though the increasing specializations of labour, trade and mediation have contributed to changes in the mechanism of hierarchical discrimination and the ways in which social privilege and governance are constructed and managed. Even so, the Messianic privilege of leadership remains deeply inscribed in the cultural psychology of westernism, even through its democratic incarnation. At the height of the 9/11 wars this privilege was evident in the invocation of an apocalyptic vision: against the *jihadist* vision of al-Qa'ida, the democratically elected leaders of the Anglophonic Coalition of the Willing were all practising Christians. US President George Bush, Australian Prime Minister John Howard and UK Prime Minister Tony Blair had each invoked a Messianic imagery as they sought to rally their people in avenging calumny of the 9/11 attacks on America—the new Holy Land of global westernism (Lewis, 2005; Nairn and James, 2005).

Thus, the cultural politics of the present remain fixed within an hierarchical resonance that conflates a gradient of value with more recent mechanisms of social discrimination. While modern societies may have dispensed with some aspects of divine right, social privilege and the dispositions of inclusion and exclusion remain forcefully rendered by the formation of privileged knowledge—expert systems—which is another battleground within the mediated sphere of language wars. In particular, Western Europe renewed and extended the knowledge systems of earlier Classical empires like Athens and Rome, and fortified their eschatological religious knowledge systems with an innovative mode of validation—scientific rationalism and the privilege of expert knowledge. Of course particular power elites in the Christian Church positioned themselves against the challenges posed by these new expert systems, particularly in terms of Creation narratives and the behavioural controls exerted by the Church over its citizens. But as noted, all privileged groups within a social formation are susceptible to exclusion and overthrow by other groups: the social and economic privilege of the Church was grounded in specific knowledge systems which justified that privilege. Through the momentum of the Enlightenment and the rise of new social groups who could mobilize the expert systems of science and technology, the Church was forced to retreat into new zones of speciality—spirituality and social virtue. Even so, the apocalyptic narratives that are formed in the Biblical canon continue to assert themselves through innumerable cultural incarnations, including science which remains welded to the problem of being human and its relentless vision of the end. Indeed, within the pre-eminent cultural fantasy of infinite pleasure, these expert systems continue to jostle for primacy and the social privileges that are attached to its deliverance.

In this context, agriculture represents a genealogical conduit through pre-industrial, industrial and contemporary, media-based societies. The crisis conditions that emerged through the Holocene have not been erased through these phasal innovations, but perpetuated, if not accelerated. Moreover, the psycho-cultural patterns and knowledge systems that have been borne through these material conditions have also continued, forming the basis of a more recent incarnation of crisis consciousness. To underline the point, it is not that the economy of agriculture and its broad range of cultural systems were erased by industrialism or information-based economies; it is rather that the agricultural economy and many of its knowledge systems continue in various permutations through, and alongside, an accretion of new practices and modes of knowing. Thus, it is legitimate to speak of an 'advanced agricultural system' or an 'industrialized agricultural system' within other economic formations and concepts, including the economy of pleasure.

Economy of desire: economy of pleasure

While the modern media is rich with narratives and reports on the economy, only a small proportion of these stories focus on the essence of our survival—that is, our capacity to feed ourselves. As discussed above, agriculture enables the supplementary activities associated with the creation of tradable surplus. Condemned to a perpetual volition of innovation, militarism, hierarchy, population growth and the expansion of surplus value, civilizations have sought inevitably to maximize their pleasures through various means, including the transfer of displeasure to others. In this context, innovations associated with industrialism, urbanization, travel and communications are forged within a crucible of desire and a fantasy of infinite pleasure. This fantasy is mobilized through the emergence of the global mediasphere.

In the Introduction I argued that the emergence of a global mediasphere represents the convergence of particular economic, technological and cultural patterns. Through the historical volition established through the Holocene conditions of crisis, the mediasphere is constituted around multiplying knowledge systems and the amplitude of a crisis consciousness. Equally, however, the media and the mediasphere are directly engaged in the expansion of surplus value, particularly as these surpluses are translated as symbolic value. As noted above, this symbolic value (property, gold, textiles, money and so on) is evolved as a critical dimension of the hierarchical system that mobilizes trade and surplus economy. The media and communications systems more generally facilitated the expansion of trade, record keeping, property management and other transactions in desire—that is, transactions that facilitate the fantasy of pleasure and its social and economic expression.

The emergence of the mediasphere cannot, therefore, be disaggregated from economy or cultural politics, particularly as the trade of material products and services was compounded and then enhanced by a trade in symbols and symbolic value. This expansion in the trade of symbolic value is often attached to the rise in electrical media systems at the beginning of the twentieth century when advertising and branding released a more elaborate system of product dissemination and discrimination (Bourdieu, 1987). That is, through their promotion in the broadcast media, products and services were appended with new social meanings and values, many of which were situated on a social hierarchy and the class system.

For some economic and cultural historians, this historical transformation represents a shift from the economy of needs (food, shelter) to an economy of wants of desires (fashion, images, media)—a shift, that is, to a consumer society (see Humphery, 2010). This consumer society is marked by an expansion in demand and purchasing power, as everyday citizens began to pursue the pleasures that had previously been the exclusive province of social elites (Benson, 1994; Baudrillard, 1998; Rojek, 2009; Humphery, 2010).

Thus, the emergence of a consumer society is directly associated with the radical expansion of developed world wealth surpluses and value-based symbols and signs (Baudrillard, 1998). This expansion was itself facilitated by the spread of western industrial production systems which enabled the proliferation and significantly reduced cost of products and the symbols in which these products were embedded and promoted. However, while consumer products have been infused with symbolic meanings and an hierarchical social value, over the past century the media itself has emerged as a distinctive corporate industry which generated a range of cultural products formed around information, entertainment and art. That is, not only does mediation convey the ascribed meanings of particular products and services, it also presents its own news, information, imagery and narratives as consumable product—that is, as value-based cultural artefacts.

Significantly, the media and the mediasphere are formed around the production and consumption of 'appearances'—a constituted reality that proliferates through the dynamic of culture and its multiplying knowledge systems. Thus, while agriculture may be the stabilizing essence of our economy, mediation facilitates and indeed perpetuates the expansion of human desire, a desire which underwrites our fantasy of pleasure and the pursuit of these transmogriforic appearances. Embedded within these appearances and fantasies, however, are the conditions of crisis and their destabilizing effects on human consciousness.

Mediasphere and the politics of excess

Thus, it is not that these conditions or fears have worsened, but rather they have been amplified and intensified through the contiguities and networking power of globalization and the global mediasphere. Clearly, then, the global, networked media is a critical component of this economy of pleasure—along with its shadows of crisis and apocalyptic anxiety. This mediasphere is a robust space in which media and culture generate the resources of meaning and related disputes and ideological claims. Thus, and as I developed in *Language Wars* (Lewis, 2005; also Lewis and Lewis, 2009), the mediasphere is the space in which power is largely exercised through contentions over meaning, language and symbolic value: it is the place in which governments, organizations, communities and individuals rally around their conception and pursuit of pleasure against the desires of others.

Many communication scholars continue to hold faith in the capacity of the media to deliver objective and accurate information for the exercise of effective democratic governance (see Chester, 2008; McChesney, 2008; Cottle, 2009). Indeed, in the minds of many scholars, politicians, political activists and everyday citizens of the democratic world, the excesses of the social world and capitalist economy may well be constrained by a fourth estate media which takes seriously its responsibility to inform the public and protect the world from dangerous desires. According to this understanding of the (news) media, a truth might be salvaged from the deluge of mediated noise that daily floods our airways with nonsense or ideologies that confirm the privilege of power elites.

For all its laudable intent, this approach to the news media seriously underestimates the ways in which the media and mediation have become so intricately woven into contemporary knowledge systems and the cultural mediasphere. In order to unpick a truth in support of specific modes of governance, cultural agents would need to liberate themselves from the cultural cacophony of claims that constitute the entire symbolic exchange system and its mediated economy of pleasure—which is also an economy of displeasure. To put this in more familiar terms: the media and the mediasphere represent a complex compound of cultural claims and counter-claims which form the basis and fabric of contending knowledge systems and their expressive language wars. In order to critique the media, therefore, it is important to move beyond a fourth estate model and address the full implications of this amorphous but compelling mediasphere as a contingent and radial knowledge space.

To this end, the mediasphere not only facilitates the expansion and imposition of uneven systems of power, it is also an emissary and progenitor of contention, challenge and resistance. It provides the mechanisms and knowledge pathways into the cultural politics of aesthetics, narrative, information and new modes of social imagining. As already noted, the media amplifies human experience as it widens the scope of knowing and reconceptualizing our experience of the present. In a very significant way, the media brings us to the precipice of our pleasures and fears, and enlivens the processes by which we can know our crisis conditions and seek to manage and resolve them. This is not simply an exercise in reasoned adjudication and accurate information, as imagined by Thomas Carlyle's fourth estate paradigm. The mediasphere incorporates these higher aspirations within a broader ambit of images, representations and narratives that constitute the full range of our knowledge systems. Thus, the mediasphere exposes us to and integrates our knowledge systems with the conditions of crisis, as well as the cultural politics and language wars that give them form. The mediasphere provides an intricate framework for representing and comprehending our crisis conditions and the specific constitution of our crisis consciousness.

To this end, the familiar scholarly critique of a neo-liberal capitalism or 'consumer society' loses some force, particularly through the definition of excess. While we will discuss this issue in subsequent chapters, the notion of excess needs to be understood in terms of its relative relationship to a concept of surplus value. In an economic system and mediasphere which is based on surplus value, ceaseless desire and appearances, it is difficult to identify a tipping point by which surplus becomes excess. While social commentators might thereby define excess in terms of capitalist greed, warfare, religious militancy, poverty, sexual lassitude or ecological catastrophe—these conditions are marked by specific knowledge systems within the volition I have outlined above. Thus, a condition of excess is both relative and positioned, emerging through the particular group of individual's experience of pleasure as it is subsumed by some intrinsic or externally imposed displeasure. The question to be addressed, then, is where and when does surplus exceed itself?

Risk society and crisis

While we will return to this question of pleasure and excess shortly, it remains for us to consider the preceding discussions in terms of a more generalized analytical strategy.

In the remainder of this chapter, therefore, I want to work through towards a more definitive understanding of crisis which can then be applied to the empirical studies of subsequent chapters. To this end, there have been relatively few theoretical studies which directly address or conceptualize contemporary crisis conditions and their rendering through a crisis consciousness; even fewer studies examine crisis in terms of the cultural politics that are generated through the global media.

In comparable studies, however, Ulrich Beck (1992, 1999, 2008) and Anthony Giddens (1990, 1999) have drawn attention to issues of crisis which they define more specifically as conditions of 'risk'. Simon Cottle (2009) has adapted Beck's framework in his specific studies of the news media and crisis, arguing that a full understanding of crisis-risk necessarily implicates the media. Cottle's one misgiving about Beck's claim that we have moved into a new historical phase called 'global risk society' is that Beck pays insufficient attention to the role of the media in the formation of this 'second modernity'. Even so, Cottle's analysis of the contemporary news reporting of crisis is largely a supplement to Beck's theory, and confirms a more generalized view that the world is hurtling towards some grand but unspecified abyss. The news and major news organizations are largely responsible for this situation, as they have sponsored a perspective of the world that supports neo-liberalist principles, the avarice of social elites and the general neglect of shared social problems. In many respects, Cottle's account of risk society and the deficiency of the media parallels those critics of contemporary consumer society who focus on cultural excess as the primary pathway to global doom. As noted above, these critics seek the restoration of a fourth estate principle by which the news media presents objective information to a democratically constituted public sphere. Within this perspective, Cottle (2009: 25) refers to global society's negative structural conditions as 'crisis realism'—a recognition that globalization generates negative and often 'unintended consequences'.

In fact, Beck's own work on 'risk society' (1992) and later 'global risk society' (1999) has provided a template for the study of the negative consequences of globalization and its phasal distinctions. Rejecting the amorphousness of concepts like 'postmodernism', Beck describes the current phase of globalization as the 'second modernity'. In an interview with Danillo Zolo, Beck succinctly defines his thesis in the following terms:

Now, at the end of the millennium, we are confronted with, what I call a 'modernization of modernization' or 'reflexive', 'second' modernity where basic assumptions, limitations, and contradictions of modernity itself are being questioned and reflected upon. That relates to key problems of modern politics. Enlightenment based on modernity is challenged by five processes: globalization, individualization, unemployment/underemployment, gender revolution and, last but not least, global risks (as the ecological crisis and the breakdown of global financial markets). I think there is a new kind of capitalism, a new kind of economy, a new kind of global order, a new kind of personal life coming into being, all of which differ from earlier phases of social development. So we do need, sociologically and politically, a new frame of reference.

(Cited in Zolo, 2010)

Thus, while the first phase of Enlightenment modernity believed that society would exercise reason and thus be able to control all social risk, the second modernity is characterized by the recognition that such ideals were fanciful. Thus, the earlier phase of the Enlightenment and industrial modernity is superseded by the emergence of 'risk' society that is characterized by an endemic and somewhat pessimistic social knowledge about predominant global conditions of risk. In a sense, these conditions of risk represent the rupture between an attempt to control the future and the unintended consequences of that project (Beck, 1999: 3). Along with other global sociologists like Anthony Giddens (1990, 1999), Beck sought to develop a parallel political theory which explains the dissolution of radical politics and the emergence of a new and broadly inclusive neo-liberal economic pragmatism which has come to dominate western (and hence global) geo-political conditions. Both Beck and Giddens regard the decline of the political Left and Right as a new form of global capitalism that has come to form a major economic and ideological orthodoxy.

According to Beck the media is responsible for the misreporting of social and political issues, leading to a reflexive state of knowledge, 'non-knowledge', information and ;disinformation' (Beck, 2000: xiv). Within this complex field of knowing and not-knowing, Beck argues that the new phase of modernity has created a radical shift in the ways in which modern societies organize themselves and their institutions; rather than the economic episteme (knowledge system) being structured around the production and distribution of 'goods', the new society is organized around the production and distribution of 'bads'—that is, the negative effects of globalization. This new mode of production contravenes the capacity of the nation-state and state-based governments to control and steer the economy and their embedded institutions. Thus, it is the very fact that societies have created security-controlling institutions which gives rise to the pervasive sense of danger.

Globalization, in fact, contributes to the multiplication of risk factors and the interdependence of global scale insecurities around military conflict, climate change or economic crisis. What becomes increasingly clear, particularly through the lens of the trans-national media, is that state-based governments can no longer (if ever) 'control the uncontrollable'; for Beck, the most revolutionary aspect of this new 'anomie' is the capacity of the mass media to 'stage' the world and create globally constituted perceptions of risk (Beck, 2008). Such views are shared by other sociologists, who describe globalization variously as 'savage' (Nairn and James, 2005), 'chaos' (McNair, 2006), 'mythic' (Hafez, 2007) or the 'globalization of nothing' (Ritzer, 2003).

Indeed, Beck's consternation about crumbling social knowledge and platforms of critique is shared by numerous scholars, including those neo-Baudrillardians who lament 'the acceleration of just about everything' (Gleick, 2004). To this end, scholars like Simon Cottle confirm Beck's perspective of globalization, arguing that the benefits and possibilities of trans-national modes of governance and cultural exchange are shadowed by the exponential expansion of negative consequences and a media generated insecurity that insists on misinformation over the interests of global citizens. Translating these negative consequences as 'crisis', Cottle claims that 'Global crises are an integral part of the global age, its dark side' (Cottle, 2009: 24).

Limitations of Beck's approach

Both Beck and Cottle have made a significant contribution to the study of crisis and risk in a globalizing society. However, Cottle's approach disaggregates social knowledge from the world of action. Cottle's focus on media reporting and the possibilities for 'accurate' representation fundamentally distort the mechanisms by which humans know their world and engage in the cultural dynamic of meaning-making. This approach to crisis also conceives of the media as merely a conduit for the distribution of elite interests, untruths and ideologies, which is a significant underestimation of the complexities by which the media, as a set of relationships, contributes to social knowledge. Like many other journalism scholars, Cottle confirms a fourth estate model, which is set within the simple truth-untruth dichotomy. From the perspective of my own studies, this dichotomy merely bookends the range and variability of media discourses and the means by which information is transferred as knowledge—that is, where the accumulated matters of the world are refurbished through human consciousness and desires. As already noted, the focus on a fourth estate model of news reporting limits our understanding of narrative formations and the complexion and complexity of the global mediasphere.

Beyond this, Ulrich Beck's 'risk' and 'global risk' thesis has gained considerable popularity, particularly as it offers a relatively straightforward explanation for the decline in Left and Right politics and the ascent of the neo-liberalist economic paradigm. The general fallibility of this approach, however, rests upon the idea that everything, including all knowledge, is compounded and conflated by unintended consequences or risk. While working from an entirely different theoretical and disciplinary base, Beck appears to arrive at a Baudrillardian conclusion that all things in the world are largely uncontrollable. Even the state and governments have lost control of the economy, and with the perpetual shifts in meaning and the circulatory conditions of insecurity and reflexivity, there seems little hope for the species and the planet. For Beck, and numerous other theorists of globalization, including Cottle, the only hope rests with the utopian prayer of cosmopolitan world governance—an effective reinvigoration of the Enlightenment solutions of state-based democracy.

For all its value, there are significant problems with Beck's notion of unintended consequences. The idea that governments can no longer 'control the uncontrollable' is, of course, a clever but somewhat vacuous declamation. The suggestion is that governments and various forms of social management are no longer feasible since everything is a contingency of an aleatory disorder which is hurtling us towards a social and environmental abyss. Leaving aside the very obvious empirical evidence about governmental power and the pervasiveness of governmental and managerial systems in contemporary societies, we might nevertheless locate Beck's vision within the broader narrative history of Holocene apocalypse—the same 'end of the world' narratives that pervade religious, scientific and fictional discourses throughout agricultural history. Beck's vision, however, is divined as a disinterested account of contemporary social politics and the ways in which the world is fragmenting through the exercise of neo-liberalist economics and its consumerist ethos.

Ultimately, Beck argues, this economic excess and the collapse of political critique are accidents of globalization, unintended consequences that are generated through the processes of modernization. In many respects, this framework parenthesizes a cultural politics that is replete with intentionality and the process by which individuals and groups seek to assert themselves and their interests over others. In effect, Beck's reading parenthesizes the vast history of language wars, violence and hierarchical systems which determine the processes of exclusion and inclusion, enforced through the transfer of displeasure. That is, the notion of unintended consequences subsumes the displeasures of others within a gradient of dangerous desires. Beck's proclamation of social chaos not only neutralizes the agency of powerful human groups, it also negates the agency or 'expressivities' of resistant and reformative agents who operate within a context of language wars, crisis and social change. As noted in the earlier discussions of this chapter, the Holocene is characterized by a perpetuity of innovation, including political innovations generated through resistance and the active pursuit of desires that transgress a given political hegemony or ideological orthodoxy. For Beck and many others who have focused narrowly on the modern/premodern dichotomy, the human volition to surplus value, self-interest, hierarchy and militarism can only ever be an unfortunate accident of history (see Badiou, 2005).

Transformation, in fact, is catalysed through distinctive assertions of interest and the attempt to realign existing conditions, particularly as they are exercised around prevailing hierarchical institutions. While these changes may be fortified through unexpected inputs, they are not the predicate of unintended consequences, nor miraculous 'events', as Alain Badiou (2005) has described it. They are rather due to an alignment of desires, which necessarily produce contention and effects. Beck's emphasis on the overarching omnipotence of the neo-liberal orthodoxy *as* globalization seriously limits the force and possibilities— the positive consequences—of crisis and change. That is, Beck and many others who have taken an interest in 'crisis' seem not to appreciate the ways in which culture and politics connect human desire through the precarious interface of pleasure and displeasure.

Jacques Lacan: desire at the pleasure-displeasure interface

Thus, the consumer society, risk society and fourth estate model of the media, the news media in particular, seriously underestimates the force and significance of pleasure in the formation of the global mediasphere. Indeed, a political critique which views pleasure as either irrelevant or frivolous misconstrues the role of pleasure as a fundamental human driver (Rojek, 2009). Jacques Lacan provides, perhaps, the most well-developed theory of this pleasure-displeasure nexus. While Lacan's theories were developed essentially as a framework for psychoanalytic therapy, his reworking of Freud's theories of desire and death nevertheless present a valuable pathway for our understanding of the relationship between crisis conditions and crisis consciousness. In particular, Lacan's interest in the ways in which consciousness is formed in language provides a valuable insight into the ways in which the underlying conditions of our animality—in particular our fears and desires—are expressed through the transformative engagements between humans' unconscious (pre-language) and conscious (in language) state of being.

As many of his contemporary critics noted, Freud had considerable trouble explaining the pleasure-death principle, and especially the mechanisms by which humans are motivated by 'death' rather than 'life' (see Ragland, 1995). Lacan's reappraisal of the principles, however, transferred the death driver into a more elaborate theory of *jouissance* or 'pleasure excess'. For Lacan, the experience of *jouissance* rendered the subject incapable of releasing him or herself from a desire that had evolved as 'displeasure': thus, for example, the abandoned lover cannot release himself from the object of his desire. Lacan (1977, 1998) argues, in fact, that the subject has no clear substance at all, being the predicate of language rules and the historical object of the condition and actions of desire. Following Freud, Lacan claims that there are three major and overlapping conditions that define the human psyche: the Real, the Imaginary and the Symbolic Order. While using a range of concepts to describe these conditions, Lacan outlines the three major categories in terms of a division between the Ego (the imaginary state of integrated being) and the subject (the self that is entirely a contingency of language). As we will explore, this division is important for Lacan, as it illustrates a substantial divide in the human psyche between the ways in which an individual imagines him or her self (the fantasy of being integrated and whole), and the ways in which the individual actually functions within the context of language and other people (the Other).

For Lacan, it is only as an infant in the condition of 'the Real' that an individual can be truly integrated or 'natural'. When an individual is in the state of sense-based infancy, needs are absolute and unconditioned by the complexity of language and linguistically formed fantasy. While this entrance into language forever removes us from the Real, creating the condition of its loss ('lack' or 'absence'), the Real nevertheless continues to exert a powerful influence over us since it is the reference by which all life proceeds and returns. It is, for example, the ever-present reminder of our materiality and hence the fulcrum that divides life and death. That is, as we move into the experiences of language, sexual maturity and adulthood, the Real remains a spectral presence in our psyche, both teasing and tormenting us with the knowledge that we have lost that wholeness, that fullness of our material being: it is this reminder of our materiality that is also a reminder of our mortality so the Real is both pleasing and horrifying.

In this sense, the Real lays the foundations for the fundamental contradictions that characterize and plague human experience and the
human psyche. The fullness of the Real provides for us a sense of completeness, but also the deep sense of loss as the individual moves into the
more complex world of language. Beyond this, Lacan also sees the Real
as the embryo and essence of *jouissance*, a state of bliss which exceeds
prohibition and the constraints of language. This is not just the form
of pleasure that exists within the frame of social sanction and linguistic appellation; it is rather a sensate condition that cannot be described
in language. In a series of seminars presented between 1959 and 1960,
'The ethics of psychoanalysis', Lacan argued that *jouissance* transcends
the socially inscribed prohibitions by which an individual is compelled
to limit his or her pleasure in order to maintain the social order. According to Lacan this excess of pleasure leads not to more pleasure but a
condition of confluence where pleasure and pain become indistinguishable. The subject, in fact, is left in a state of suffering by which she or he
is re-engaged with the condition of the Real. The subject's desires, that
is, exceed any capacity for satisfaction.

The Real, therefore, as a complete state of being, can only ever be
ephemeral for adults who must otherwise live their lives within the aegis
and complex ordering of language. Between the Real and this Symbolic
Order, however, an individual also experiences the condition called the
Imaginary Order. The Imaginary, in fact, marks the transition of the
individual from pure 'needs' to what Lacan calls the state of 'demand'.
Unlike needs, which can be met, Lacan's notion of demand suggests that
this dimension of the human experience is ongoing, self-centred and
can never, ultimately, be satisfied. As the transition condition between
the Real and the Symbolic, the Imaginary is a state by which a child
recognizes that she or he is not a part of the mother's body, but is a
separate entity to all other objects. The Imaginary facilitates the emergence of a fantasy of self or Ego, which is formed out of a complex mix
of a deep sense of separation, narcissism and anxiety. This sense of lack,
which is at the core of the Imaginary, remains significant throughout an
individual's life, even though it is precipitated in terms of the psycho-
sexual developmental stage called the 'mirror-phase'. Thus, a child looks
into a mirror and imagines that she or he is looking at a complete and
integrated subject; in fact, she or he 'mis-recognizes' the figure in the
mirror and ultimately the imagined self in order to compensate for the
loss of nature and completeness. This process of self-supplementation or
fantasy of oneself is facilitated by the presence of 'others' or 'otherness'
by which an individual absorbs the language, style, look, products and

practices of other social beings. As we will discuss below, it is a significant part of a consumer economy and the mechanisms of mediated and popular culture.

In this way, the Imaginary Order, which is formed around fantasy and the trauma of loss, becomes immersed in the Symbolic Order, which Lacan regards as the big Other of language and social regulation. In a sense, we might see the Imaginary and the Symbolic as two sides of the same condition, as they both contribute to the stimulation of human desire which is in perpetual tension with the materiality and pre-lingual fortitude of the Real. Thus, for Lacan, desire and Eros are not expressions of physical or natural expression; rather, desire is propitiated through fantasy and organized through the regulatory and symbolic power of the big Other—law, ritual, imagery, narratives, practices and hierarchies that are created and imposed by others. Even our unconscious, including our unconscious desires, cannot be regarded as our own since everything is bound up with a fantasy of reality that is ultimately externally bound to culture and cultural ideologies. The ultimate failure of desire to accomplish and complete the self in full contact with the Real indicates that the objective of fantasy and desire is not completion at all: it is rather to reproduce itself in the perpetual tension between Imaginary, Symbolic and the Real. It is in this state of openness that individuals remain set within the conjunction of trauma and pleasure, the condition that Lacan and others regard as the ontological imperative of human existence.

Lacan and culture

Lacan's theories have been adapted in many ways and for many different models of cultural analysis. Roland Barthes, Michel de Certeau, Deleuze and Guatarri, Alain Badiou and Slavoj Zizek have all adapted Lacanian concepts in order to explain the cultural politics of desire and its social expression. While these adaptations are all nuanced and distinct, they share an interest in the ways in which desire, pleasure and suffering are interconnected. In particular, they recognize that an excess of desire necessarily endangers the effects of pleasure: and that *jouissance* may express itself socially and culturally, as well as individually. As already noted in our discussion of the media, Jean Baudrillard has integrated this idea into a general theory of contemporary culture. In *Symbolic Exchange and Death* (1993) and *Seduction* (1991), Baudrillard argues that the social aggregation of desire has significantly changed the structure and character of the modern capitalist economy.[2] According to Baudrillard, the economic system that is based on the exchange of goods and services has become entirely transformed as a system of transmuted desire and 'symbolic' exchange. Through a complicated transferral, human agents redirect their libido from other humans into symbolically conflated media images. Desire for sex, in other words, is reconferred as desire for the symbolic layering of goods and services. However, as this desire can never be satisfied, the whole of the economic exchange system becomes a circulatory process of libidinal dissatisfaction: the symbols and images are transformed as 'simulacra', an 'imitation of an imitation', which can only refer to itself and not to the products and real world it formerly represented. The proliferation of signs and simulacra in an ever-expanding media environment has largely transformed the human psyche such that the symbolic is now regarded as an unfolding and unyielding hyperreality. While the differences between Baudrillard and Lacan have been well canvassed (see Mahoney, 2009), the confluence of perspective remains significant.

> Lacan is right: Language does not convey meaning. It stands in place of meaning. But the effects produced are not effects of structure, but seduction effects. Not a law which regulates the play of signifiers, but a rule which ordains the play of appearances.
>
> (Baudrillard, 1990: 6)

This 'play of appearances' or 'hyperreality' suggests that the political, semiotic and cultural particulates and patterns that contribute to the formation of meaning are washed into a general monad of meaninglessness and representational absence. Baudrillard's pessimistic vision, nevertheless, alerts us to the processes by which libido and desire become integrated into the capitalist consumer economy through the power of generalized mediation. For Baudrillard, there is no meaning beyond this alignment of simulacra, and the surrender of sex and seduction to the force of infinite exposure. Important as it is, this perspective dilutes the characteristics of meaning-making and desire, and the ways in which social hierarchy continues to marshal mediation through a complex set of cultural systems we might call *mediatocracy*—that is, the hegemonic ordering of the symbolic.

As Slavoj Zizek (see Zizek, 2006) frequently reminds us, however, the Symbolic Order is not, and can never be, a complete coverage; the gaps and absences that lie across and through the Symbolic Order, therefore, leave space for various forms of human challenge and psycho-cultural transformation. This is precisely why cultures are dynamic and complex, particularly through the evolution of the agrarian systems into the present. Lacan explains that the Imaginary connects the Real and the Symbolic Order through a complex association of fantasy. The desire for the fulfilment and completion of the self may be constituted around libido in Lacan's scheme, but the drive to pleasure is more generally articulated through a fantasy of human bonds, love, inclusion and an infinitely unfolding, yet ultimately insatiable, demand for something other than the self. The Imaginary, therefore, works towards and against the order that is formed around language (the Symbolic) because this order can never be complete and is as much the expression of pleasure as displeasure. Conceiving of this process in broader social and cultural terms, the fantasy of completeness is always a contingency of the 'language' or Symbolic Order that is generated through the media: the media gives us a sense of order and satisfaction, as it stimulates our desires and provides for us a fantasy of completeness; simultaneously, however, the media is deftly shifting our perceptions as the completeness we imagine is simply an appearance, a representation of something that seems to be present but which is actually absent. Ultimately, therefore, the media is both a source of pleasure and displeasure (*jouissance*) as its systems of knowledge, as Martin Heidegger warned, can never escape this oscillation, being both real or noumenal, and infinitely deceptive.[3]

Given the fundamental nature of these drivers, it is not surprising that the amplification that is mobilized through modern mediation generates equally complex, and frequently contradictory, epistemological systems. These systems, however, are not politically neutral but constitute a series of cultural processes that form perpetually around language wars that are fought over a hierarchical terrain of inclusion and pleasure—exclusion and displeasure. This terrain is neither entirely symbolic, nor entirely material; rather it is the conflated zone of conditions and consciousness, a zone in which the Symbolic Order seeks to complete itself but where alternative cultural forces work the gaps and fissures in order to realign their effects. Within this terrain—that space I am abbreviating as the mediasphere—the play of appearances is riven by an insidious disposition to fear and violence, dispositions that become institutionalized through the schematic differentiation of groups and individuals. Nor indeed are these hierarchies benign or accidental; they are inscribed in the survival systems that are themselves constituted around an agrarianist foundation by which demands and desires are infinite, but resources are not. They are, that is, inscribed in the war of language and the systems of militarization that continue to threaten pleasure with displeasure, as they subject specific human groups to privation and suffering, and imperative of the excesses articulated by others.

From excess to crisis in the globalizing mediasphere

The preceding discussion can be summarized in the following terms.

1. Contemporary crisis conditions and crisis consciousness have deep genealogical roots reaching back to the end of the Pleistocene and the emergence of agrarianism. Through this genealogy, a pervasive cultural dynamic of change and innovation has contributed to the emergence of new and increasingly complex systems of communication, language and knowledge. These systems have amplified human dispositions of desire and fear, drawing them together through the interface of crisis conditions and crisis consciousness.
2. Lacan adds to this historical analysis, arguing that humans are motivated by desire, but this desire is fundamentally incapable of being satisfied—first, because it is founded on loss, fear and a fantasy of self; second, because the amorphousness of this desire expresses and transforms itself as a desire for other individuals, products and symbols, all of which exist outside the self, and third, because the acquisition of pleasure, which is founded on a fantasy of pleasure and a symbolic order that perpetually asserts itself over the self, inevitably tilts the subject towards excess and displeasure (*jouissance*).
3. The pleasure that exceeds prohibition and returns the individual to a full confrontation of the Real (sensate animality that exists outside language) will always be confronting and displeasurable, as it exposes us to the limits of our material and mortal self—our death and the loss upon which our fundamental being is constructed.
4. At this point, our historical analysis and Lacan's psychoanalytic model converge around the cultural politics of crisis. While Lacan was interested in defining the underlying pattern of human desire and the experience of pleasure/displeasure, cultural theory applies these ideas to the study of social organization and the ways in which meaning and power are formed: that is, through the formation of language wars.
5. In particular, this underlying pattern of human animality—desire for pleasure, fear of loss and *jouissance* through excess—is amplified through the contemporary media. The processes of mediation and the mediasphere become the meeting place for the self and others. It is where the Imaginary (fantasy and the amorphousness of

desire) assembles itself and encounters the orderly imposition of concentrated power (ideology, coercion). This engagement between the
Imaginary and the orderly volition of power and language exposes
social groups to the possibilities of crisis, change and creative innovations. Crisis and transformation, therefore, are of themselves neither
necessarily good nor necessarily bad. Rather, these transformations
are situated within the interests of particular social groups and their
claims to pleasure and province of knowledge.

The consonance between Lacan's psychoanalysis and our more general cultural theory of crisis is formed around this interconnectedness
of desire-fear, and pleasure-displeasure. Inevitably, the question that is
often asked of Lacanian analysis has relevance for our own theory of
crisis: at what point does pleasure exceed itself to form this amorphous
state of displeasure? Lacan's response is simple enough: the line of excess
occurs as the subject pursues pleasure beyond the prohibitions established by the Symbolic Order. This pursuit inevitably exposes the fantasy
of wholeness that drives the pursuit, and the 'dissatisfaction' that is
inscribed in desire reveals itself. In our more general cultural theory the
notion of 'excess' actually is implicated in the experience of pleasure
since it is the shadow of pleasure's own finitude: that is, in the ending
of the pleasure experience.

   This finitude is, of course, perpetually obscured by the fantasies that
propel desire. In the context of an economy of pleasure, in particular, the pursuit of surplus value leads inevitably to the condition of
excess where displeasure is formed through the outbreak of language
wars. This means that excess emerges through the pursuit of a surplus
value that is conceived, like desire, as self-generating and necessarily
infinite, even though the physical resources that support economy and
culture are not. Indeed, the contradiction between infinite desire and
material-ecological finitude is marked through the allegorical exploration of excess, most spectacularly in end of the world narratives and
religious-ethical cosmologies. Excess, therefore, is not simply calculable
or set within a specific discursive framework. Rather, excess exposes itself
in the underlying condition of our fantasies and desires—through the
pursuit of products and pleasures beyond any purpose or constraint that
is not simply an expression of its own self-validating volition, *desirer pour
desirer*. Displeasure, that is, emerges out of the cauldron of demands that
pursue surplus that is indistinguishable from the damage it creates. And
even though we may try perpetually to annul this displeasure, through

the regeneration of our desires or its transferral to others, it nevertheless awakens us to the raw and unrelenting light of our fantasies and the morbid fact of its sepulchral finitude.

The theme of excess is a prevalent dramatic driver in Holocene religious mythology, narrative and ethical philosophy. From Aristotle's 'fatal flaw' thesis to the political excesses of Macbeth and the irrevocable imagining of Jay Gatsby, fictional narratives have been replete with protagonists and antagonists who dared too much. Under this 'extremity of the skies', characters like Joseph Conrad's Marlow have contemplated the desires that lead to calamity and ultimately annihilation. Marlow, in his catatonic ruminations despairs of our 'civilization' with 'a policeman on every corner' and our well-rehearsed 'monkey tricks'. For Marlow it is only in the extreme pursuit of our desires, personified in the character of Kurtz, that our true humanity is revealed. The presence of European civilization in the heart of the African darkness exposes us to the naked and unremitting fact of our being: the pretty rags of our civilization are simply cast away 'by the first good shake'. Yet in the horror of this truth, this extreme, it is only 'the idea' that is redemptive.

> The conquering of the earth, which mostly means taking it away from those who have a different complexion or slightly flatter nose than ourselves, is not a pretty thing when you look at it too much. What redeems it is only the idea. An idea at the back of it; not a sentimental pretence but an idea. An unselfish belief in the idea—something you can set up. and bow down before and offer a sacrifice to.
>
> (Conrad: 1969: 9)

While Marlow is contemplating this 'conquering of the earth' specifically in terms of the European colonization and the spread of industrial modernism, we are able to extend the thinking in terms of the more general spread of the Holocene crisis and its various modes of innovative adaptation. In this sense, 'the conquest' continues through globalization and the broad reach of the mediasphere. Francis Ford Coppola's re-rendering of Conrad's novel in *Apocalypse Now!* (1979) represents the genealogical density of this crisis and the meagre prayer that sustains our hope. Crisis thus becomes the metaphor for the ongoing and radical rupture that is associated with this conquest and its broad transformative encapsulation of the Earth, along with its anthropogenic and ecological systems.

Crisis model

Figure 1.1 provides a summary of the formation of crisis conditions. The first column refers to the continuities of being human, underlying conditions which are shared by most individuals. The second column represents the social and cultural expression of these continuities. The double arrow connecting these two columns refers to various forms of mediation, including personal and technological channels. The arrow indicates that this transference is two-way, leading from the personal to the cultural and vice versa. In many respects, these columns represent the processes by which culture itself is formed (Lewis, 2008); they emphasize the dynamics of meaning-formation in terms of power and the clustering of meanings through various forms of social hierarchy and ideology.

The second column also makes clear that these patterns are always a contingency of cultural politics and tensions constituted as language

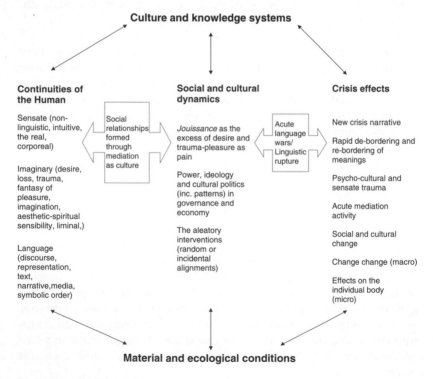

Figure 1.1   Crisis model.

wars; these tensions are themselves formed in terms of the pleasure-pain nexus which is a fundamental driver in human personal and collective expressivities. The patterns are also subject to the destabilizing effects of aleatory interventions. When the instability of these patterns and language wars becomes acute, linguistic rupture occurs in the form of crisis. And as noted, these ruptures will be transferred through a second pathway into specific effects: these effects will return in various ways through a new crisis narrative to effect a new set of cultural patterns. At the outer rim of these columns are two defining signifiers of crisis and crisis conditions: the ecological—material context—and the cultural knowledge systems that link individuals and groups to their ecology. These linkages are constituted over space and time. These transformations are neither of themselves good nor bad. In most cases, however, crisis involves some level of damage and suffering associated with the pleasure-displeasure nexus.

2
Grand Fraud: New Capitalism, Fantasy and Financial Crisis

> Now, as there are many actions, arts, and sciences, their ends also are many; the end of the medical art is health, that of shipbuilding a vessel, that of strategy victory, that of economics wealth.
>
> Aristotle, *Nicomachean Ethics, Book 1* (350 BC)

> Those who charge usury are in the same position as those controlled by the devil's influence. This is because they claim that usury is the same as commerce. However, GOD permits commerce, and prohibits usury. Thus, whoever heeds this commandment from his Lord, and refrains from usury, he may keep his past earnings, and his judgment rests with GOD. As for those who persist in usury, they incur Hell, wherein they abide forever.
>
> *The Qu'ran* (2: 275)

The swallowing monster

There is a recurring motif in African Bantu mythology. At around 500 AD the Bantu had established themselves as the dominant ethnic group in much of the coast-to-coast regions of southern Africa. Through the development of iron technology and a range of economic and cultural innovations associated with agriculture, the Bantu were undergoing significant economic and cultural transformation. Indeed, by 500 AD the Bantu of West Africa had established several large urban centres, including Djenne-Djeno which, with a population of 20,000 people, was larger than most European townships at the time. As we noted in Chapter 1, the development of these sorts of major agricultural and urban civilizations was associated with various kinds of social, economic and cultural rupture—crises that demanded significant cosmological, narrative and political adaptation.

The convergence of these conditions contributed to the formation of new knowledge systems by which the Bantu sought to secure their survival and lifestyles. As Aristotle notes in his writings on economy and ethics, these survival processes were layered by what he calls 'the good life'—an accretion of ethics and harmonious social existence. In the pursuit of wealth or 'surplus value', however, the Bantu like all other agricultural civilizations became caught within the complex social modalities of hierarchy and its strategic deployment of inclusion and exclusion. Thus, the good life and social harmony were contingencies of other economic and social-cultural mechanisms, particularly as different clans and social units sought to maximize their own pleasures by the transferral of displeasure to others.

As we also noted in Chapter 1, this volition towards the infinite pursuit of surplus value to the exclusion of others leads inevitably to the generation of 'excess' and ultimately the *jouissance* that circulates through the pleasure-displeasure interface. Michael Sendel (1998, 2009) makes this very point in his discussion of the recent Global Financial Crisis (GFC); according to Sendel, economic self-interest can never be disaggregated from greed or excess since both are the prerequisite of a market capitalism which perpetually defers issues of ethics or collective responsibility. While we will return later in the chapter to discuss market triumphalism and the GFC, Sendel's comments might equally apply to an agrarian mercantile society where excess only reveals itself in terms of these generated displeasures and the shadow that they cast through various forms of cultural anxiety, including visions of the apocalypse. Thus, 'excess' becomes the Grand Other of surplus—that dangerous condition by which a human group populates, fights or consumes itself out of existence. Like the agrarian Abrahamite myths of the Eastern Mediterranean, many of the Bantu narratives are replete with these same anxieties about excess and social destruction.

Specifically, Bantu mythology tells of a deadly 'swallowing monster' who raids and pillages villages, devouring everything in its path—crops, livestock and humans. While there may be many different interpretations of the swallowing monster motif, it is very clear that the monster has an allegorical function, drawing together many of the desires, anxieties and ethical propositions that beset agricultural cultures. It isn't surprising, therefore, that the motif of the swallowing monster is present in many early agrarian religious and mythic narratives. In the Bantu story, a swallowing monster called Khodumodumo is marauding across the countryside, destroying villages and eating all the livestock and people he can find. In a particular part of the region, Khodumodumo enters a narrow mountain pass and begins to attack the people who live in a cluster of villages on the fertile valley floor. Once inside the closed valley, Khodumodumo grows larger and larger as he attacks and devours goats, dogs, cattle and people. A pregnant woman is mesmerized by the horror. She watches the men's iron-tipped spears shatter and twist as they strike the monster's hoary skin. Children, women and men are seized and dropped whole from Khodumodumo's claws into his distended and horrible gut. As Khodumodumo approaches the pregnant woman, she stumbles and falls into an ash heap, disappearing from the monster's view. Eventually, Khodumodumo has slaughtered all the people and other living creatures in the villages, and he turns to leave the valley through the narrow pass. Now, however, he is too bloated with food to exit, and his engorged frame becomes trapped between the cliffs at the neck of the valley. Exhausted from his murderous violence and gorging, Khodumodumo lays down his enormous body and falls asleep in the warm, setting sun.

The pregnant woman, who had escaped the slaughter, sees the monster sleeping. She washes off the ash and lies down by the river where she gives birth to a son. Still terrified by the monster, the woman leaves the infant for a moment and climbs upon a wall to see whether the monster is still sleeping. When she returns to her baby, however, she finds a fully grown man in his place: 'Where is my son?' she asks, and the man tells her that he is indeed her son. The young man has powerful arms. He takes his slaughtered father's spears and sharpens them all through the night. As the sun is rising, the man goes to the pass and climbs across Khodumodumo's mountainous body. When he is near the monster's throat, the young warrior strikes his spear deep into the skin beneath Khodumodumo's ear. The monster wakes, screaming with pain. He tries to swallow the man, but the young warrior is too nimble and the monster is still trapped by his engorged body. The warrior tears his spears down Khodumodumo's body, opening a huge wound in his gut and releasing blood onto the valley floor. The monster struggles but the deep wounds finally drain him of life, allowing all the people he had devoured to slide out of his gut into the new day. The young man is then named chief of the village, and his bloodline will rule for evermore.

Modern monsters

As Claude Levi-Strauss informs us, such myths can be usefully understood in terms of a social group's attempts to resolve its own internal tensions and anxieties. And while there may be many interpretations of the swallowing monster myth, we can certainly recognize that the dramatic narrative is shaped by the dangers of excess and the need for control and social authority. As central figures in agricultural societies' lore and mythology, such monsters frequently represent the dangers associated with any form of excessive pleasure, particularly when it is linked to dangerous others and the illegitimate exercise of 'unnatural' power. In this sense, nature is realigned with human social sustainability and harmony in order to create a balance and clear lineage between god, nature and human society. Unlike the hunter-gatherer conceptions of nature and natural ancestry, agrarian societies like the Bantu create a cosmological order in which humans seek to control nature through the imagining and mimicry of god's will. Otherness and its grotesque rapacity—excess pleasure, consumption, violence—is conjured as the ultimate rupture to this natural order. However, this otherness is, as Lacan notes, simply a mirror and misrecognition of the self, which in this case means the settled and harmonious Bantu community. Otherness is not simply the interventions perpetrated by actual out-siders, or even an imaginary of these others: it is, also, the fear that someone or some group within the community's own ranks might pur-sue pleasures beyond the unspecified parameters of value and their intrinsic hierarchical order. This would simply be unnatural. Indeed, the Bantu story's happy ending suggests that a resolution to the crisis has been accomplished by the installation of a line of authority that is miraculous, (and hence godly), heroic and natural. This naturalness is intensified, like the Christian myth, of an immaculate birth which transports humankind beyond the apocalypse into a new and more wonderful period of authority and law. Thus, the rebirth of the village and the people is symbolic of a new history, a new beginning in which a new cosmologically ordained lineage can rightfully impose itself over the excesses associated with external threat and internal vulnerabil-ity. The 'end of the world' vision that the story presents is reconciled through this renewal of nature and natural authority.

The swallowing monster motif appears in innumerable other agrar-ian cultures, including the mythologies of Native North Americans (Kamiah monster), Pacific Islanders (Pouahaokai), Abrahamic cultures (Jonah and God's swallowing fish), the Chinese (the dragon), and Anglo-Saxon people (Grendel in *Beowulf*). Each of these stories warns against the corruption of nature and the pursuit of desires that are 'unnatu-ral', disruptive, unethical or simply unsustainable. The stories are also embedded in an ideology that naturalizes a particular source of power, either through the authority of god, familial lineage or the prowess of the outstanding male (the *extra*man, as Nietzsche calls it). It is this authority, this social ordering, that ensures against excess and the over-reach of human desires. In the end, authority and social stability are restored through legitimate power and the legitimate restoration of authority and orderly value accumulation (wealth).

Very clearly, and as we noted in the previous chapter, these new knowledge systems associated with agriculture provide a basis for divinely sanctioned modes of human governance, the ascension of the individual within an hierarchical mass, militarism and the ideol-ogy of sovereign power. In the Bantu and other swallowing monster stories, these hierarchical and militarist systems, which are designed to control human excess, are frequently woven through sexual narra-tives by which bodies are gendered and fortified through desire and kinship. Against the emergence of mass populations, individualist and masculine heroism is thus constituted as a source of power and symbolic order; femininity appears as the conduit of masculine ascension and the normative pre-eminence of male desire. In this way, sex, property and violence are welded through narratives of fear and desire which often mobilize human innovation at the precipice of personal and commu-nity annihilation. In the Anglo-Saxon story of *Beowulf,* the swallowing monster Grendel is borne out of the monstrous sexuality of his dragon mother through the lineage of the Abrahamic religious figure of Cain. In the *Beowulf* manuscript, the monster's mother is depicted as living beneath a lake, a motif which Freudians regard as archetypically female. And certainly, in the 2007 film version of the legend (*Beowulf,* Robert Zemeckis, 2007), the lake dragon is steeped in sexual mystique and a potency that scholars of the original text believed was the iteration of virginal purity and the first woman (see Nitzsche, 1990).

Thus, the sexual intensity and apocalyptic dangers associated with female otherness and sexual potency are subdued within the power of ordained male authority. These motifs have morphed somewhat and been reformulated through the economic and cultural innovations of industrialism, the Enlightenment and the rise of new knowledge sys-tems. Even so, in films like *Jaws* (Steven Spielberg, 1975) the motif of the swallowing monster is revivified through familiar anxieties over the pursuit of pleasure, wealth and legitimate (male) authority. In this case, the swallowing monster is a giant-sized great white shark which terror-izes a small tourist resort island in New England. The 'rogue' shark's attacks represent the random but pervasive power of nature to impose itself over human order and the social pursuit of pleasure. Significantly, the attack is also directed at the tourism industry and leisure (Rojek,

2009) which are the symbolic acme of America's cultural pre-eminence in the global economy of pleasure. From the security of wealth and power, these pleasure-seekers are suddenly cast back into the shadow of threat, a shadow which lurks perpetually in the darker spaces of their consciousness.

And indeed, Spielberg's art recognizes this very point. The giant shark is appended by a sense of insidious evil which threatens the harmony, order and livelihood of the town. In this way, the random attacks of nature expose the Aristotelian dualism that distinguishes the mere survival of beings (economy) from the ethically ennobled condition of 'the good life'. Thus, while the town mayor attempts to suppress the shark attack story to avoid disrupting the town's economy of pleasure, the police chief, Mike Brody, seeks to redeem the people through an heroic act of eradication. The shark, in this sense, becomes appended by the human imagining of good and evil; its status as nature resonates, like Herman Melville's Moby Dick, with Biblical symbology. Indeed, the spectral power of the shark fortified by the confused and amplified responses of the townspeople who, like the people of Nineveh in the Book of Jonah, are confounded by imaginings of the shark's evil and apocalyptic intent. Spielberg generates this apocalyptic force through the libidinal imagery of bare bodies and the sexual freedoms that symbolize the pleasure economy. Indeed, the shark's first victim appears like a sacrificial virgin, bathing naked in the water, her youthful body enlivened by alcohol, sensuality and the prospects of sexual ecstasy.

The town and all its libidinal and materialist calumny is restored to order by the 'only rational person on this island'. Significantly, the heroic police chief, Mike Brody, kills the shark and eliminates the threat on American Independence Day, confirming the ideological potency of American culture and the primacy of the pleasure economy. Even so, the anxieties and fears that drive the film's dramatic tensions are not entirely resolved, as audiences are lured back to the cinema in a series of increasingly extravagant accounts of the same conflux of pleasures and dangers. Spielberg's *Jaws* series, in fact, reminds us that the threat of nature is as much a manifestation of our own intrinsic nature as it is the spectre of external threat. While we seek perpetually to secure and distance ourselves from the random imposition of natural conditions, the swallowing monster might simply reveal itself as the destructive force of excess and the illegitimate (non-ethical) exercise of social power.

Mike Brody is the agent of reason and a technological fortitude that saves the island people and their economy of pleasure: this rational power imposes itself over the excesses of the island's pleasure practices and industry. Clearly, however, the fear that the *Jaws* films elicits in its audiences has a deep lineage in the Holocene agricultural cultures. In other swallowing monster films this fear expresses itself in cannibal anxieties by which excess is expressed as a kind of rapacious madness. Films like *Cannibal Holocaust* (Ruggero Deodato, 1980), *Children of the Corn* (Fritz Kiersch, 1984) and the Hannibal Lecter series (Micheal Mann, 1986; Jonathan Demme, 1991; Ridley Scott, 2001; Peter Webber, 2006) conjure this sense of an extreme human evil. This evil is formed within a sexual excess that expresses itself in the extremes of fleshly devourment—a metaphor that represents the extension of our desires into a fantasy of infinite power and pleasure. Along with the whole lineage of vampire movies that are again resurgent in the popular, Gothic imaginary, the cannibal films articulate the most basic anxiety about human 'appetite' and the essence of our deeper nature. Thus, while the American Film Industry voted Hannibal Lecter the 'most memorable villain in film history', the popular imagining of cannibals and vampires reflects a deeper cultural anxiety about the un-layering of our inner being, our animal being: exposed in the mediasphre, this intrinsic swallowing monster of our intrinsic nature confronts us and the means by which we propagate our civil selves and the imagining of the Aristotelian good life.

This contention between essential nature and a good life drives the dramatic force of more recent swallowing monster films like *Magalodon* (David Wroth, 2002). However, unlike *Jaws* or the cannibal films, the *Megalodon* monster is more clearly the effect of humans' own excessive practices and ecological interventions. This more recent incarnation of the swallowing monster, a perversion of a prehistoric shark species, has been created by human over-population and consumption practices that are directly associated with damage to natural life systems. Thus, a prehistoric shark called Carcharodon megalodon is released by the environmental delinquency of a major mining company that is seeking oil below the Earth's crust. In an allegory of excessive human interventions in nature, the film *Megalodon* interrogates the modern world's obsession with technological innovation and the exploitation of fossil fuels. Drilling deeper than any other oil rig in history, the oil rig Colossus ruptures the membrane that separates Holocene life systems from the subterranean Jurassic core. The rupture of the deep fault lines beneath the sea releases the giant Megalodon sharks, which have continued to exist in a sealed oceanic basin beneath the Earth's crust.

The allegorical force of the film not only exposes our deep anxieties about excessive economic exploitation of nature, it also betrays our fears about being both greater and less than nature—indeed, of being both part of nature, but ultimately outside nature (see Chapter 5). This double anxiety parallels the Frankenstein myth by which humans seek to perfect themselves as the pinnacle of nature, only to have these interventions return to destroy them. Mary Shelley's famous novel, *Dr Frankenstein,* along with its labyrinth of sci-fi and fantasy antecedents, however, also has its roots in agrarian mythologies, including the Abrahamic religions. Consider, for example, the story of Babel in which a community seeks ultimate wisdom and bliss through the construction of a tower that will take them to heaven. Nature, in the image of God, rejects this technological intervention in heaven, smashing the tower into pieces and sending humans scuttling across all corners of the Earth. The point here, and this theme is pursued in Alejandro González Iñárritu's filmic allusion to the Biblical story (*Babel,* 2006), is that human desire is never proportionate because humans have released themselves from their deep immersion in nature. Having removed themselves from the ontological base of their animality, that is, humans have surrounded themselves with other humans and a technological system constructed over their desire for power and pleasure. The swallowing monster represents the outbreak of these desires and their contingent fears: the fantasy of human conquest over the monster (their own monstrousness) is merely a validation of the symbolic order that grounds that desire in the social hierarchy.

Militarism and the evolution of global trading systems

As noted, swallowing monster narratives are pervasive across early and industrialized agrarian cultures. In many respects, they are part of a broader cultural dialogue, which inscribes imaginings of infinite pleasure and perpetual progress with a darker vision of excess and apocalyptic disaster. In most cases, salvation takes the form of an heroic order that is ordained by some greater good or miraculous being. The good life, as Aristotle conceives of it, is restored against the unravelling force of an internal or external rogue nature. This resolution, however, is never complete, and the good life perpetually evades our grasp as it so easily becomes confused within a volition of desire and the darkling spaces of excess and danger.

As we outlined in Chapter 1, this desire for pleasure—and fear of its loss—is articulated in the economic and social innovations associated with formation of surplus value. The production and control of this value, particularly as it becomes increasingly transformed as symbolic value, information and knowledge, contributed to the emergence of individualism, social hierarchy, power, trade and militarist modes of governance. While my argument has been that these innovations are entirely interdependent, many historians argue for the primacy of one or other of these changes in determining human progress and the rise of civilization. Kenneth Clark (1969), for example, in his canonical text, *Civilization*, argues that it is the refinement of the human mind, particularly as it is expressed in art and architecture, that separates advanced human societies from primitivism. The great civilizations, Clark maintains, are characterized by the wealth of their art and ideas, which are the supreme articulation of the human mind.

While not denying the importance of aesthetics and technology, many economic historians claim that it is the innovation of trade that provides the real impetus for human progress through agriculturalism to modern global capitalism. In their account of world economic growth, such historians correlate the expansion of trade with social improvements, including advances in urban infrastructure, the arts, public health, domestic comforts and nutrition. In his history of global trade, *A Splendid Exchange* (2008), William Bernstein argues that communities, nations and empires have always had to choose to 'trade, raid or protect'. The most successful civilizations, according to Bernstein, are those populous and urbanized social organizations that choose commerce and trade over militarized modes of theft. Citing Ancient Greece, the medieval Muslim societies of the Middle East and modern Holland, Bernstein notes that these communities were able to sustain large populations and a substantially affluent lifestyle through the aegis of trans-territorial trade. Through trading companies like the Dutch East Indies Company, for example, Holland generated considerable wealth for the imperial state while providing a diverse range of new products for the domestic market. The same, of course, would be said of the British Raj in India which imported a range of products into England, including pepper, spices, scents, textiles, gemstones and furnishings for the new urban dwellings of the rising British middle classes. Bernstein's analysis insists that social groups that adopted the 'raid' or 'protection' options could only expect ephemeral success, since the only true source of wealth in the modern economy was constituted around product value and commerce.

Bernstein's analysis, like numerous others, simply misrepresents the history of civilizational violence and the historical interdependence of military and social organization. Of course, 'raiding' is generally not a sustainable economic mode since it requires perpetual mobility and ongoing violence, which in turn limit community stability. However, it is very clear that all of the large and powerful Holocene urban cities and empires were sustained by internal and external military force. Indeed, the trading networks that spread across Europe, Asia and ultimately the world were defended by imperial militarism: the larger the empire, the larger and more powerful the military system that supported it. Moreover, while Bernstein seeks to heroize the entrepreneurial and individualist instincts of the small-scale merchant in history, his account underestimates the importance of empire itself in establishing trade networks. Even countries like Holland established a brutal regime of exploitation and colonial administration, which enabled the Dutch East Indies Company and its various appendages to conduct their work. Conveniently, Bernstein also overlooks the fact that the most profitably traded commodity for the East Indies Company during the eighteenth and nineteenth centuries was opium, a substance which implicated societal problems of addiction, as well as laying the foundations for today's global trade in illegal narcotics.

Even more telling, Bernstein's lionization seeks to remove trade and traders from the insidious practices of trade in munitions and human bodies. Continuing into the present, these highly profitable areas of trade were established through the aggregation of human populations and settlement, both of which are the predicate of trade and surplus value. The demand for cheap labour, human sacrifice, sexual enslavement, military personnel and entertainment encouraged most of the pre-industrial empires, along with several industrial empires, to engage in the trade of human bodies. While the idea of enslavement has lost favour with many industrialized societies, the hierarchical discrimination of traded labour value has not. Across all Holocene agrarian cultures, in fact, trade in labour is a critical part of the hierarchical system and the military framework by which human groups are governed and controlled. Very clearly, the civilizations that Bernstein praises constructed their wealth around the trade and control of labour, especially through the social management of female sexuality and reproductive capacities, as well as the physical strength of young men.

Bernstein's account of civilization and history is designed to disaggregate trade from its political and cultural context. According to Bernstein and other economic historians, trade is as much a moral project, as an economic benefit that draws all humankind towards development and an improved standard of living. This image of trade as a neutral and universally positive human pursuit, in fact, is deeply embedded in an ideological historical imagining that decontaminates commerce and its association with hierarchical, oppressive and violent social systems. Indeed, even if we distinguish between earlier agricultural civilizations and the rise of European liberal capitalism from the sixteenth century, we can see very clearly that the expansion of trade across the globe is fostered through a politics of oppression, exploitation and control. As noted above, the hierarchies become more complicated as the territories expand, but commerce is never neutral: it is intrinsically woven through the fabric of competition and the rise of purposeful elites (Plate 2.1).

Plate 2.1   The rise of Western European industrial trading systems as represented in the great Victorian trading houses on the River Thames in London.
Photograph by Jeff Lewis.

Thus, the desires and pleasures that accumulate around Europe's increasing wealth and power during the period of western globalization are inevitably and necessarily inscribed by the suffering of others—those 'others' upon whose bodies, labours, culture and territories this new wealth of the European middle classes is convened. Thus, while Adam Smith, John Stuart Mill and other British liberals commended the virtues of labour and self-fulfilment, the actual functioning of industrial trade created at least as many victims as victors.

Edward Said (1993) makes this point in his critique of Jane Austen's *Mansfield Park*. According to Said, Austen's novel is informed by a dialectical ordering of the world that privileges the liberation and social pleasures of the new English mercantile classes over the misery and humiliation of African slaves. Thus, the cultural and political liberation of Austen's middle-class characters, including her women, is simply a reordering of England's social elite: the middle-class merchants rising against the old landed aristocracy. Mansfield Park, the Antiguan plantation upon which the protagonists' liberation is founded, is also the silent spectre of abject human misery. Sitting in the background of the novel's social intrigue, the moral and ideological ambiguity of Mansfield's slave labour force is never interrogated.

We must first take stock of *Mansfield Park*'s prefigurations of a later English history as registered in fiction. The Bertrams' usable colony in *Mansfield Park* can be read as pointing forward to Charles Gould's San Tomé mine in *Nostromo*, or to the Wilcoxes' Imperial and West African Rubber company in Forster's *Howard's End*, or to any of these distant but convenient treasure spots in *Great Expectations*, Jean Rhys's *Wide Sargasso Sea, Heart of Darkness*—resources to be visited, talked about, described, or appreciated for domestic reasons, for local metropolitan benefit. If we think ahead to these other novels, Sir Thomas's Antigua readily acquires a slightly greater density than the discrete, reticent appearances it makes in the pages of *Mansfield Park*.

(Said, 1993: 112)

While Said's account of the western literary tradition and its assumptions about 'the Orient' has evolved as a canon for postcolonial studies, a number of critics have leapt to Austen's defence (for example, White, 2006; Warriq, 2007). According to these critiques, Said simply overstates the case and in doing so underestimates the significant contribution of authors like Jane Austen, E. M. Forster and Joseph Conrad to the evolution of western liberatory politics, which provide the foundation for universal human rights and decolonization.

In either case, Said's account of the world and its imperialist base directs our attention to a deeper ambiguity about the formation of global capitalism and the double entry matrix of pleasure and displeasure. In essence, the expansion of capitalist trade into the broader reaches of global territories is presaged by a complicated cultural imaginary that attaches itself to a fundamental human desire for pleasure. Said's point is simply that these pursuits are implicated in the transfer of displeasure, and that the hierarchical system that is assumed in the principles and practices of trade are intrinsically political.

Not surprisingly, civilizations and their militarized trading systems cannot define their own limits or conditions of excess. Industrial Europe's expansion into the powerful Asian empires like India and China replicates the imperial patterns that had dominated agricultural history, including the history of the east. Industrialization, which incorporated new ballistic systems, provided an exponential advantage for the expansion of westernist modes of economy and commerce across the globe (Johnson, 2005). While this new system was clearly advantageous for the elite social groups of Europe, the imposition of colonial rule in extraneous territories created a major crisis of culture, economy and governance for the conquered peoples. This was especially the case for pre-existing empires in the near and far east which had already established powerful governmental, urban and military systems. In most cases, in fact, colonial administrators imposed a European superstructure over the existing hierarchies. Members of the local elite would maintain their privilege and power if they subscribed to the colonist's will and performed their bidding.

In Indonesia, for example, the Dutch overlords appointed many members of the Indonesian elite into senior public roles. Sultanic and other aristocratic families were especially favoured in order to secure social stability and a sense of structured legitimacy. In Bali, for example, the Dutch administrators formalized the caste system, creating new laws about inter-caste marriage and the maintenance of social privilege (Lewis and Lewis, 2009). The aim of this formalization was to create an orderly system of social control and maintain the alignment of labour and taxes. Using the high caste officials as formal emissaries and tax collectors, the Dutch were able to deflect any forms of peasant or worker agitation through the local governance structures. This model, of course, was also used by the British in India where the Raj became tantamount to a new imperial overlord. The caste system, thereby, became embedded through a new form of global aristocracy that was managed and controlled by the interests of merchants and mercantilism.

In *Heart of Darkness* one of Joseph Conrad's primary narrator-characters, Marlow, speaks redemptively about 'the idea' behind colonialism. Without specifying, this idea is the notion of progression and moral enlightenment associated with civilization. Drawing humankind away from the brute superstition of 'darkness', civilization fortifies the idea of humanism, which we might conceive more generally as the more benign side of Social Darwinism. Conceived by philosophers like Herbert Spencer and developed more broadly after the publication of Darwin's *On the Origin of Species* (orig. 1859) and *The Ascent of Man, and Selection in Relation to Sex* (orig. 1871), Social Darwinism provided a moral base for imperial ambitions. Elaborated through British Utilitarianism and the idea that human self-interest is the most forceful reason for human co-operation and 'the good', the moral component of British colonial expansion convinced itself that trade would necessarily deliver moral and cultural progress to the primitive peoples of the world. As the 'fittest' civilization, Britain (and concessionally other European colonists) had an obligation, if not a divinely sanctioned right, to impose themselves and their knowledge systems on other parts of the world.

Thus, while Cortez and Pizarro had marched across the Americas behind the Christian Cross, the Moguls behind the sword of Mohammed, and Ashoka the sacred visage of Buddha, the British slaughtered their foe and plundered palaces under the mantra of Enlightenment, westernism and science. In the end, of course, it all meant the same thing: the export of displeasure for the import of pleasure. And in a way, this is precisely the point that is often missed in debates about Edward Said and his account of western cultural imperialism. In his vigorous attacks on European Enlightenment and reciprocal defence of its victims, Said inadvertently restored the dualism he sought to deconstruct (east-west divide); in so doing, Said critically parenthesized the ideological and human atrocities that shaped the great Asian empires (Lewis, 2008). In many respects, this is also the fallibility of many current-day apologists of those cultures that have become victim to the political and military interests of American-western economic and political domination. That is, the defenders of the non-western cultures and creeds are tempted to overstate the value and ideological integrity of the dominated groups.

Bernstein's account of the history of trade, in this context, seriously misreads the interdependence of culture, militarism and commerce. The ideological force of Bernstein's claim is grounded, of course, in the same utilitarian framework that supported westernist modes of globalization and which continue into the present, particularly under the banner of what has become popularly dubbed 'free market' or 'neo-liberal' economics. In this broader conceit, trade is the enabling system for a broader communalist structure as it connects people from vastly different social, ethnic and political realms. Again, this is the 'idea' about which Marlow speaks—the centre of a complicated knowledge system which draws humans into a dynamic cultural and community contiguity. Like Marx's dream of a proletariat world community, the imaginary of the capitalist ideal is a network of interacting parts, a system of shared understanding by which competition is the mere appendix of our more substantially grounded and mutual economic surplus and pleasure.

Symbolic trade and the new global economy

This utopian imaginary of global trade has become even more pronounced as tradable commodities have become more densely symbolized. As we noted in the previous chapter, this process of 'Symbolic Exchange' was fostered through the innovations associated with language, representation and the media. Thus, a product's capacity to attract value from a given market was enhanced by its perceived social value; the integration of this perceived social value through symbolization encouraged a higher price. More broadly, producers and traders recognized that symbols could themselves be conceived as products for market consumption. The most powerful of these consumable symbols included image-based entertainment, music, information, fashion, self-adornment and finance.

As we also noted in Chapter 1, a number of theorists have seen this mode of Symbolic Exchange as a critical definer in a new type of economy, one that is based on wants, images, libido and pleasure beyond basic needs. As the essence of consumer capitalism, this image-based economy rises in the early part of the twentieth century and ultimately eclipses the more bordered trading system that was based on an increasingly inefficient strategy of colonial conquest and state-based administration of extraneous territories. Thus, in seeking to increase trade volumes and surplus value, global economic elites have tended to create a greater porousness and ambiguity around national borders. During the course of the twentieth century, these free market elites have become less bound to the colonial model of empire and state, preferring instead to create their exchange without the encumbrance of government regulations or controls that might limit their capacity to access and exploit local resources, markets or labour. Decolonization, at this level, enabled many of these global-focused producers and traders to by-pass cumbersome governmental policies and bureaucracies which may be motivated by something other than profit. For global trade, in fact, government is only valuable when it fosters trade and provides military or other security systems when required.

This is particularly the case for the trade in symbols, images and information which move almost instantaneously across borders. Indeed, as the pleasure economy supplements and enhances the older trading systems of agricultural and industrial products, the cultural politics of trade also morphs, shifting from a colonial to a more subtle and pervasive system of hierarchy and discrimination. In this sense, the labour of bodies becomes more subtly enmeshed in processes of imagining and consumption, particularly through the mobilization of libido and youthful (especially female) sexuality. In this way, colonial structures give way to the following:

1. First, the engagement of cheap, lower skilled labour in poorer parts of the world and the concomitant rise in the global exchange of high skill labour. As Karl Marx outlined, capitalism seeks perpetually to reduce its manufacturing costs, and so globalization processes have enabled agricultural and industrial producers to create their goods in low cost areas of the world. At the same time, richer countries have sought to maximize their capital and skill base, leading to significant international competition for higher skilled and technical labour.
2. Second, the imperative to growth and the rise of media-based industries have contributed to the embedding of labour in the sexual power of consumption. Labour and consumption, therefore, converge around sexuality and desire, as youthful (especially female) bodies become the composite of design, product, promotion and sale. Sex, that is, becomes the weld of the commercial system.

In this latter instance, mass reproduction of the female image and the formation of the 'housewife' as a consuming agent created a new locus for sexual and economic gratification (Miller, 1995; Sassatelli, 2007). The libidinal effect of the female body, that is, became culturally intensified through the 'democratization' of consumption, and the centralization of the household as a consuming unit (Lewis, 2008; Humphery, 2010). Through this 'ecstasy of communication', Baudrillard sees desire as the primary economic driver.

Increasingly, all seduction, all manner of enticement – which is always a highly *ritualized* process – is effaced behind a *naturalized* sexual imperative, behind the immediate and imperative realization of desire. Our center of gravity has been displaced towards a libidinal economy concerned with only the naturalization of desire, a desire dedicated to drives, or to a machine-like functioning, but above all, to the imaginary of repression and liberation. Henceforth one no longer says: 'You have a soul and it must be saved', but: 'You have a sex, and you must put it to good use'. 'You have an unconscious, and you must let the id speak'. 'You have a libido and you must expend it'....

(Baudrillard, 1990: 38)

Like Lacan, who conceives of desire in terms of the human fantasy of 'completeness', Baudrillard recognizes that the human pursuit of sexual (as *symbolic*) pleasure can never be satisfied but must forever replicate itself in the act of desiring. This means that the individual's pursuit of sexual or consumer pleasure is always dependent upon others. Thus, while these 'others' are both the object of desire and the source of the fantasy by which desire is to be satisfied, an individual can never experience that completion she or he so desires—because that completeness only exists in others who can never be the self. Others are not only the object of desire, they are also the source of its impediment. Moreover, others are the fabric by which the hierarchical social system obstructs and controls pleasure, as it locates individuals and their desires on the broad hierarchy of social privilege. Completeness, in this sense, can only operate within the ephemera of fantasy.

To situate this point in terms of our history of trade, it means that the image-based economy of pleasure is both facilitated and limited by this process of desire and its libidinal essence. Individuals and social groups function to maximize their pleasure and privilege, while encountering the competitive and manipulative aspirations of others who are doing the same thing. Thus, even in the expanded terrain of the global exchange of symbols, particular social groups, especially elites, manipulate the economic order in accordance with their own interests and advantages. Moving beyond simple colonization or imperial militarism, these elites maximize their pleasure through the production and distribution of representational products and processes that are constituted around the transformed libido of their consuming markets. In this way, the ideal of global trade and world economic community is fostered by the spread of consumerism and the ideals of self-interest, utilitarianism and a standardized ideology of market choice.

This concept of a market of free thinking and free choosing con-sumer agents is a critical addendum to Bernstein's history of trade. Within the evolving economy of pleasure, which is fostered around symbols and libido, the concept of 'free market' reinvigorates the idea of a shared (global) human consciousness forged around the pursuit of pleasure. The new Symbolic Order governing the economy of pleasure is conceived, therefore, as an imaginary that celebrates trade and global capitalism as the inheritance of true civilization—a universal expression of our true humanity. This reinvigoration of nineteenth-century liber-alism (vaguely dubbed neo-liberalism) has become a primary driver in national and trans-national modes of economic management and gov-ernment policy. Within this ideological mind-scape, free trade and the market are canonized against the prospect of human doom, violence and calumny; competition and hierarchy are simply the side-effect of a more generative social and species progression. In this way, Bernstein's account of history is conceived through this very ideal, a perspec-tive which synthesizes all that is good about the commercial exchange system, and excludes all that is bad.

Baudrillard's sense of this new economy, however, differs somewhat from the neo-liberalist evangelism, certainly inasmuch as he acknowl-edges the persistence of 'the bad' in terms of social, if not ecological, limits. To this end, the Symbolic Order with which the law of free market economics accords is not a complete coverage, but is replete with its own inconsistencies and fallibilities. While a number of commentators have seen Baudrillard's perspective as pessimistic, or even nihilistic, he never-theless alerts us to the ways in which the circulatory system of this new global hyper-economy falters within its own un-bordered conditions of excess; the limits, that is, are immanent within the very pursuit of plea-sure. Thus, even within a symbol-based economy that is liberated from the heavy materials of industrial trade and its equally heavy engage-ment with European military colonialism, the limits are self-inscribed by the fantasy of pleasure upon which it is based. For Baudrillard this Symbolic Order is itself constituted around an incomplete or ambigu-ous imaginary, which can never permit the conditions of ideology and law to form a unitary system. Indeed, this is precisely Foucault's point when he notes that power always begets its own equal force of challenge. As Baudrillard himself notes through his Gnostic sensibilities, good will necessarily stimulate its own opposition.

Does not [the] secret disobedience of a group to its own principles, this profound immorality and duplicity, reflect a universal order? We need to reawaken the principle of Evil active in Manicheism and all the great mythologies in order to affirm, against the principle of Good, not exactly the supremacy of Evil, but the fundamental duplicity that demands that any order exists only to be disobeyed, attacked, exceeded and dismantled.

(Baudrillard, 1990b: 77)

While Baudrillard overstates the degree to which the economy of signs and pleasures has overtaken all other economic and commercial forms, he nevertheless directs us towards the complexity of the circulatory system and the ultimate contingency by which its benefits and displeasures are formed. To this end, Baudrillard's own apocalyptic discourse might have presaged the great financial calamity that emerged in 2007, a calamity which Karl Marx had also imagined in his teleological prophesy in *Das Kapital* and *The Communist Manifesto*.

Releasing the monster: the greedy Gekko

Thus, the GFC that struck America and other parts of the developed world from around 2007 was delivered through a remarkably familiar discourse of doom—another iteration of 'the end of the world' scenario. In 2008 the visionaries claimed that for the first time in world history the *global* economy contracted; its two largest economies, Japan and the USA, shrank by around 4 per cent and 6 per cent, respectively (US Bureau of Economic Analysis, 2010). According to the International Monetary Fund, the radical decline in industrial output amongst developed world economies has led to the deepest recession since the Great Depression of 1932:

The continuation of financial crisis, as policies failed to dispel uncertainty, has caused asset values to fall sharply across advanced and emerging economies, decreasing household wealth and thereby putting downward pressure on consumer demand. In addition, the associated high level of uncertainty has prompted households and businesses to postpone expectations, reducing demand for consumer and capital goods. At the same time, widespread disruptions to credit are constraining household spending and curtailing production and trade.

(IMF, 2009: 2)

In 2009 the newly elected President of the United States, Barack Obama, linked the GFC and Global Recession to the pride of the American Union and the noble imperatives of a 'just war'. Circuitously, but deliberately, the President bound his rhetoric of economic struggle to the virtues of America's collective destiny. In his call to arms against the vicissitudes of economic hard times, Obama invoked a sense of deep history and the heroic project of nation and civilization.

> History reminds us that at every moment of economic upheaval and transformation, the nation has responded with bold action and big ideas. In the midst of civil war, we laid railroad tracks from one coast to another that spurred commerce and industry. From the turmoil of the Industrial Revolution came public high schools that prepared our citizens for a new age. In the wake of war and depression, the GI Bill sent a generation to college and created the largest middle-class in history. And a twilight struggle for freedom led to a nation of highways, an American on the moon, and an explosion of technology that still shapes our world.
>
> (Obama, 2009: 3)

And while attempting to draw down the calamities of one war, the war in Iraq, Obama was increasing America's engagement in Afghanistan and Pakistan, the continuing frontline of America's 'war on terror'.

Obama's call to arms is not dissimilar to the Bantu story of the 'swallowing monster'. Indeed, 'greed' has been one of the most widely applied epithets and explanations for the GFC. Kevin Rudd, the Prime Minister of Australia, argued consistently that

> If you want a definition of social injustice this was it in brutal colour—millions of innocent workers losing their jobs because a few thousand financial executives around the world surrendered any pretence of social responsibility in their blind pursuit of absolute greed.
>
> (Rudd, 2009)

Rudd's raillery echoed a great deal of the public anger over the excesses of Wall Street and the global financial services sector. The Wall Street moguls were now monsters, swallowing monsters, who had unchained their greed through decades of deregulation and the apotheosis of unrestrained avarice. As the sub-prime property market collapsed in 2007 and the impact of loan defaults was felt across America and much of the world, many of the critics of this unrestrained and deregulated financial sector recalled the words of Gordon Gekko, the rabid stockbroker in Oliver Stone's 1987 film *Wall Street:*

[G]reed, for lack of a better word, is good. Greed is right, greed works. Greed clarifies, cuts through, and captures the essence of the evolutionary spirit. Greed, in all of its forms; greed for life, for money, for love, knowledge has marked the upward surge of mankind.

Stone, of course, is presenting Gekko's hyperbole as a mild parody of the American free market ethos, particularly in the wake of the 1987 stock market collapse. But the crash of 1987, along with its prescience and memory, was rapidly erased and the ethos of unregulated trade and perpetual economic growth was restored with even greater intensity and conviction. In effect, this speedy recovery from the Wall Street-global collapse—along with the equally resonant collapse of the Berlin Wall and Soviet communism in 1991—seemed to convince the world that the New York stock market was in fact *the* invincible wall: there could be no other. Global capitalism and the expansion of trade, particularly financial trade, could no longer be hindered by the reservations of public good or the mechanisms of social responsibility. Greed was good, and the swallowing monster was off the leash.

Neo-liberalism and the fantasy of infinite pleasure

The 1987 Wall Street stock market collapse was ultimately regarded as a blip on the computer screen that represented a new form of global trade. The networked computer, in particular, with its capacity for instantaneous data transfer had become an integral tool for the production and transfer of value. Enormous profits could be conjured through the rise and fall of stock prices and the value of national currencies. The 1987 crash, it was ultimately declared, was an effect of this rapid transfer process and the complicated psychology that drives share values up and down. When trading occurred 'on the floor' of the stock market, intrinsic material and human inhibitors could delay the movement of the prices; however, the immediacy of computer trade largely erased these inhibitors as the lure of instantaneous digital lighting seemed to intensify the trading thrill and the imperative of speed. Indeed, it is generally agreed that the 1987 crash was caused by the increased interconnection of global markets, combined with the newly developed American practice of 'programmed trading'—a system of buying and selling that was coded into particular traders' computer systems. The 1987 crash, therefore, is now regarded as an effect of these new technological innovations, as much as any weakness in the market fundamentals or the system of capitalist exchange itself. That is to say, the flaw in this increasingly globalized and computerized trading system was in the mode of representation and symbolic exchange, rather than in the underlying mechanisms by which the economy continued to grow and individuals in the developed world continued to prosper. Even so, there remains a peculiarity in the 1987 Black Monday crash which various commentators claim to be the system's point of chaos (Taleb, 2007).

It is also important to note that this crash occurred at a particular moment in history when the divide between Left and Right politics was being deconstructed. During the 1980s, major political parties in the Anglophonic developed world largely capitulated to the idea that particular government policies that protected local manufacturers from international competition constituted a significant hindrance to global free trade. Leftist, social democratic and liberal democratic parties which were the traditional supporters of local industry and the local labour force largely surrendered to the idea that free trade and free markets were the ultimate source of an efficient national economy, economic growth and prosperity (Lash and Urry, 1987; Giddens, 1994).

Even Leftist intellectuals in the English-speaking world capitulated to the 'end of the Old Left' thesis, as international communism collapsed and western world Labour parties adopted a new style and a new paradigm of deregulation. As noted earlier in this chapter, political analysts like Anthony Giddens and others in the London-based 'Polity Bureau' embraced a new Left conception which celebrated personal development, Do-It-Yourself and creative communalism. As the old industrial working class declined, concepts like universal human rights, equal opportunity, anti-discrimination, environmental sustainability and refugee advocacy softened the old socialist model. The economy of pleasure and its libidinal essence were thus integrated into a new cultural politics of freedom which inevitably became woven through an imagining of prosperity, global free trade and deregulation.

This was particularly significant in a period which had seen the economic and cultural decline of England in the 1970s and early 1980s, and its revitalization under the conservative neo-liberalist Prime Ministership of Margaret Thatcher. This economic revitalization, extended through the Blair and Brown governments, was achieved largely through policies linked to the liberalization of markets, deregulation of labour, the sale of public assets and utilities, and the promotion of international trade in manufactured goods. As economic growth rates were stalling in Anglophonic countries during the later 1970s and early 1980s, many East and South East Asian economies were beginning to surge. A combination of cheap labour, new and more efficient industrial machinery and a free market model was producing significant economic achievements for countries like Japan, Taiwan, South Korea and Singapore. The global media at the time was replete with stories of the Asian tiger economies and an imaginary of threat to westernist cultural and capitalist primacy.

In countries like Australia, which had protected its manufacturing and finance sectors, the new competitors were creating considerable panic, such that the then Labour government Treasurer, Paul Keating, warned that Australia was rapidly becoming a 'banana republic', and Australians 'the poor white trash of Asia' (see Love, 2008). Thus, the value of trade, privatization of public assets and deregulation became a mantra for all sides of politics during the 1980s into the 1990s. In this context the merging of economic models became fostered through the general rubric of 'neo-liberalism', a convergent ideology which commended high levels of consumption and the de-bordering of national economies. In what is sometimes also called 'economic globalization', neo-liberalism has emerged over recent decades as an almost unassailable ethos, being promoted by most economists as economic nirvana, the salvation of the world.

Neo-liberalism as salvation discourse

At least until very recently and the emergence of the GFC (see below), 'neo-liberalism' represented the revival of the 'original' liberalist principles that evolved in association with European industrial capitalism during the eighteenth and nineteenth centuries. British philosophers from Adam Smith to John Stuart Mill argued that 'freedom' and prosperity were intricately linked through the capacity of the individual to pursue his or her own self-interest. Social and moral progress would naturally flow from individual self-fulfilment, not simply because of the aggregate effect of combined individual wealth but because this aggregation contributed to a sense of mutual destiny and belonging. This principle was also the effect of free trade and open markets.

According to free market economists like Milton Friedman (1982), economic liberalism was the basis for human progress and especially the advances of political freedom and democracy. For Friedman and others, these fundamental liberalist principles have been contaminated by various forms of Marxist and socialist conceptions of 'the state' and government. According to these older socialist ideals, governments should do more than provide security and the mechanisms for law and social control; they should also provide a broader scope of security through education, health, welfare, industry protection, labour protection and income redistribution. For free marketeers, like Friedman, these public interventions seriously distort markets, creating the conditions for vast inefficiencies in production and labour. Welfare, in particular, created a condition of artificial security which weakened competitiveness and innovation, contributing to a culture of social lethargy, insularity and disincentive. As Philipp Genschel (2004) notes, economic globalization lay at the centre of these discussions with free market economists insisting that the welfare state was an aberration in the general progression of capitalism. Social welfare, in fact, was the cause of the boom-bust economic cycle as it distorted the psychological patterns required for confidence and growth. As Genschel puts it:

Globalization was the Western European crisis of the 1990s. The red menace has disappeared with the implosion of the Soviet empire and public attention turned to the dangers connected to the final triumph of capitalism. The increasing internationalization of the economy was seized on as a particular cause for concern. It appeared to endanger the balance of power between economy and polity.... The globalization of markets seemed to leave governments with no choice but to pursue neoliberal policies. Good government became synonymous with market friendly government.... Competitive party democracy stagnated because global competition left no room for leftist economic policy alternatives. The corporatist foundation of the welfare state was at risk because (mobile) capital, thanks to its new international exit options, no longer needed state support to force wage restraint and discipline on (immobile) labour.

(Genschel, 2004: 613–614)

This increasing globalization of trade, finance and labour, however, was not affected in the economic policies of the developed world, but became integrated into international development discourses as well. Indeed, the neo-liberalist discourse is often traced to John Williamson's notion of a 'Washington Consensus', a term coined by Williamson in 1989/1990 to describe the policy recommendations of major international economists working in Washington DC. Representing organizations like the International Monetary Fund (IMF), the World

Bank and the US Treasury Department, these economists prescribed a range of policies designed to assist developing countries, particularly in Latin America, work their way out of economic crisis. These policies included:

- Fiscal discipline.
- A redirection of public expenditure priorities towards fields offering both high economic returns and the potential to improve income distribution, such as primary health care, primary education and infrastructure.
- Tax reform (to lower marginal rates and broaden the tax base).
- Interest rate liberalization.
- A competitive exchange rate.
- Trade liberalization.
- Liberalization of inflows of foreign direct investment.
- Privatization.
- Deregulation (to abolish barriers to entry and exit).
- Secure property rights.

As noted, these policies had already become naturalized in economic and political discourses in western developed nations by the time of the Washington Consensus. However, Williamson's phrase gave traction to the rising force of economic globalization and the free market/free trade policies of the west and its financial institutions. Quite notably, organizations like the World Bank and the IMF, whose charter relates directly to international development and the ultimate goal of increased global trade, increasingly attached these policies as conditions of borrowing and investment in developing countries.

Neo-liberalism as ideology

The ascent of free market neo-liberalism can be explained, in part, through the failure of Soviet economics and ideology, and the tapering of the western world's economic growth rates, especially as they were measured against the rising tigers of East and South East Asia. Inefficient welfare systems and expensive labour costs in the developed world were blamed for this tapering, even though the drive to innovate continued to marshal new modes of economic activity, particularly in the symbolic, entertainment and information sectors. This crisis of stagnation, however, can be further explained in terms of Karl Marx's principles of 'capital accumulation', whereby the excessive concentration of wealth in one place leads necessarily to its redirection as investment to another. In this way, capital necessarily flows, like water, away from the nodes towards areas of capital vacuum where infrastructure is underdeveloped and labour is cheap. In many respects, the expansion of investment and currency exchange has been driven precisely by this mechanism: as a supplement to direct trade of commodities and manufactured goods, corporations have also invested their accumulated capital—including borrowed capital—in those areas of the world economy that are likely to grow and generate surplus value. Along with many other things, economic globalization has been constructed on this web of accumulation and redirection of capital.

Thus, while western states were entranced by the imagined threat of Soviet ideology and nuclear militarism, a more spectral challenge was emerging from within the west's own privilege and principles. Governments, corporations and other economic agents in the advanced world, therefore, broadened their focus and practices in order to accommodate the continued demand for expanded markets, production sources and investment models. Accompanying this shift in policy and practices, of course, were shifts in thinking, knowledge and discourse. While Anthony Giddens and others conceive of these shifts in terms of 'reflexivity' or self-analysis, they are more broadly constituted around an ideological seepage by which neo-liberalism appears as the welcome stranger, the *new* liberalism that emerges from the dust of our experimental dalliance with welfare and socialist protectionism.

Indeed, at the end of history, as Francis Fukuyama (1993) described the fall of the Berlin Wall, the enemy within revealed itself as a failure of our own principles of freedom, or at least the failure to respect the very freedom upon which economic capitalism and its prosperity had been founded. Milton Friedman's (1982) account of this foundation in *Freedom and Capitalism* assumed a canonical status for free market economists, political thinkers and policy makers on the Right. In this context, neo-liberalism conflated the political and economic discourses of freedom, marshalling the post-Soviet euphoria into a universalizing and self-validating ideology that could explain the death of communism in terms of the natural impetus of human self-actualization and the ascent of economic rationalism and the basic tenets of democracy. Particularly in the USA, where labour politics had never achieved the same status as in Europe and where freedom was embedded in the national psyche, the Cold War victory simply fortified the country's superpower centricity. As Table 2.1 indicates, the rationalism of the liberal and neo-liberal ideology could be simply tabulated.

Table 2.1   Growth in national GDP by 2000 international million $ value

Country	1500	1870	1913	1950	1973	2000
France	11,000	72,000	72,100	220,402	683,965	1,600.00
UK	2815	100,1200	224,614	347,850	675,914	1,108,568
USA		98,374	517,383	1,455,916	3,536,662	7,394,598
China	61,8000	189,740	241,344	239,903	740,048	3,873,352
India	60,500	134,882	204,231	222,222	494,812	1,702,812

Source: Adapted by author from Maddison (2003).

As the table reveals the USA led the charge for international development and prosperity during the early part of the twentieth century;
while Europe was destroying itself with two world wars, the USA's relative security enabled it to continue to industrialize and out-compete its
trading partners and commercial rivals.

As Hirst and Thompson (1999) and Maddison (2003) point out, the
period prior to the First World War matches the current period of
globalization, at least in terms of volumes of trade and trans-national
movement of capital. What is also clear is that this form of globalization
declined during the middle years of the twentieth century, only to be
revived over the past two decades. With the Soviet threat removed and
the increasing prosperity of Asia and now Latin America, neo-liberalism
has provided the ideological impetus for a new burst of globalization
and the proliferation of free trade and labour agreements across the
world. Emerging at a time of economic recession in the west, however,
neo-liberalism established itself as a crisis discourse that was designed to
create a rallying point for recovery and the re-establishment of western,
especially American, economic primacy.

More recently, however, the (re-)emergence of China and India as
economic powers is revitalizing anxieties about American and western
primacy. With China's economy set to overtake Japan during 2010 as
the world's second largest economy, the force of rationalist discourse is
again faltering. Table 2.2 reveals that OECD economic growth rates are
relatively low when measured against the booming economies of India
and China. In this light, Samuel Huntington's (1993) notorious 'clash
of civilizations' thesis represents an ideological 'call to arms'; at least
inasmuch as the conception of 'the west' is identified as a fortress for
these high principles of liberal capitalism and democratic freedom. The
threat posed by 'the east', at least in terms of Huntington's thesis, is
not simply constituted around economics, but is imagined in terms of a

Table 2.2 Growth in US public debt in billions of US$

Year	Public Debt: Total US Debt in Billions US$	Approx. % of GDP
2000	5776	58
2001	5662	56
2002	5943	59
2003	6405	60
2004	6997	63
2005	7596	62
2006	8170	65
2007	8680	66
2008	9229	70
2009	10,699	83
2010	12,311	94
2011 (est.)	15,673.9	98
2012 (est.)	16,565.7	104

Source: Adapted by the author from US Treasury, http://www.treasurydirect.gov/NP/NPGateway.

cultural antagonism that would entirely shift the axis of world history and geo-political processes. For many, this challenge is expressed in the attacks of 9/11 whereby America, as the spearhead of the west, was assaulted at its ideological core. In the words of the American president of the time, George W. Bush, this attack was perpetrated against 'our very way of life'—on freedom, libidinal consumerism and democracy which are the epicentre of the neo-liberal ideology. In essence, the war on terror is in a very profound way an ideological language war, which is grounded in the very notion of 'America' (Lewis, 2005).

Neo-liberal rhetoric and OECD economic performance

While there was a surge in the adoption of free market policies in various parts of the developed world during the 1980s, these policies are remarkably mixed. The powerful rhetoric of neo-liberalism, in fact, has been frequently fused with more politically pragmatic and parochial economic policies in those western states that have been the free market's greatest advocates—particularly for the developed world's poorer trading partners. The administration of George W. Bush (2001–2009), for example, evolved as the most indebted and high spending US administrations of all previous history. The small government, deregulation rhetoric, thereby, collapsed as Bush sought to impose his ideological will across his own and most other nations. In the period from Bush's inauguration until the end of his presidency (2001–2009), government expenditure in the USA increased exponentially. Under the pressure of the GFC, recession and continued American military commitments in Afghanistan and elsewhere, the Obama administration has continued this pattern of government spending and debt, with much of the borrowed money deriving from China.

Certainly, the processes of deregulation and the removal of tariff barriers has generated some increases in global trade volumes and financial exchange, but governments in the developed world, particularly Anglophonic governments, have maintained remarkably high levels of economic intervention and welfare. Thus, the welfare state, while shifting somewhat in orientation, has barely changed in terms of size and aggregate government costs. Indeed, as numerous studies have indicated, the steady growth in government social expenditure in the OECD has largely stabilized at historically high levels since 1990 (DiNitto and Cummins, 2007; Day, 2008). Social expenditure has increased on average across the 28 OECD countries from 16 per cent to 21 per cent of GDP (1980–2003), including a 1 per cent total increase between 2000 and 2003; since 1990 social expenditure has exceeded real GDP growth (OECD, 2007). The GFC and the global recession (2007–2010) has generated, in fact, a new surge in government expenditure and economic intervention in an effort to stimulate economic activity. Indeed, despite claims to being a small government administration, the George W. Bush presidency radically accelerated government spending and borrowing from 2001–2008 in the USA.

The period of the 2000s also continued America's strategy of improving productivity and reducing unemployment rates through the processes of workforce casualization. By transferring full-time positions to casual and part-time, employers were able to save costs on insurance, holiday and sick pay while increasing 'flexibility', especially during periods of lower labour requirement. This strategy has led, especially in the USA, to an increase in what has been called the working poor—a system of underemployment where individuals receive very low hourly rates of pay but do not qualify for unemployment or other welfare benefits. As we will discuss in later chapters, this approach has contributed in various OECD countries to a significant increase in national poverty and inequality rates over the past two decades (OECD, 2009). Thus, the general levelling out of unemployment from its peak in the 1991 recession is due in part to these policy models; very clearly the contraction in economic growth during the 2008–2010 recession has also been most acutely experienced by people in the lowest end of the employment scale. In 2010 the unemployment rate in the USA had climbed back to around 10 per cent.

Even more telling, perhaps, has been the rise of what is now called 'middle-class welfare' in western nations. The blurring of Left-Right politics is linked to the expansion in numbers of 'swinging voters' who shift their electoral preference from one party to another, depending upon perceived personal advantage and social policy options. With both major sides of electoral politics in Anglophonic countries adopting a free trade, privatization and deregulation economic model, voting has tended to flow according to perceived personal and local benefits, however that might be defined. Contending parties often employ strategies and policies that might attract the swinging voter, particularly those who are in 'swinging' and closely contested electorates. This sort of 'vote-buying' has led to a significant increase in social benefit flows to the middle class for such things as tax concessions on investments and private health insurance, public funding for private schools, child endowments, childcare and superannuation. These policies have ultimately contributed to an extension of inequality in countries like Australia and Canada, where many social benefits payments are no longer means tested (see OECD, 2009).

Table 2.3 indicates that the neo-liberalist precepts and ideology are not clearly borne out in economic performance, at least by key indicators like productivity and economic growth. Across the OECD, productivity rates are modest and economic growth is well short of the emerging economies like India and China, and noticeably lower than in previous decades (OECD, 2009; CIA, 2010). Even so, the richest nations of the world are clearly interdependent and share key economic and cultural attributes around policy, education and technology. In democratic states where public spending continues to spiral and free trade agendas

Table 2.3 Productivity growth rates in key OECD countries

Year	Productivity Rate—Australia	Productivity Rate—UK	Productivity Rate—USA
2000	−1.2	3.4	0.1
2001	3/9	1.4	2.4
2002	1.9	2.4	3.1
2003	2.2	2.9	3
2004	1	2.1	2.4
2005	−0/2	0.9	1
2006	0.8	2.3	0.8
2007	0.8	1.7	1.4
2008	0.1	1	1.3

Source: Adapted by the author from OECD (2009).

continue to dominate, GDP growth and productivity improvements are increasing at only modest rates or are actually levelling off, as for Japan. During the 2008–2010 recession, in fact, many OECD economies contracted as GDP growth rates tumbled (CIA, 2010).

While the issues here are complex, there are several implications to consider. First, it suggests that while the free trade model clearly advantages emerging economies, in mature economies there may be an effect of capital accumulation, labour costs and decreasing opportunities for productivity improvement; this is especially problematic for manufacturing industries and the lower skilled labour force. Second, it also suggests that the policies and strategies associated with neo-liberalism are double-coded: that is, they are simply not producing the effect of diminishing government expenditure, but simply shifting expenditure into areas like military activities and middle-class welfare—including subsidies for private education, childcare and private health. Third, while free market economists might argue that the neo-liberal principles have simply been distorted by continued government interventions in the OECD states, the experience of China suggests that government interventions do not necessarily impinge on economic growth and increased trade activities. While supporting private ownership and entrepreneurialism, the Chinese government maintains strict central control.

In this context, the neo-liberal panacea for tapering growth rates in developed western states is perhaps less a solution to economic stagnation, so much as it is simply an ideological screen that simply obscures the crisis that is enmeshed within the conditions of capital accumulation and economic prosperity. Thus, while the mediasphere is replete with self-absorbed cultural promulgation of choice and freedom, the neo-liberal narrative is simply obscuring the complex codings of our economic fantasies. This crisis, in fact, is inscribed in the over-production and over-consumption of the hierarchical, economic global hegemony—a condition that is endemic to the swallowing monster that sits at the top of the global economic pile. Thus, while its proponents might conjure this system as the striking hero of the swallowing monster story, it is really a condition that perpetually besets this excess of pleasure. The essential problem for this westernist model of economic development is that it is tending to bloat and suffocate its own innovations, leading to the transposition of its capital from the centre to other less heavily capitalized and developed regions of the world. This habit of securing advantage through the mobilization of larger populations is now being fostered through globalizing knowledge systems, and an ideology which believes that the pursuit and acquisition of pleasure is fundamentally infinite. It simply is a matter of conjuring the security of more people working for the *right* cause—this means more people, more resources, more consumers and more soldiers.

Neo-liberalism, thereby, conceives of itself as a trans-national ideology, one which liberates economies from the walls of their nation-state. In its most profound imagining, the world will be constituted around trading cities and agricultural regions, all working for the common good of economic and political freedom, global peace and competitive but mutual prosperity. For innumerable critics, however, this imagining falsifies the true intent of neo-liberalism, which is the sustained advantage of the rich over the poor. This advantage is not only manifest across global terrains; it is also set within the conditions of local-national culture, economy and politics. For its critics, neo-liberalism merely extends the insider-outsider organizational principles upon which hierarchical capitalism is structured. For Michael Sendel (2009) neo-liberalism's market triumphalism is not simply a problem of excess greed, but rather the deficiency of ethics and collective responsibility. Capitalism is, by its very essence, an economic system that is founded on self-interest and 'greed'. Thus, while the market might be an efficient mechanism for trading shares or agricultural products, it is entirely inappropriate for the management and provision of public good—health, education, the environment. Henry Giroux (2008) translates such concerns into a more direct ideological polemic, arguing that

> Under neoliberalism everything is for sale or is plundered for profit. Public lands are looted by logging companies or corporate ranchers; politicians willingly hand the public's airwaves over to broadcasters and large corporate interests without a dime going into the public trust; corporations drive the nation's energy policies, and the war industries give war profiteering a new meaning as the government hands out contracts without any competitive bidding.
>
> (Giroux, 2008: 2)

For scholars like Giroux, neo-liberalism actually seeks to expunge the status and value of the public, public responsibility and social welfare.

Anti-globalization: counter neo-liberalism

Henry Giroux speaks for many scholars and public critics of neo-liberalism, particularly in terms of its association with what is generally called 'economic globalization'. Parenthesizing the complex cultural politics associated with increased global contiguities, economic globalization focuses on and supports the increased flow of goods, finance and labour across national borders. By and large, economic globalization is fostered by three major first world institutions—large trans-national (or 'multi-national') corporations; development and finance agencies, such as the IMF, the World Bank and the Asian Development Bank (Japan); intergovernmental agencies and trans-national policy organizations such as the World Trade Organization and the Group of 8 (now 20). While we will examine a number of the development functions of these institutions in later chapters, it is worth noting here that anti-globalization groups frequently target these organizations as the source and symbolic centre of economic globalization. According to these critics, economic globalization is the cause of many of the problems of the developing world, which remains trapped in the wake of western imperialism and ongoing practices of economic exploitation.

Quite bluntly, anti-globalization and decolonization political dissidents, in fact, regard globalization as the invisible continuity of colonization; in this context, neo-liberal policies and principles are responsible for developing world poverty, injustice, warfare, political instability and ecological disaster. Economic globalization and its supporting institutions are also the focus of developed world trade union concerns over national and international labour issues. In particular, national policies which reduce trade barriers and tariffs open industry to competition from lower cost economies. The net effect has been the reduction in wages and conditions for the first world industries, as local companies try to compete with their lower cost counterparts. Even more telling is the closure or offshore transposition of local manufacturers, especially in labour-intensive industries like textiles. Indeed, even as the first world economies try to adjust by shifting to new high skill areas like computing, media or information service industries requiring high levels of education and training, lower cost countries like India are able to out-manoeuvre their first world competitors and offer a cheaper service on equal gradients of technical capacity (Rodrik and Subramanian, 2006).

In this sense, the 'swallowing monster' is perceived by anti-globalizationists to be unrestrained pursuit of private profit, free markets and growth at all costs. This criticism of neo-liberalism, which bundles together all the world's woes and places them at the feet of major trans-national corporations, is regarded by the advocates of free trade as generally unjustified. Indeed, this is the point of John Williamson, whose term the 'Washington Consensus' has become equated with neo-liberalism and the source of all that is wrong with free trade models. According to Williamson (2000, 2002), it is precisely this opposition which creates the sense in which there is an integrated ideology of neo-liberalism: 'Audiences the world over seem to believe that this signifies a set of neoliberal policies that have been imposed on hapless countries by the Washington-based international financial institutions and have led them to crisis and misery. There are people who cannot utter the term without foaming at the mouth' (Williamson, 2002: 7).

We might agree, therefore, that 'neo-liberalism' is above all other things an ideology that is propagated or mediated through the more generalized fantasy of infinite pleasure. Packed within that fantasy are a range of ideological and policy discourses which bear little consistency and even less consensus—Washington or otherwise. Indeed, over the past decade the anti-globalization movement has itself been forced to recognize that free trade and neo-liberalist policies have not been universally abominable, particularly as many millions of people in India, China and Central America have moved above the poverty line as a direct effect of expanded trade and high levels of economic growth. Particular areas of the anti-globalization movement, thereby, have shifted the emphasis of their activism from Nike sweat-shops to sustainable development, human rights, Fair Trade and issues of global warming. Along these lines, anti-globalizationists challenge the claim that neo-liberalism and prosperity will necessarily generate greater personal and political freedoms. Critics of economic globalization argue that the double-digit growth rates have not improved China's abysmal record on human rights, nor its despotic and centralist model of government. While Chinese economic growth has many winners, there are also continuing accounts of inhumane working conditions, social oppression, torture and the base denial of rights (Angle and Svenson, 2001; Flanagan, 2006).

Equally telling, the free trade framework enshrined in the principles of the World Trade Organization continues to be compromised by national interest, especially around agricultural policy and various forms of militarism. America, Japan and the European Community retain strong agricultural protectionist policies which are designed to secure their local industries against competition from lower cost producers— most of which are from the developing world. Thus, while exposing their own highly sophisticated and technologically advanced manufacturing and service industries to international competition, wealthy countries deploy a range of tariff and subsidy mechanisms to support their agricultural producers who might otherwise compete poorly in an international marketplace. While we will take this issue up in later chapters, this slippage in the neo-liberal organizational order is generally linked to the political power of the agricultural lobby in developed nations, as well as circuitous arguments about the need for a domestic primary production industry. As Paidang Carmody points out, 'U.S. cotton farmers now receive three times more in subsidies than total U.S. Aid to sub-Saharan Africa' (Carmody, 2005: 98).

Moreover, countries like the USA have engaged in various forms of resource wars, particularly over oil, in order to protect their military power and consumer lifestyles. There are certainly many critics who believe that the American led wars in Afghanistan and Iraq were motivated by a desire to control important oil supplies (see DiGeorgia, 2005; Kaldor et al., 2007). Very clearly, the blow-out in America's public debt and this remarkable distortion in the ideological force of neo-liberalism is directly linked to the policy on oil security, a policy that Francis Fukuyama regards as the cornerstone of George W. Bush's framework of neo-conservatism. According to Fukuyama, neo-conservatism represents a distortion of the political centre by the Right. Opposing the polarities of Left and Right, Fukuyama rails against the excesses of conservatism, which are characterized by over-reaching government intervention and a vision of global domination. While Americans are not 'imperialist by nature', the Iraq War represents a 'costly intervention' and savage failure in American foreign policy.

> Neoconservatism, whatever its complex roots, has become indelibly associated with concepts like coercive regime change, unilateralism and American hegemony. What is needed now are new ideas, neither neoconservative nor realist, for how America is to relate to the rest of the world—ideas that retain the neoconservative belief in the universality of human rights, but without its illusions about the efficacy of American power and hegemony to bring these ends about.
>
> (Fukuyama, 2006)

For Fukuyama and other members of the political Right in America, therefore, neo-liberalism is neither realist nor utilitarian, but is a base for the generation of innovation and new ideas.

In this sense, Fukuyama is claiming that neo-liberalism is not an ideology, as such, but is simply an approach to economy and governance that has its roots in the rise of democracy. Oliver Hartwich (2009a, 2009b) supports this view, arguing that the whole concept of 'neo-liberalism' has been perverted by late twentieth-century critics of free trade. According to Hartwich, it is the modern media and opponents of free trade who have created an ideological monster out of market economics, particularly in the context of the GFC which they seek to blame on deregulation and unethical financial practices. These practices are not a part of liberal economics at all, Hartwich claims, except in the imagining of radical anti-globalization activists and an unthinking media.

Global financial crisis

The battle-lines that have been drawn between neo-liberalism and anti-globalization are largely determined by different ideological readings of world politics, social infrastructure and international development. Each side of this ideological divide accuses the other of marshalling the media and deploying particular rhetorical strategies to support their respective claims. Across the borders of this divide, however, are diverse policies and perspectives, all of which contribute to the inconsistencies that characterize national, trans-national and global economic systems. Globalization scholars have described these inconsistencies in terms of 'the end of organized capitalism' (Lash and Urry, 1987), the 'globalization of nothing' (Ritzer, 2003) and 'liquid modernity' (Bauman, 2000). But even these accounts tend to obscure somewhat the patterns and discourses that comprise the cultural politics of economy and in particular the ways in which pleasure and crisis are formed within the global mediasphere.

Indeed, the GFC and related recessions exposed the underlying fantasy around which the modern economy is formed. In seeking to explain the dramatic rupture in the international loan system and subsequent collapse in stock market values and economic growth, western-based economists, journalists and public officials invoked a familiar apocalyptic vision—the end of neo-liberalism, end of greed and even the end of capitalism, as we know it. The media, which is the clarion of crisis, generated volumes of dire warning, sending terror through the hearts of investors, workers and home-owners across the developed world. As in earlier recessional conditions, this pandemic of fear precipitated significant shifts in government rhetoric and policy emphasis. In a sudden reversal, the rhetoric of free market economics was modulated through a reinvocation of Keynesian government intervention and the virtues of economic regulation.

Of course, and as we have noted, first world governments never actually retreated from the economy, as the neo-liberalist ideology demanded: they simply shifted the focus and emphasis of public spending. Even so, the GFC now provided a more overt and dignified reason for action and the government's direct intervention in the productive capacity of the economy. Billions and even trillions of dollars were suddenly poured into stagnating national economies in order to curb slowing production, collapsing investment infrastructure and rising rates of unemployment. The economy of pleasure was itself under siege and governments could now offer the media a discursive crisis hook—'The worst recession since the 1930s'.

As with the horrors of 9/11, the apocalypse revealed itself once again. The mediasphere rattled itself into action and governments presented themselves as Saviour, the agency of good over evil. Democratic governments, in particular, whose primary *raison d'être* is public security, invoked an even higher authority than economic neo-liberalism: that is, the grand ideology of government itself and its heroic capacity to save the nation. Like the miraculous warrior in the Bantu myth, governments fortified themselves and the unsuspecting public against the rapacious beast of financial markets, bankers and greed.

Speaking at the World Economic Forum in Davos, in 2009, former British Prime Minister, Tony Blair, declared an end to the sorts of international greed that had sponsored the sub-prime real estate collapse in America. According to Blair, claims of the end to capitalism were largely premature: it was simply the financial system that needed to be rebuked, reformed and restored. Thus, in a very Aristotelian move, Blair invoked the moral drivers that might restore the global good life through the control of unethical and unregulated greed. *New York Times* correspondent, Floyd Norris, who attended the Davos conference, also noted:

> Another vote for globalization came from former President Bill Clinton, who emphasized that 'we have to get out of this together' and said it was important for China to continue buying Treasury bonds to finance a recovery that would allow Americans to resume buying Chinese exports.
>
> (Norris, 2010)

Clinton's declaration that we must 'get out of this together' not only confirms the intricacies of global commerce and the rising power of China, it also betrays the deeper anxieties about American indebtedness and the complex problems associated with capital accumulation. The peculiarity of the agricultural systems has always been their reliance on growth and the interdependence of trade, capital (surplus value) and labour. This interdependence, however, is shaped by co-operation and collectivism within the delicate framework of competition and hierarchical frames of exclusion. Clinton's importunation that we must work together simply restates the horribly obvious fact of Holocene economies that we both rely on one another and are beset by a volition that tears us apart. While the players and emphasis has changed, the general volition of these economies has not.

Indeed, in order to explain the GFC numerous economists, journalists and public officials seized upon the dualism which distinguishes between the 'real economy' and its shadowy financial declension. For Blair, Clinton and innumerable others it is this shadowland of finance and investment which has caused so many problems for the 'real' economy. Dubious lending practices, greed and the failure of ethics and regulation sowed the seeds of temptation, leading many Wall Street mavericks into the Gomorrah of sub-prime (less than ideal) realty.

The distinction between the virtual and real economies has become allegorized in terms of an imagined distinction between Wall Street and Main Street—the idea that trade in stocks, derivatives, currencies and bonds is somehow distinguishable from the 'real' economy where material things like houses, automobiles, food and widgets are traded. As a new orthodoxy, this dualism has been frequently reported by finance economists like Michael Darda:

> The Treasury bailout plan to recapitalize the U.S. banking system may help the U.S. avoid a deep and protracted recession. But even if the plan succeeds, it almost surely will not prevent a recession. The major reason for this is that the credit markets have been under incredible stress for well over a year, and have recently taken a significant turn for the worse. During the last two weeks, the spread between Libor (the cost of borrowing between banks) and the rates on zero-risk Treasury bills exploded to more than 300 basis points, the widest gap since October 1987. This kind of stress reflects fear and a lack of trust among banks, which will be reflected in the real economy with a lag.
>
> (Darda, 2008)

As many commentators have noted, Libor, which is the rates at which banks borrow from one another through the multiplication effect on a deposit, is at the centre of the financial crisis. Thus, while the 'real economy' involves the trade of actual products, Libor denotes the following process: a percentage of a deposited sum becomes available for a bank to lend to other banks; this loan becomes a 'deposit' of which a certain percentage is available to lend on to another bank; this sum is then available for further lending and so on. Thus, while government regulation requires a certain portion of each deposit to be held within the bank, the remainder is loaned on: the original dollar deposit, let's say, may multiply in value through the network of loans to become nine or ten dollars. If there is a run on the bank, and these sums have to be paid back, there is an immediate liquidity problem, that is, the money simply doesn't exist, except as a debt. This is precisely what happened with the sub-prime real estate crash where borrowers were loaned money that could not be paid back and depositors, panicked by news reports of bad loans, suddenly wanted to withdraw their money from the banks. In a distinct sense, the sub-prime crash and the ensuing GFC represent a clash of knowledge systems whereby the imagining of infinite pleasure was propagated by various media fantasies—these fantasies collapsed when they encountered the other, more overriding imaginary that held the whole financial system together.

While Tony Blair and others might have it otherwise, this invisible web of borrowing and lending is enmeshed within the whole economic system. Indeed and as noted, the economic drive to surplus value entirely welds the trade in products to the trade in symbols—of which debt and finance are central components. As the agricultural economy has evolved through industrialism and capitalist symbolization, this weld has become even more intractable, particularly through the evolution of an imaginary of infinite pleasure and the dislocation of humans from the agricultural source of their survival. Humans, while retaining an umbilical connection to agriculture and other life systems, have nevertheless participated in the transformation of their symbolic environment, especially through the innovations that produce surplus value. Thus, as property mutated through its integration with hierarchical systems of power and social distinction, new innovations altered the way it could be represented and transacted—from land to labouring bodies, trinkets, money and finance. The symbolic debts and investments associated with finance may in some respects be self-referencing, but they are nevertheless constituted as 'surplus value' or capital, and hence are always linked to the conditions of property.

Indeed, within an economy of desire, the act of borrowing enables individuals and social groups to pursue the fantasy of infinite pleasure and the multiplying effects of economic growth. Remarkably, the 'greed' or 'excess' that many commentators see as the essence of the GFC is never adequately defined, except in terms of effects. Bill Clinton's exaltation of collective salvation, thereby, seems counter-intuitive, particularly as he insists on the use of Treasury Bonds (government loans) to drive the bailout. Thus, while railing against the excesses of Libor and loans to people who couldn't afford repayments, public figures like Bill Clinton nevertheless encourage the continuation of government borrowing as a panacea to the disaster.

To this extent, Marxist description of capital accumulation needs to be supplemented by the idea of pleasure accumulation which manifests itself in terms of the accumulation of debt and displeasure. America's high standard of living, in this sense, reflects the problems of sustainability within a globally constituted competitive framework that is necessarily constituted on the fantasy of infinite pleasure—even for those who can obviously not afford to pay for it.

Within the ambit of the global mediasphere which propagates and sustains itself through fantasies, the idea that the real economy is divisible from the symbolic economy is entirely illogical. Inevitably, the system stings itself as displeasure is driven into the material lives of everyday consumers—especially the poor. The sub-prime real estate collapse is one spectacular manifestation of this instability. The radical accretion of the global credit system from the 1980s facilitated an almost unpunctuated expansion in debt and debt-driven economic growth. Along with many other citizens of the advanced world, a significant number of America's poorest people were enticed into high levels of debt by a fantasy of progressive pleasure. This fantasy and commensurate desire were fortified and validated by an ethos of a deficit lifestyle. Beginning with the credit card system, this ineluctable progression to deficit led eventually to the dream of 'home ownership' and its associated *entrée* into true citizenship, the community from which the American poor have often felt excluded.

The truth, of course, is that the poor are never excluded from the capitalist web: they are, rather, its very foundation. This is not merely to repeat Marx's point about the exploitation of labour in the production process (which is and remains entirely valid). It is rather to note also that 'the poor' are a significant symbolic category which mobilizes the whole hierarchical system and its forward momentum. As well as being a specific category of people living under certain material conditions, the poor represent a point of cultural reference or comparison, providing the drivers for consumer-based symbolic exchange. To expand on this point, the poor are regarded as the baseline in a hierarchical cultural comparison that is constructed around human imaginings of *relative* power, status, ideology, values and ritualized belief. Thus, the category of 'the poor' is more than an expression of what Pierre Bourdieu has called distinctions: it is a psycho-cultural label that assists members of a society identify themselves against other social agents and hence build their own sense of identity. The fantasies, which are enabled by credit, materialize in a reflexive, self-identity by which people recreate themselves in the car they drive or the house they own—even when it is the bank that holds the tile and the individual borrower, the debt. In this way, the poor can avoid the self-definer of being poor. Thus, the condition of 'being poor' is not simply a measurable and material condition; it is also that bleak sociological 'Other' who stimulates a more broadly diffused desire for progress and pleasure. It is this condition of otherness that mobilizes the desire to be someone or something else other than 'poor'.

More than anything else, therefore, the GFC represents the interconnection of these two symbolic systems: first, Libor and the processes by which debt multiplies itself through the 'hyperreal' of networked financial systems; and second, the fantasy of infinite pleasure which is both the primary driver of the 'macro' economy and the inculcation of hierarchical knowledge systems into the lives and fantasies of all cultural agents within a social group. In both cases, we might usefully describe these symbolic systems as 'media' since both are conveyed through widely dispersed communication systems, and both contribute to the shaping of the symbolic fabric by which cultures construct meaning, value and knowledge. In this sense, it is not simply that the media contributed to the dispersal of information and panic about the subprime collapse and the run on banks. Nor indeed, is it simply the case that the media enabled the playing out of the anti- and pro-finance regulation debates that have followed. Rather, finance and the symbolic economy is a critical and functioning part of mediation and the formation of our knowledge systems. As much as anything else, therefore, the GFC is a manifestation of the media and the ways in which our economy of pleasure and related knowledge systems have evolved.

3
Reckless Desire: Love, Sexuality and Infinite Bliss

Ho, the rose having curled its sweet leaves for the world
Takes delight in the motion its petals keep up,
As they laugh to the wind as it laughs from the west.
                    Sappho, 'Song of the Rose', sixth century BC

Pentheus: Where women have the delight of the grape-cluster
at a feast, I say that none of their rites is healthy any longer.
                    Euripides, *The Bacchae*, 405 BC

Got the old pill, got the new pill,
Got the blue pill, got the green pill—
Gets my girl humpin' like a man...
                    Claudia, 'Thrills', 2010

Fantasy shopping

In his treatise on the 'frailty of human bonds', Zygmunt Bauman claims that for modern societies love is eclipsed by power, and desire is eclipsed by spontaneous urges: 'As far as love is concerned, possession, power, fusion and disenchantment are the Four Horsemen of the Apocalypse' (Bauman, 2003: 8). For Bauman and numerous other sociologists of contemporary sexuality, the vision of the end emerges in a condition of crisis: love and desire become the 'fear and trembling' of the advanced world's emotional, reproductive and sexual insecurity.[1] More than anything else, the sexual and erotic desires that were associated with 'lust', as the counterforce of love, have been reconditioned by a society that has grown increasingly intolerant of the deferral of gratification. In a context of cultural and economic urgency, love has become subsumed by a more exigent volition to pleasure. As outlined

in previous chapters, this volition and the fantasy of infinite pleasure compounds love and desire in the densely mediated conditions of
consumerism and the pursuit of pleasure through the pursuit of purchase. In Bauman's terms, desire has become trammelled up into the
needs of perpetual acceleration and the imperatives of spontaneous,
consumer urges.

> In its orthodox renditions, desire needs tending and grooming,
> involving protracted care, difficult bargaining with no forgone resolu-
> tion, some hard choices and a few painful compromises—but worst of
> all a delay in satisfaction, no doubt the sacrifice most abhorred in our
> world of speed and acceleration.... When guided by 'wish'... 'sexual'
> partnership follows the pattern of shopping and calls for nothing
> more than the skills of an average, moderately experienced con-
> sumer. Like other consumer goods, partnership is for consumption
> on-the-spot.
>
> (Bauman, 2003: 12)

Like Jean Baudrillard's (1990) regretful account of the end of 'seduction',
Bauman conceives of the instantaneous gratification of sexual wishes as
the deflation of desire—a contraction which subsumes human sexuality within the deeper conditioning of cultural acceleration and radical
consumerism.

In Eurpides' ancient Greek tragedy, *The Bacchae*, King Pentheus bans
the women of Thebes from engaging in the worship rituals of Dionysus,
the god of music, wine and sensuality. As retribution, Dionysus addles
Pentheus' mind and lures him into the forest where the women are per-
forming their ecstatic rites. Knowing that the King secretly desires to
see the worshippers, the androgenous Dionysus dresses Pentheus in the
clothing of the female Maenad, divine followers of the Bacchus cult.
Pentheus goes to the forest dressed in fawn skins and bearing a thyrsus;
in their own psychic and Bacchanalian ecstasy, however, the women of
Thebes attack Pentheus and tear him to pieces.

In *The Birth of Tragedy* (orig. 1872) Friedrich Nietzsche viewed the
Greek drama, and Dionysian ritual more generally, as one side of a cultural dualism that has always characterized human society—the divide
between the formlessness of sense and sensuality, against the structures
of rational and orderly cognition. Dionysus represents human sense and
desire, while his brother-god, Apollo, represents light and reason. For
Nietzsche and others, humans and human cultures must work within
this dualism, not only for the perfection of art but for the enhancement

of civilization. In denying the formless beauty of desire and sensuality, Pentheus is denying an essential component of his humanity: he is thus destroyed by the beauty he denies but secretly covets.

For Zygmunt Bauman contemporary culture has moved further towards a Bacchanalian vision, tipping out the more restrained and orderly Apollonian condition. Anxieties over the power of sexuality, desire and the (female) body to overwhelm rationality and order have been evident, therefore, in western cultural imaginings through classical civilization, the Enlightenment and into the present. We might confirm Bauman's apocalyptic anxiety in the emergence of new forms of sexual excess and crime that have appeared in many economically developed societies over the past several decades. In an Australian regional court in 2009, for example, a female school teacher was convicted of the 'sexual penetration' of two adolescent males, one aged 14 and the other 17. While the relevant law refers to 'sexual penetration', in this instance the woman who was penetrated is regarded as the perpetrator of the crime. According to the evidence, the music teacher sent the younger boy over a thousand text messages and had performed sexual acts in front of her victims before having sexual intercourse with them (Williams, 2009). In keeping with many other legal jurisdictions around the world, the Australian legislation treats all humans under the age of 18 as 'children' who cannot legally give their consent for having sex with people who are more than 2 years older than themselves.

In the same year, it's been estimated that around 33 million people worldwide are living with HIV-AIDS, including over two million children; since 1981 over 21 million people have died from AIDS, leaving around 14 million children orphaned (UNAIDS, 2009). With the Global Financial Crisis (GFC) moderating in 2010, US consumers spent around $8 billion on cosmetics and around $7 billion on perfume. The American Plastic Surgery Industry research body reported on their website that approximately 11.7 million cosmetic procedures were conducted during 2009. These procedures included three million botox treatments, 400,000 breast augmentations, 200,000 breast reductions, 200,000 abdomen reductions and nearly 1.5 million laser hair removal treatments. Significant increases have been recorded for a relatively new cosmetic procedures—labial reduction surgery (labioplasty). While the amputation and modification of damaged labia, especially after childbirth, have been conducted for many decades, these procedures are now being conducted on pre-partum women who are seeking a cosmetic or aesthetic enhancement of their genitalia. In particular, women who are seeking these enhancements report a sense of embarrassment about the size or extant nature of their labia, especially when wearing revealing or tight fitting clothing like bikinis. Women also report embarrassment when undressing in front of sexual partners, especially casual sex encounters (Braun, 2005). At the same time, the British National Health Service has reported that as many as 500 girls undergo backyard genital mutilation surgery each year in the UK. According to *The London Times*—

> Despite having been outlawed in 1985, female circumcision is still practised in British African communities, in some cases on girls as young as 5. Police have been unable to bring a single prosecution even though they suspect that community elders are being flown from the Horn of Africa to carry out the procedures.
>
> (Kerbaj, 2009)

Defenders of the practice argue candidly that they see no difference between the genital surgery conducted on Muslim immigrant girls and the expensive cosmetic surgeries being undertaken by non-Muslims— they are both designed to enhance a woman's beauty, however that might be culturally inscribed (Essén and Johnsdotter, 2004).

Whether by the transmission of diseases like HIV or the pursuit of bodily ideals and beauty, desire is problematized through the convergence of cultural and personal conceptions of crisis—a crisis of wanting. Leaving aside Bauman's distinction between a rich and a consumerist mode of 'desire', we can return to Jacques Lacan's claim that human sexuality is largely formed around fantasy; these fantasies are themselves animated by the contrary dispositions of desire and loss. As noted in Chapter 1, Lacan believes that human sex drives are unlike the drives of other species, at least inasmuch as they are characterized by a form of fantasy-based onanism rather than instinctual demands for reproduction. This onanism, however, is not simply solipsistic and self-pleasuring: it is a profoundly and intricately formed inter-weaving of self and society, an expressive mode which intricately connects the subject to his or her culture. In many respects, that is, the body of the subject is the meeting place of history, the site in which mind and sense converge around an experiential moment that draws all evolutionary and cultural history into the primary expression of selfhood—the moment of desire.

Desire, therefore, is not simply a physiological, psychological or chemical action; nor is it an exclusively self-formulating and private expression of lust or reproductive urges. Nor simply can desire be de-fused from the past, present and future by which an individual engages with others through the articulation of politics, culture, institutions and power. It is not the course of love alone, nor the transcendent stimuli of intimacy, poetry, drugs or music. It is all of this, gathered around the sexuo-cultural totem that is formed in the fantasy of infinite pleasure, life and the manifestation of incumbent dangers and displeasures.

Desire and the mediasphere

Given its ontological force, therefore, sex is frequently represented in terms of crisis conditions and the volition of a mediated crisis consciousness. This crisis is shaped within the insolubility of sex's great contradiction—the desire for someone or something that exists *outside* the body of the desiring agent. Baudrillard and Bauman define this crisis in terms of a loss ('seduction' and rich 'desire' respectively) that is embedded in a much deeper and broader cultural rupture and transformation. Sexuality and libido are at the centre of an individual's personal experiences, and sense of personal destiny and life values; but they are also central to the ways in which cultures define themselves and explore the dimensions of their collective being—their standardized values, belief systems and sense of collective identity.

For contemporary cultures, the formation of this collective sensibility and crisis consciousness is clearly a contingency of mediation within the globalizing mediasphere. Along with violence and conflict, in fact, sex is a primary driver in a broad range of representational and narrative texts. While sex and libido have always been essential components of human ritual and narrative life, they are present in the widest range of contemporary media—popular music, fashion, TV, advertising, art, film, photography and even the news and other information media which frequently conflate sex with various informational narratives, including sport, politics and even warfare. The Abu Ghraib photographs that appeared during the American occupation of Iraq, for example, both literally and metaphorically exposed the ways in which sex and desire project themselves into the most basic of human conditions and modes of expressive violence (Lewis and Lewis, 2006b).

As noted in previous chapters, the enhancement of agricultural and industrial economies through symbolic exchange systems is formed around the integration of products and images via the mutual stimulation of libido and consumer wants. Again, while I would not accept their respective conclusions, both Bauman and Baudrillard recognize that this integration of sex and economic consumption is shaped by a complicated engagement of mediation and the hierarchical structuring of capitalist economics. As we also noted in the previous chapters of this book, power is both the conduit and catalyst of this exchange system: power in this context circulates around access to the resources of mediation, as well as the economic and cultural value that is integrated into sex and sexualized bodies.

There is, of course, nothing new about the social contingency of sex and power: agricultural economies have structured their reproductive and libidinal relationships around the contract of gender, inter-marriage and the transfer of property. In contemporary cultures, however, the media forms the creative web that is both the conduit for the exchange of product and sexuality, as well as the sticky entrapment by which power imposes itself on human relationships. In his own account of the *History of Sexuality,* Michel Foucault alerts us to the ubiquity of power and the means by which it stimulates and represses the libidinal engagement of bodies—'because it is produced at every instant, at every point, or moreover in every relation between one point and another. Power is everywhere' (Foucault, 1981: 22).

Working through the mediasphere, therefore, this ubiquity of power enables and shapes the knowledge systems that have formed around economic and sexual exchange. The media, therefore, is critically implicated in the conflation of desire and displeasure (*jouissance*) which are expressed through these knowledge systems and the fantasy of infinite pleasure. In a culture that now defines and privileges itself in terms of political, consumer and sexual 'freedom', this fantasy inevitably generates its own mirror image of disappointment or loss—its own agitated and restless spectre of unattainability.

Thus, while commentators like Zygmunt Bauman and Jean Baudrillard might nostalgically bemoan the surrender of seduction or rich desire, they are essentially marking the terrain of crisis by which the 'sexual revolution' and the pursuit of infinite economic growth encounter one another in a sound studio, bedroom or back-street bar— the terrain in which the skin and the fantasy conspire against the midnight air and the inevitability of farewell. In other words, commentators like Baudrillard and Bauman have sought to demarcate the trajectory of a sexual revolution that now encourages the proliferation of sexual imaging and transient sexual partnering against the repressive power of state sanctioned and enduring heterosexual marriage. The crisis of contemporary sex and sexual relationships falls somewhere within the triad of sometimes disjunctive and sometimes conjunctive cultural trajectories—that is, between control and repression, the infinite pursuit of sexual pleasure, and the drive to consumer accumulation.

Marriage, kinship and the family

The Lacanian conception of sex and sexual relationships can be connected to the anxieties of people like Zygmunt Bauman through a range of social indicators, particularly around human reproduction, marriage and the family. These social indicators are often translated into a simpler and more integrated discourse of 'family crisis'—the effect of what has become popularly called the sexual revolution. This discourse, of course, has its own structured knowledge and ideological systems which are generated through a cultural politics in which sex, desire and the body are the primary polemical sites.

Beginning in the western world in the 1960s, this revolution has enabled a greater diversity of sexual expression beyond the simple parameters of monogamous, heterosexual marriage (see Pallotta-Chiarolli, 2010). Through the progress of this revolution, however, new concerns have arisen about the pressures that are now associated with liberation, particularly around sexual performance, early-age sexual activity, gender identity and faith in love. In this context, there is also an increasing anxiety amongst social commentators about the proliferation of sexual partnering and sexual imaging that contribute to bodily dissatisfaction, excess consumerism and transmission of sex-based infections. Indeed, it is precisely this question of 'excess' that drives much of the critique of contemporary sexuality and sexual practices. For Bauman and Baudrillard, it may be that the sexual revolution has simply exceeded itself—that it has simply gone 'too far'.

At the centre of many of these anxieties is the 'family'. For most agricultural and industrial societies the family, in fact, has been the primary social framework and institution for the management of libido, reproduction and populations. The emergence of heterosexual monogamy as an organizing archetype has a long and complicated history. Through the rise of agrarianism, human societies have shaped their families through various permutations of polygamy and monogamy, multiple wives or multiple husbands, and sometimes a mix of both (Foucault, 1981; Forbes, 2005). While monogamy was practised by some cultures, its emergence as an imposed, legal system of marriage in the modern sense is more directly associated with Western Europe and sovereign Catholicism. Indeed, while the Biblical stories of the Middle East were often constituted around polygamous social structures, the Catholic Church in Europe began to impose a more distinctly monogamous model over its subjects during the medieval period. While many explanations have been offered to explain this social and cultural innovation, it is commonly felt that monogamy provided for rulers and social governors a more acute method of social control, particularly around the legal transfer and management of property and inheritance.

Applying the force of the sovereign and divine lineage to civil justice, European medieval legal processes were invoked to ensure the effective transfer of property and reproductive order. Medieval magisterial records reveal the importance of contractual arrangements in marriage and family maintenance. Property and money are exchanged in various forms of betrothal: any breach results in fines and restoration. The following excerpt from magisterial records in Kent demonstrates clearly that the sovereign has a vested interest in the control of human bodies and their desires; gender is problematized through the threat to marriage and its imagining of social responsibility and monogamy.

> Henry Cook of Trotteslyve (Kent) and his wife were summoned because each has turned away from the other and they do not live together. Both appear in person. And Henry then alleged that he did not know why his wife left him but she behaved as badly as possible towards him, with contumelious words and other evil deeds, as he asserts. His [unnamed] wife said that her said husband loved several other women and therefore had a malevolent mind towards her, and she could not go on living with Henry on account of his cruelty. Finally both of them swore after touching the gospels that they would live together in future and give each other the usual conjugal services ('suffragia'), and that she [blank left for name] will now be humble and 'familiaris' with her husband and not fighting, contumelious or insulting; and that the husband will treat his wife with marital affection from now on.
>
> (orig. 1347, Johnson, 1948: 974)

During the late nineteenth and early twentieth centuries, the new sociological disciplines, led by people like Max Weber, suggested that the rise of modern capitalist economics was linked to this same religious and political base. While focusing on Protestantism, Weber nevertheless argued that the rise of capitalist individualism could be traced to the embedding of social and political practices within the more intensified, modern monogamous family (orig. 1905, Weber, 2002). Writing in the late nineteenth century, Friedrich Engels claimed that monogamy in 'sex-love' was clearly developed through capitalism's emphasis on individualism and free choice. According to Engels (1902), the 'love match' became a significant part of individual rights and the ideology of freedom.

This view has been more recently corroborated by Alan Macfarlane in *The Culture of Capitalism* (1987). According to Macfarlane, western societies adopted new modes of kinship and marriage ritual that replaced communalism with a much stronger and more intense expression of individual choice. In this context, the emergence of romantic love as the core of ritualized matrimony and reproduction was, therefore, an inevitable consequence of the rise of capitalism and its 'vicious' subordination of the interests of the group by the interests of the individual. To a degree, this same argument is central to the critique of numerous socialist and radical feminists who claim that there is an alignment of capitalist and patriarchal ideologies in the rise of the modern marriage and the oppression of women. Thus, as capitalists seek to oppress the proletariat through the exploitation of labour, it also mobilizes patriarchal power in order to oppress women's bodies, labour and reproductive capacity. Through both physical coercion and the force of patriarchal ideology, women's lives are constrained by the needs of men. According to many feminists, this mode of oppression continues into the present day, as gendered social systems continue to constrain women's income, career prospects and sexual experiences.

While far less focused on the issues of class and gender, Michel Foucault (1981) nevertheless argues that the modern family and the conditions of normalized heterosexual marriage were constituted around the modern state and its strategic management of increasing populations. Thus, it is not so much capitalism and its vaguely articulated ideology of control which best characterizes modern sexuality, but rather the emergence of the modern state itself which has a vested interest in stimulating an optimum level of social libido. Thus, the *modern* state employs various strategies to both stimulate libido and control it through the modulation of sexual discourse. In this way, the formal discourses that are generated through social science, health, population studies, religious teaching and social taboos are integrated with a broad range of mediated and less visible social conversations in order to form this complex system of modulation.

In *The History of Sexuality Volume One*, Foucault makes clear that the state had a vested interest in social and personal libido: too little and the populations would be repressed and fail adequately to reproduce; too much and the population might be distracted from other social and economic functions, including work and warfare. Running parallel to Engels' account of heterosexual monogamy, Foucault insists that the state quite consciously propagated normative social behaviours which were more easily controlled than a broader and more liberated mode of sexual practice. In this way, the state has marked the territory of sexuality, as it excludes (even criminalizes) sexual practices that lie outside its ambit—non-marital, gay, transgenderist and so on. In a recent example of this transformation, the Indonesian state has enacted new anti-pornography laws that cast doubt on the legal status of homosexuality and transgenderism, which have been a significant part of community and sexual practice for centuries (Lewis and Lewis, 2009).

Foucault's account of romantic love and the authorization of heterosexual marriage accords with socialist and feminist perspectives. These studies situate the concept of 'ideal love' within an instrumental history that identifies social bonds with external social and institutional forces. And while we might have some misgivings about this instrumentalism, it is nevertheless clear that industrial modernism has necessarily been formed through a considerable crisis of sex, family and kinship. The simple fracturing of geographically contained community and the reformulation of society in mass urban spaces undoubtedly contributed to this reshaping of social relationships and especially the availability of prospective partners. Little doubt, too, greater social and spatial mobilities created new opportunities for social variance, and alternative values and practices. Occurring throughout the period of industrialization, the increasing congregation of people in cities provided a further screen for cultural innovation, including innovations around sexual practice and partnering. Liberated somewhat from the surveillance and controls exerted by village, familial and religious authorities, individuals were able to exercise greater choice over their partners and sexual activities. The urban working classes, in particular, were able to choose partners for passion or love, while the rising middle classes were also exploring the possibilities of 'love matches', though these remained largely situated within their own social group.

Thus, the literature of love that emerges through middle-class writings in England, for example (Jane Austen, the Brontes, George Eliot), represented a new class formation, its passions and self-obsession. In the refinement of female desire, these cultivated novels contrasted somewhat with the proliferation, in the nineteenth century especially, of popular pornography. Rising literacy rates among the working classes enabled the expansion of sexually explicit texts and the literary genre of the 'penny-terrible'. Thus, the eighteenth-century porn novels like *Memories of a Woman of Pleasure—Fanny Hill* (John Cleland, orig. 1748–1749) provided a template for the rise of racy and sexually explicit texts that proliferated during the nineteenth century. Iain McCalman (1984) claims that the increasing demand for pornography in the nineteenth century is attributable not only to the widening of literacy but also an increasing individualism. While this increasing individualism may be linked to urbanization and capitalism, it is also a condition of mechanization and the impact of industrial alienation. Certainly, the erotica associated with romantic writers like Keats, Byron and Swinburne may be viewed as a reaction to the mechanistic and instrumental brutality of the new industrial cities—but pornography and erotica must surely have played a similar role for the less well-educated or culturally refined members of the new industrializing states of Europe (Brulotte and Phillips, 2006).

In any case, state authorities sought to control and censor the obscene and anti-Christian tenor of many of these erotic and pornographic texts. Certainly in England, the state imposed itself on human desires and sexual practices, as new laws banned pornography and 'sodomy' (including male homosexuality) which were deemed immoral and hence threatened the fabric of monogamy and the heterosexual family (Weeks, 1981). In Foucault's reading, the state demanded a stable family setting for nurture and preparation of new generations for work, warfare, taxation, reproduction and other state duties. Laws prohibiting homosexuality, polygamy and marital desertion, along with fault-based divorce laws, were designed to maintain family cohesion, durability and order within an increasingly complex urban life. As noted, however, the pressure for change, fostered through the increasing volition of individualism, consumerism, women's liberation and the availability of new contraceptive technologies eventually produced changes in social attitudes and practices, as well as government policy—especially around no-fault divorce, equal opportunity and the relaxation of censorship laws. For social conservatives, these changes were of themselves a crisis, while for more progressive thinkers, they represented the foundations of a true sexual revolution.

Contemporary family

Very clearly, these transformations are centred upon the sexual and civic status of women, particularly women's role in the household, work, public life, parenting and as sexual agents. And while it is important to emphasize the active political and cultural pursuit of these changes, it is equally important to acknowledge the transformative effects of women's role in the macro-volition of an economy of pleasure. Specifically, in an economy that demands constant growth and innovation, women and women's bodies have been conscripted into the symbolic exchange system in three distinct ways—first, as working agents who have expanded the economic skill base and available labour; second, as consumers within the restless momentum of an economy that requires ever-expanding populations and markets; and third as sexual stimulants whereby the female body is culturally fetishized for the sale of itself and products.

In particular, the convergence of media industries, a culture of pleasure and the need for a constantly expanding market of consumers have contributed significantly to the mobilization of women and women's bodies within the symbolic core of the new economy. Into the present, therefore, women's bodies have become the primary agents of these changes and especially the ways in which love, family, sex and relationships are conceived and constructed. The promulgation of new sexualities, sexual identities and formations of 'the family' is therefore a manifestation of constituent individual choices; however, it is also evidence of more aggregate cultural patterns and flows, including an imagining of an infinite pleasure which is shadowed only by the anxieties of displeasure within the mediated crisis consciousness.

Thus, if an aim of radical feminism and socialist critique was to deconstruct the love ideal, monogamy, gender and the sexually constraining family, then it may well have achieved its goals. According to Eurostat (OECD, 2008 see Figure 3.1), marriage rates in all major OECD countries have declined dramatically since the 1970s, with even religious countries like the USA experiencing a 25 per cent decline,

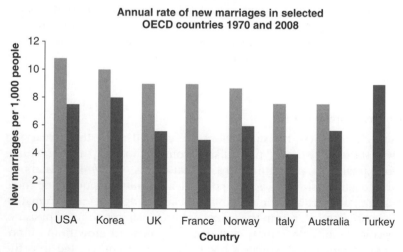

Figure 3.1   Annual rate of new marriages in OECD countries.

and more secular nations like the Netherlands having fallen more than 50 per cent.

These figures are partly explained by significant increases in the average age at which individuals now marry, and by an increasing proportion of people who are deciding not to marry at all but prefer de facto cohabitation. The figures do not include, for example, those people in Australia and New Zealand who cohabit and enjoy the same legal rights and privileges as married couples. The radical decline in marriage, however, is also due in part to an increasing proportion of the population who are preferring to remain single, or who are engaged in 'alternative' sexual relationships.

The OECD research also notes that for those countries that introduced no-fault divorce in the 1970s, there was a radical upswing in divorce rates, presumably because of backlog demand. This is the case in the 1980s when particular countries like South Korea introduced no-fault divorce in keeping with the country's economic and social modernization. Even so, as the Eurostat figures demonstrate, divorce rates remain high in economically advanced nations.

As indicated in Figure 3.2, the average duration of marriage has also declined markedly in many nations. In the USA, for example, the average length of a marriage is a little less than 10 years, the lowest in the developed world (OECD, 2008; NCFMR, 2010). The duration figure for first marriages is considerably lower, at around 8 years. While the marriage duration figure for predominantly Catholic countries is somewhat

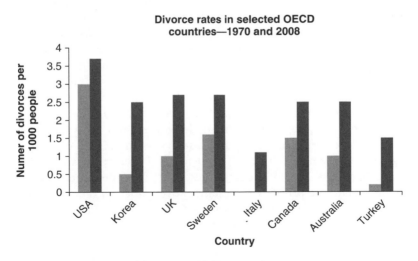

Figure 3.2 Annual rate of divorce in OECD countries.

higher (especially Portugal), this is partly due to the Church's prohibitions on divorce and partly due to variable attitudes towards the most commonly cited reasons for separation, including attitudes to sexual frequency, infidelity, familial security and child-rearing. It has been conjectured, for example, that Americans are less tolerant of sexual infidelity in marriage than some European countries; this intolerance might partly explain the high rate of divorce and relative brevity of marriage in the USA (Amato and Previti, 2003; Fine and Harvey, 2006; Hills and Todd, 2008).

Infidelity in marriage

It is fair to say that sex and sexuality permeates much of the modern media. While the news and information media often report the sorts of statistics outlined above, sex is a primary driver in many entertainment texts, particularly through melodrama and public intrigue with celebrity relationships, marriage, infidelity and divorce (Rojek, 2004; Turner, 2004; Lewis, 2008). As the normative pattern of human sexual relationships, marriage and its challenges have also been a central narrative motif in fictional texts. Evolving through nineteenth-century British and European literature, in particular, modern media narratives have developed specific genres in order to explore and dramatize the experience of contemporary erotica, marriage and the family. Thus, as the transformation of sexual relationships and the crisis of marriage have created a discursive rupture, TV texts, in particular, have sought to narratize the moral and gendered battles that are so evident in everyday life. Programmes like *Sex in the City* and *Desperate Housewives* have been discussed by many public and academic commentators in terms of 'comedy of manners': that is, a form of social critique which reveals underlying social and moral tensions through the narratization of new forms of sexuality, identity and relational practices.

Thus, while *Sex in the City* has been regarded as a frank and quite revolutionary exposé of modern single women and their sexual and emotional explorations, *Desperate Housewives* is an account of marriage and family life in which libido, infidelity and divorce are the primary dramatic drivers. While of course these texts are entertainments, they also articulate the private circumstances that underpin the statistics we have cited above. In particular, *Desperate Housewives* and various other mid-life phase TV narratives examine the ways in which marriage breakdown and divorce constitute the spectre of displeasure that threatens all committed sexual unions. And if divorce is the sword of Damocles that hangs over marriage, then trust, sexual performance and fidelity are often viewed as the horsehair that holds the sword in place.

In this context, sexual engagement with someone outside the marriage is regarded as an assault on the integrity, history and deep values that are anchored in the ideal and the vow of monogamy—not simply an independent choice or action exercised by an independent being. Even without the framework of religion or state sanction, extramarital sex appears to be a primary breach in the cultural status, social arrangement and personal contract upon which contemporary marriage remains grounded. Indeed, it has become increasingly clear since the powerful surge of the sexual revolution that the ideal of enduring, monogamous marriage is no longer the responsibility of religion and state: rather, marriage is sustained through the imagining of romantic love and an infinite pleasure fortified by sexual bliss and a mutually sustaining consumerist lifestyle. The great romantic films and TV programmes that still issue from the Hollywood commercial imagining remains fixed by a fantasy of enduring love and erotic bliss. The problem is that when the marriage falters, it is not only the deficiency of the respective partner that is at fault—it is the imagining of love itself. Within the still pervasive mediated fantasy of enduring, monogamous love, the ideal seems strangely discordant as it encounters the 10-year limit by which time the love and the marriage, especially in the USA, have usually collapsed. This discord explains, at least in part, the cynicism or crisis consciousness that has become increasingly associated, not only with marriage, but with love.

While research on the reasons for divorce abound, sexual infidelity is amongst the most commonly cited reasons for marriage dissolution. In a broad empirical study on American divorce, Amato and Previti note:

> Infidelity was the most commonly reported cause, followed by incompatibility, drinking or drug use, and growing apart. People's specific reasons for divorcing varied with gender, social class, and life course variables. Former husbands and wives were more likely to blame their ex-spouses than themselves for the problems that led to the divorce. Former husbands and wives claimed, however, that women were more likely to have initiated the divorce.
>
> (Amato and Previti, 2003: 692)

As numerous other commentators have noted, however, the act of infidelity may not of itself be the central cause of a relationship problem, but may be merely a symptom of alienation which then breaks the bond of monogamy and the ideal of romantic bliss. Indeed, in this most private dimension of people's lives, it is very difficult to obtain accounts of marriage and sexuality that are not clouded by a subject's personal perspective, ambivalence, confusion or even preference for untruth. As many researchers in the field of human relationships and sexuality concede, people tend to lie about sex, sexual performance and sexual activities—especially around issues of infidelity and alternative sexual attractions. Indeed, the very word 'infidelity' suggests the normative status of 'fidelity'—it may be quite difficult, even in anonymous surveys, for an individual to 'confess' to an aberration, particularly as this is the moral implication of the researcher, the research and the question itself.

This heuristic problem merely confirms Lacan's assertion that sex and desire are largely predicated upon fantasy and the problematics of pleasure and its spectral displeasure. Thus, the data on sexual frequency (the number of times in a week a couple has sex) and sexual engagement with persons other than their primary partner are notoriously unreliable—if only because sex is itself a conflux of contending dispositions, psycho-emotional needs, moral framing, expectations, hormonal flows, fantasies, imaginings, contexts, and states of body and mind. Thus, figures on the incidence of sexual infidelity vary quite markedly: significantly, some recent American studies suggests that as many as 70 per cent of wives and 72 per cent of husbands have had sex with a person other than their primary partner during the course of a marriage (Hite, 2000, 2006; Praver, 2006).

While there may be contentions over the rate of extramarital sex, it is very clearly an increasing trend, even with couples that cohabit rather than formally marry. Along with the high rate of divorce, these high rates of extramarital sex contribute to an escalating sense of sexual crisis in America and other first world societies (Hite, 2006; Herzog, 2008). Indeed, the agitated and pervasive presence of infidelity in narrative and celebrity texts seems to fortify a broader, public sense of crisis in which infidelity is a clandestine but powerful spectre that lies within the shadowy souls of all human spouses. As Judith Treas and Deidre Giesen note, this increasing propensity for couples to engage in extramarital sex occurs within a highly disjunctive context in which the expectation of newly-weds is that their marriage will be sexually exclusive and a view by up to 90 per cent of Americans that extramarital sex is 'wrong' (Treas and Giesen, 2000: 48). According to Treas and Giesen, this form of disapproval is articulated within many American states which retain sanctions against 'adultery': those who engage in extramarital sex may forfeit 'the right to vote, serve alcohol, practice law, adopt children or raise their own children' (Treas and Giesen, 2000: 48). And all this in a country in which *Sex in the City* and *Desperate Housewives* attract massive television audiences.

While these laws are largely unenforced, they indicate the enduring aspiration of state and religious apparatuses to impose themselves on the personal lives of citizens, even as social attitudes have transmogrified and state powers have been refocused. Very clearly, however, child-rearing remains critical to these powers. The emergence of the single parent family in everyday life and textual narratives continues to generate deep anxieties and ambivalence in advanced societies (Usdansky, 2009). According to Dafoe Whitehead and David Popenoe (2006, 2009), only 20 per cent of children were raised in single-parent families in 1960, while in 2009 this figure was 54 per cent (Whitehead and Popenoe, 2009). Combined with the dramatic rise in mixed parent families and cohabitant families, the increase in especially fatherless families has created considerable changes in the ways in which marriage, kinship and family relationships and institutions function. According to Whitehead and Popenoe (2006), Americans are less accepting of the realities of this situation and persist with social fantasies and policies on marriage that contribute to relatively higher levels of child poverty and teenage pregnancy than in Scandinavian countries. Thus, while only 65 per cent of women in Sweden marry, 85 per cent of American women marry; this higher marriage rate in itself contributes to a higher divorce rate in America, as well as the related problems of psychological and emotional trauma. Scandinavians, it would seem, are more accepting of the transient nature of sexual relationships and have a stronger fabric of public funding and social support for child-rearing outside of formal marriage and family contexts. Child-rearing, that is, is seen in Scandinavia as a state responsibility more so than it is in America where the model of the formal family persists in fantasy and public policy.

The wider impact of these social changes, however, is being experienced by younger people themselves. According to most recent studies on marriage and family, it is now only a very small minority of teenagers who believe that marriage is likely to produce greater sexual and emotional fulfilment than other forms of lifestyle, including cohabitation or individual living arrangements (Whitehead and Popenoe, 2009). The research indicates further that only half the teenagers in America believe that child-rearing within marriage is in any way superior or more valuable than child-rearing outside marriage. This benign view of child-rearing and divorce lifestyles is supported through highly popular narrative texts like *Two and a Half Men*, in which single parenting, divorce and free sexual associations are represented in a positive way. Thus, if there is a widening cultural scepticism about the capacity of love to frame an enduring marriage, there appears less cynicism about the ways in which sexual pleasure might be explored and enjoyed—at least on television.

Indeed, the discourse of sex and love has shifted from the virginal, standardized monogamous marriage to a more amorphous mix of enduring love, cohabitation, marriage, relationships and sexual fulfilment. Family and children are no longer set within the narrow framework of marriage, but float more freely through various relational and open permutations, including alternative relationships, single parenting, lesbian *in vitro* and trans-national adoption. Through her ageing and the passing of her fertility capacity, the celebrity performer Madonna created an international controversy over her adoption of two children from the African nation of Malawi. While it is generally recognized that the celebrity pop star paid millions of dollars to the Malawi government, and the child's care community, this trans-national adoption raises many ethical and ideological questions about the direction of the sexual revolution. Once an icon of 1980s' popular female liberation, Madonna expressed her social and economic privilege and maternal desires through the effective purchase of another human body. In a manner that resonates with colonial enslavements, Madonna's actions both intensify the blackness of her adopted child as it restates her power and primacy within an American dominated mediasphere and economy of pleasure—an economy that necessarily evinces itself through innovations in sexuality and familial relationships.

Girl power

The socially conservative US administration of George W. Bush (2001–2008) sought to reverse the sexual transformations that have been taking place in the world. In her own account of America's sexual crisis, Dagmar Herzog (2008) points to Bush's attempts to restore chastity and pre-marital sexual abstinence in the USA and other nations dependent on US aid. In an attempt to reverse the trajectory of sexual liberation discussed above, the Bush administration spent $120 million on abstinence before marriage programmes in its first year in office. After 4 years in office, the cumulative figure was around $1 billion, with nearly half of all public schools teaching abstinence. At the same time, abstinence programmes were also being exported to developing world contexts, largely through HIV-AIDS prevention programmes. As a condition of receiving funding, foreign governments had to teach abstinence as the key preventative strategy (Herzog, 2008).

The purpose of both the domestic and international programmes was to restore the symbolic status and virtues of monogamous, heterosexual marriage and to stabilize the family. Very clearly, the ideal of virgin marriage accords with an older form of fertility and reproductive controls associated with property inheritance: in a patriarchal system fathers protected their power and inheritance rights through the security of their genetic lineage. A woman's sexual fidelity and virginal status ensured a clear genetic lineage and hence was an important political and military strategy for the propertied classes.

These control strategies were necessary, it would seem, as men regarded themselves as sexual predators who could be easily tempted into all forms of sexual activities, seductions and reproductive seeding. Thus, supported by various forms of religious precepts and erotic fantasies. virginity marriage maintained itself as a cultural fantasy well into the twentieth century. However, through the rise of secularism, symbolic exchange, Freudian psychoanalysis, women's emancipation and the surging power of sense-based media, the sexual revolution ultimately subsumed the status of virginity, replacing it with a new fantasy of enduring love and sexual fulfilment. Virginity and pre-marital abstinence, in this sense, became impugned as 'old-fashioned' and 'repressive sexism': what was okay for males should now be okay for females.

As noted in previous chapters, the fantasy of infinite pleasure inevitably conscripted female and youth markets into the matrix of the economic exchange system. As noted above the so-called sexual revolution was due in large part to this expansion in the economic role of women and youth, and the cultural and economic deployment of their erotic sensibilities within a new market (and labour) sphere. Thus, in an economy that is shaped by desire, symbolic imagery and various forms of social mobility, new subject-consumers were generated in order to drive the imperatives of economic growth and its underlying pleasure imaginary. The collusion between romantic love and erotica was sustained, therefore, through fantasy, especially as they were propitiated through various modes of mediation. Women's sex, while always a primary driver in agricultural and industrial cultures, became transfigured through the proliferation of choice, narrative and erotic imagery.

In this context, 'third wave' feminism, which focuses on the free sexual expressivity of women, collides with the greater instrumentalism of 'second wave' feminism, which focuses on the patriarchal suppression of women, women's right to work and the need for women (and men) to be de-gendered—or at least to have their socially inscribed symbols of gender neutralized. Even without the 'wave' labels, this clash of gender knowledge systems is common in academic, public and popular discourses, including various forms of representation in the mediasphere. These clashes, however, are not simply a matter of work against family, or love against casual sex. Rather, the emergence of new female subjectivities is besieged by deeper and more powerful psycho-cultural contradictions and contentions, contentions that affect a more profound sense of emotional satisfaction and state of being.

In the online environment, these challenges and debates around the new female subject have proliferated. The Web 2.0 and mobile devices, for example, have taken the Internet into more expansive realms of interactivity, providing new forums for the exploration and expression of gender sensibilities across a bewildering array of sexual possibilities. Online dating and other modes of social networking are often constituted around female sexuality and the prospects of sexual choice. Among the more provocative of these social networking sites is an interactive blog written by English woman Abby Lee. Lee's autobiography of liberated sexual adventures parallels a whole industry of female generated pornography, another new expressivity of the female subject. Lee's blog, *Woman with a One-tracked Mind*, details the author's appetite for casual sex and her various techniques of seduction and gratification. True or fictionalized, the blog proved very popular with women with similar sexual interests and practices; not surprisingly Lee was able to convert her sexual narratives into a consumable 'novel' which generated considerable market interest and personal profit.

Yet even within the Madonna and Abby Lee world of sexual assertiveness, women continue to wonder about men and their own prospects for attracting a substantial boyfriend or even life partner with whom they will find emotional and erotic satisfaction. Within this dualism, the condition of 'being single' looms as either an honourable (new) female status, or a spectral crisis which gnaws at self-esteem and a sense of social visibility. Even Carrie, who is the perpetual single in *Sex in the City*, is prompted to ask in one of the episodes:

> I couldn't help but wonder, when did being single become the modern day equivalent of being a leper?...Then I had a frightening thought, maybe I was the one who had been faking it. All these years faking to myself that I was happy being single.

Thus, the re-ascription of male bachelorhood as a genuine female life option is interrogated in ways that betray a certain kind of emotional uncertainty, even through the propagation of choice (see Whitehead, 2003; Whitehead and Popenoe, 2006).

This emotional and psychological dissatisfaction is often associated with a broader cultural pattern of communal and interpersonal disconnection. Thus, the crisis discourses that are generated around sex, sexual relationships and the family are not simply the emissaries of the surrender of seduction or rich erotica—they are mobilized through the very essence of gender and the ways in which women's sexuality has been released in the first world and the economy of desire. In this sense, the aphorism that 'sex is shopping' becomes redolent within the crisis of love.

An end to marriage: what men really want?

The question inevitably arises: is the pleasure economy, which constitutes itself around individual needs and the perpetual reinvigoration of desire and innovation, ultimately incompatible with romantic love, durable relationships and marriage? If this economy, which requires perpetual growth, innovation and change, is merely the mirror image of the new sexual ethic, do we simply change partners, the way we change socks or hairstyles? Will our loyalty to a breakfast cereal brand prove more durable than our loyalty to a sexual partner—or even to our own children? Does the incompatibility between durable love and economy of desire merely expose some ultimate incompatibility between men and women?

These questions have certainly been raised by a culture that is not merely obsessed with sex, but whose very survival—its economy and culture—is bound to the conditions of insatiable desire and the fantasy of infinite pleasure. Esther Perel (2006), among innumerable other female authors and commentators, has attempted to reconcile the contending demands of erotica and durable love by advocating increased marital independence. In her account of psychological therapy sessions conducted with couples, Perel claims that the comforts and security of marriage are fundamentally incompatible with the excitement and recklessness of sexual desire. The only solution to this discord is a certain kind of sexual ruthlessness in marriage, whereby the partners become individuals who resist a temptation to frequent and excessive communication, and an 'intimacy' that exposes each of the partner's private fantasies and sexual independence.

This Do-It-Yourself advocacy echoes much of the sentiment of Anthony Giddens' panegyric on sexuality in modern societies, *The Transformation of Intimacy* (1992). Giddens uses the idea of intimacy in a different way to Perel, arguing that intimacy is the essence of all erotica and mutual titillation, rather than a suffocating blanket of perpetual communication, as Perel defines it. Like Perel, however, Giddens interrogates the underlying assumptions of marriage and seeks to deconstruct the institutional dimensions of partnering through a more heightened sense of independence and choice. Giddens argues that institutional modes of marriage create financial and emotional dependency, a condition which inevitably inhibits true eroticism, intimacy and even love. In a normative gesture against marriage and the ideals of durable romantic love, Giddens advocates a new form of relational intimacy that is constituted around independent and autonomous lifestyles. For Giddens, the ideals of a longevitous mode of cohabitation and financial dependence are merely atavistic, creating an image of intimacy that is little more than a political charade: real intimacy evolves around political choice, autonomy and the perpetual risk of change.

This view of marriage as political failure is shared by numerous other commentators who advocate a more honest and courageous reappraisal of contemporary culture and its relational requirements. In *Sex in the Future* (2000) Robin Baker expands on these arguments, claiming that new reproductive technologies will enable the more complete expression of humans' underlying sexual biology. The demands of reproduction and nurture, Baker claims, have suppressed our sexual nature, leading to a complex of largely incongruent social institutions and practices. Humans' essential biological need for multiple sexual partners and sexual change will be released as women, in particular, are liberated from the demands of reproduction, nurture and family. Thus, genetic selection and *in vitro* technologies will allow both genders to explore and enjoy their sexuality, facilitating new kinds of relationships and modes of sexual experience. Sex in the future, Baker claims, will resolve tensions around intimacy, monogamy, erotica and durability as individuals will be free to choose a range of relational styles and partners, including partners for casual sex, friendship sex, reproduction, same gender sex and so on.

Baker's predictions of the death of the nuclear family and monogamy clearly accords with a particular lineage of second wave feminism which focused on the repressive nature of marriage and patriarchal hetero-centricism (Applewhite, 1997; Jeffreys, 2007). Paradoxically, the predictions also accord with a frequently cited male fantasy about sexual freedom beyond the institution of marriage and familial responsibility.

The resurgent popularity of 'swinger' culture (Gould, 2000; Cooper, 2004; Moore, 2007) and multiple partner relationships (Pallotta-Chiarolli, 2010) in western societies is symptomatic of the changes that Barker and others presage. While younger people may experiment with multiple partner casual sex, swinger culture facilitates sexual partnering between individuals who are often involved in a long-term couple relationship, including marriage. While swinging has been practised in gay and heterosexual communities over time and in various cultures, it has become increasingly popular in western societies, as couples seek to reconcile committed love relationships with adventure and extraneous sexual excitement. House parties and mass attendance 'balls' in public venues have evolved as places where couples engage in partner swapping and group sex. While the focus of these parties is heterosexual, single women are often also invited to attend and woman to woman sex is either tolerated or actively encouraged. Over recent years, holiday resorts have also been established in countries like France, Italy and Jamaica where often naked vacationers engage in a range of recreational activities involving sex with other couples and single women.

Multiple partner relationships are also becoming increasingly common in economically developed societies. While TV series like *Big Love* represent one version of these polygamous lifestyles—a sub-branch of American Mormonism—there are numerous variants and constituencies, some involving cohabitation and others a form of commuter partnering with individuals spending time in separate houses with alternative partners (Pallotta-Chiarolli, 2010). While many of these multiple partner relationships involve one woman and two men, they are also comprised of one man and two or three women. In some cultural groups, like Australian Aborigines, these relational styles have been blended with traditional modes of polygamy where males often had two or three wives. Similarly, migrant groups from some polygamous Muslim countries continue the practice beyond the sight of their new country's legal purview (*National Geographic*, 2010).

Proponents of these new relational forms express a general dissatisfaction with both conventional, monogamous marriage and the alternative of serial, casual sex. Echoing Esther Perel's (2006) concerns over the incompatibility of marriage and desire, swingers in particular seek to reconcile this discord through the separation of their ongoing love and more light-weight or 'fun' engagements with other people. For both multiple partner spouses and swingers, the conventional marriage is often seen as an artifice or pretence of monogamy where people simply lie about their extramarital relations: when these lies are exposed, the marriage often collapses under the weight of truth.

As we have noted, however, the most common of these new social arrangements is the formation of the especially fatherless, single parent household. In this context, the utopian vision of a new world sexual order can appear rather grim. Poor, single mothers, in particular, battle the double duress of emotional and sexual alienation—effects of masculo-centric freedoms and residual patriarchal irresponsibility. While we will discuss this condition more fully in terms of the globalization of poverty (see Chapter 4), it is certainly worth noting that the vaunting celebration of male sexual liberation advocated by Giddens, Baker and others, and the broader social deconstruction of marriage and marital security, is neither universally welcomed nor advantageous. Certainly, a number of feminist and other public commentators concede that the deconstruction of marriage has come at a cost; specifically, the ideology of male responsibility that was inscribed in patriarchy has been jettisoned and replaced by a state-imposed responsibility that many men resent. As marriages dissolve, this legal zone of male responsibility and familial rights has become an intense emotional battleground which can often leave single mothers in a state of financial insecurity or destitution.

Masculine revivalism?

Peter Cattaneo's cult movie *Young People Fucking* (2006) gives voice to many of the issues surrounding new sexualities, relationship styles and sexual practices. In particular, the film addresses the issues associated with libidinal atrophy in longer term relationships. While one longer term couple featured in the film seeks to reawaken their sexual passions through experimentations with new sexual activities—toys, leathers, anal sex—another couple experiments with the introduction of a third sexual partner. An ex-couple are aroused by their current unfamiliarity; another two friends attempt to have sex with one another, despite their previous lack of sexual interest and strong bonds 'as friends'. All of these vignettes focus on the ongoing dichotomy between desire and enduring love, in particular the ways in which desire diminishes within many longer term relationships. While each of these vignettes offers its own idiosyncratic solution to the 'problem', each is conditional to the fantasy and primacy of love.

And indeed, there seems little evidence that social transience and the rejection of durable love provides the best template of life satisfaction for the majority of modern humans. In an increasingly transient world, many people still seem to need the ideal of durable love and long-term relationships in order to sustain their fantasies of pleasure, reproduction and social completion. Perhaps, as Esther Perel (2006) notes, we need the spice and danger of sexual passion, as well as the security of durable and committed love: and it is this discord in and of itself which sustains us. To complicate matters even further, recent health research shows that individuals who are in long-term relationships—marriage, de facto, heterosexual, multiple partner or same-sex—have much better all-round health outcomes than people who are single or in a state of perpetual relationship transience (ASPE, 2007). To this extent, it seems to matter very little whether the long-term stable relationship is institutionally sanctioned and described as 'marriage' so long as it is loving and durable.

The Viagra revolution

A common gender stereotype claims that men have greater difficulty with commitment, intimacy and monogamy, and men are more sexually precipitative than women. According to the same stereotyping, men are less emotionally communicative and emotionally intelligent than women (Brackett et al., 2003; Rojek, 2009). These stereotypes are supported, to some degree, by survey data, particularly data generated around sexual attitudes, experience and marketing. Certain kinds of media texts are gender-focused, suggesting a patterned distinction between the ways men and women relate to the world. Indeed, during the 1990s particular gender commentary shifted away from 'equality as equivalence' and advocated equality as the free articulation of difference. Along with third wave feminist discourses, popular commentary reinvigorated debate around gender difference by defining equality and equal rights not through cultural sharing but through mutual respect for these differences. Books like *Men are from Mars, Women are from Venus* (Gray, 1992) amplified and to a degree caricatured these discussions. Similarly, advertising began to promote products through new images of female power, opposing it to slapstick male buffoonery (Parkin, 2007). There was almost a collective and global sigh of relief when the media, advertising media especially, began to free itself from the seriousness of women's liberation advocacy based on gender equivalences and image homogenization. Within a post-political correctness environment, advertising gave itself permission to present men as voyeuristically playful and desiring, while women were given full permission to be sensuous, alluring, sometimes sexually assertive and sexually ideal.

Of course, this revival of stereotypes, even through cult films like *Fight Club*, masked the considerable diversity that has evolved in advanced world gender culture. Indeed, while *Fight Club* (Fincher, 1999) has been seriously promulgated in terms of new forms of masculine self-awareness and the restoration of male genderism so long suppressed by second wave feminism (for example, Giroux and Szeman, 2001; Wager, 2005), such films more broadly are signifiers of the complex conditions through which sex and gender identity are being transformed and negotiated. For all their methodological deficiencies, pop surveys like the 'American Sex Survey' (Langer, 2004) and the 'Global Better Sex Survey' (Mulhall et al., 2008) give us a sense of the way the popular imagination is engaged in these problematic transformations. Using a phone-in survey for the 'American Sex Survey', the US-based ABC News claimed that around 20 per cent more men than women 'enjoyed sex a great deal' and around 30 per cent more men than women 'thought about sex every day'. The poll also showed that men on average have many more sexual partners than women at a ratio of about 2:1, although the ratio is closer to 5:1 for individuals who have had more than 20 sexual partners (that is, five times more men than women have had more than 20 sexual partners). Twenty-five per cent of women had only one sexual partner, while only 12 per cent of men fell into that category. Men are nearly three times as likely to have looked at online sex porn, and twice as many men as women report that they have an orgasm every time they have sex. Forty-two per cent of men have had 'first date' sex, while the figure is 17 per cent for women. And men are twice as likely as women to condone and engage in sex without commitment (casual sex).

This image of a robust male sexuality needs to be mediated against the profound anxieties that many men experience over sexual performance, erectile dysfunction and libidinal decline associated with ageing. While there is an increasing interest in heterosexual masculinity in the 'men's movement', the majority of scholarly focus on masculinity and male sexuality has been generated either vicariously through feminist literature or more directly through queer and gay men's studies. In her analysis of 'sex in crisis' and evangelist religions in the USA, Dagmar Herzog argues that the erectile dysfunction drug, Viagra, has re-energized the sexual power of men, both personally and politically. Against the background of excessive media stimulations and sexual imagery, along with an increasingly competitive economic environment where there is less and less time for sex and family, the emergence of Viagra merely intensified the sense that sex is a surfacial function of the body. Rather than discussions around sexual pleasure and fulfilment, sex has become a source of profound anxiety and even despair for most Americans. Viagra enabled therapists and the public to regard male sexual problems as first and foremost

> ... originating in the body. Forget your unhappy childhood or unhappy prior relationships. Sex was about *now*. Male sexuality was increasingly interpreted as something mechanical, as though, at least for the purposes of performance, emotions played only a minor role.
> (Herzog, 2008: 6)

While promoted initially as a cure for arterial dysfunction in older men, Viagra was quickly adopted by middle-aged and younger men as a recreational aphrodisiac, a performance enhancing drug. Thus, as the ancient Egyptian nobles invested their hopes in celery and Chinese rulers created alchemic concoctions of monkey brain and ginger to enhance male sexual prowess, modern science produced a chemical compound that actually enabled greater and more durable sexual performance for men (Delate et al., 2004). Since its release in 1998, nearly 35 million men worldwide have used Viagra legally and with a medical prescription; however, this figure is dwarfed by the non-prescripted distribution of the pill through developing world pharmaceutical production and distribution, and Internet sales. Even so, the performance enhancing drug has netted enormous profits for its manufacturer, the global pharmaceutical megalith Pfizer.

In a very significant way, Viagra is simply another component of the global industry that is generated around the health of a relatively elite community of first world citizens and their specific pleasures and consumerist lifestyle. Turning over around $602 billion a year, the pharmaceutical industry generates the majority of its profits through the treatment of modern conditions such as psycho-neurosis disorders (Olfson, 2009) and cardiovascular disease. According to Forbes.com (2009), seven of the top ten best-selling drugs worldwide are treatments for cholesterol or heart disease, while the remaining three are for depression (for example, Effexor) or bipolar disorders (for example, Zyprexa). According to Olfson (2009), over 27 million Americans are prescribed antidepressants each year, which is twice as many as in 1995.

In many ways, Viagra is linked to the same physiological and psychological conditions—on the one hand, it is designed to treat erectile dysfunction which is often associated with arterial problems linked to high cholesterol, low physical activity and obesity. On the other hand, the recreational use of Viagra is linked to psychological anxieties and the pursuit of 'pleasures' that cannot be delivered through 'natural' sexual performance; to this end, Viagra is a drug which is designed to promote the excesses generated through a fantasy of infinite pleasure and the global mediasphere.

Viagra and recreational sex

The lifestyles that are propagated through the first world mediasphere are, thereby, a critical component of the Viagra health intervention: that is, the fantasy of infinite pleasure and intrinsic crisis consciousness are implicated in the idea and biological manifestation of sexual dysfunction in the first world. The arterial sclerosis that is linked to overeating, fatty diets and inactivity is clearly related to western lifestyle excesses; the pursuit of sexual pleasures beyond natural physiological limits is also a manifestation of advanced world psycho-cultural knowledge systems. In a mediasphere that normalizes fantasies of excess, we might expect an epidemic of dissatisfaction and overindulgence. Viagra, in this sense, is bound to the chemically induced imaginings of pleasure.

Thus, through the subterranean networks of the Internet and the party drug scene Viagra, in fact, has morphed into a sex drug for relatively widespread use among younger and middle-aged men. In the electronic-music club scene, in particular, Viagra is being used in combination with psychotropic drugs like Ecstasy and Ice. Thus, while Ecstasy heightens rhythmic and sensual pleasures for the user, Viagra ensures an enhanced sexual performance for men. The prolonged sensual narcosis provided by Ecstasy is even more elevated through the use of Viagra by both gay and heterosexual men. In a community of casual sex partnering, in particular, a man's sexual prowess and reputation become tradable attributes in the complex exchange process of sexual partnering and pleasuring. A man who is known to be able to 'go all night' is well regarded by women who are seeking casual encounters. The same conditions apply in the male gay community, particularly in club and sauna environments. According to David Rosen:

> Urban party-going young men use it [Viagra] as part of an erotic drugfest. Known as 'poly-pharmacy', the taking of a handful of different party drugs, these drugs help counterbalance the different altered states induced during a night on the town. Taking Ecstasy or Special K (Ketamine hydrochloride) often kills the sex drive as does alcohol and cocaine. For serious party players, Viagra solves one problem. It allows a guy to party, in every sense of the word, all night.
>
> (Rosen, 2008)

Like other critics of the non-therapeutic use of Viagra, Rosen sees this chemical modification of male physiology as a symptom of a new kind of sexual politics which reduces human relationships to basic corpo-reality. Like Dagmar Herzog (2008) and Ray Moynihan (2005), Rosen believes that the demand for Viagra has been propagated by profit hun-gry pharmaceutical companies and advertisers who are preying on male anxiety and female vulnerability within a broader context of craven and competitive materialism. The richness of human relationships and sensuality are thus subsumed within the unrestrained vortex of capi-talist consumerism. This is also the point that second wave feminism has frequently made about women and the propensity of global com-merce and image-makers to objectify women as patents of male sexual performance. Thus, the intensification of the female body as 'allure-in-product', and the male body as performative slave creates a commercial aesthetic which fundamentally demeans the richness and power of human sexual sensibilities and the significance of relationships and deep desire.

'Skins', drugs and dangerous teenage sex

These criticisms of sexual enhancement drugs tend to overlook the ways in which a variety of users themselves experience pleasure. Couples in longer term relationships, for example, often use Viagra, Ecstasy and other euphoria-inducing drugs as an antidote to over-familiarity and libidinal atrophy. Just as alcohol, marijuana and other psychotropic substances have been used by various cultures in order to liberate con-sciousness from the grid of everyday experience and social controls, a new generation of 'designer' drugs has become popular with many com-munities in the developed world, especially young people engaged in nightclub, electronic and dance club culture. A range of these drugs, methamphetamines in particular, excite and extend individuals' capac-ity to be active beyond normal levels of fatigue and sleep deprivation. Thus, party drugs contribute to the all night party culture—which in some cases also involves the surrender of inhibition and a propensity for violence. Thus, while the psychotropics enhance sex and sensuality, other drugs contribute to male violence and disharmony.

Social consternation over these forms of drug taking are further heightened when the users are teenagers. Indeed, one of the most intriguing and disturbing manifestations of the transformation of a needs economy into a wants economy has been the expansion of a new social category called 'adolescence' and its prescriptive consumer mode known generally as 'youth culture'. Until very recently, adolescents were categorized generally as difficult adults whose sexuality and fertility needed especially ritualized forms of social and cultural control. When we consider the most prominent of Anglophonic love stories, *Romeo and Juliet*, we are reminded that these two Venetians were only around 12 or 13 years old. As late as the nineteenth century adolescents were being married off in order to manage libido, reproduction and property inheritance. In this historical context, concubines and mistresses of aristocrats and other wealthy men were notoriously young, often under the age of 18. People like Sir Joseph Banks, for example, the noted British botanist who sailed with Captain Cook in the late eighteenth century, freely expressed his preference for very young concubines, girls who were around the age of 13. Into the twentieth century, the last dynastical ruler of China kept over a thousand concubines, many of whom were also in their earliest teenage years. In rural Indonesia, Africa and other parts of the developing world today, adolescent girls—their fertility and inferior labour value—continue to pose a problem for parents who seek to have them married off at the earliest possible age, or in worse cases employed as sexual servants (Brown, 2001; Lewis and Lewis, 2009).

The emergence in advanced societies of 'adolescence' as a distinct social and economic category is linked to the demands of the new economy for highly trained and educated workers, home-makers and consumers. The extension of childhood into the grey category of adolescence is due in large part to the need for extended periods of education and the ever-widening need for growth and new consumers. These changes—along with the cultural centricity of individual choice, the intensification of the female body and the contraceptive pill—created a new social dilemma around sexuality and sexual divisions. While women were to be consumerized and sexualized, children still needed to be cared for, trained and educated. A social and legal line, thereby, was drawn around adolescence to mark the boundary of sexual independence, activity and capacity for choice. At that moment adolescent sexuality became enclosed within a new social discourse of il/legitimacy—and this for a group which included people whose hormonal and sexual capacity was reaching a corporeal peak.

Some national jurisdictions have seen this boundary as practically unrealistic, and so countries like Spain have set their age of sexual consent as low as 13. And indeed, while some Islamic countries have laws prohibiting pre-marital sex altogether, many developed western nations have set laws against older people having sex with people under the age of 18. Thus, while adolescents may have sex legally within their own peer-age bracket, when they cross the age line they are then subject to severe legal sanctions. For many decades these age of consent laws seemed to have had limited enforcement; more recently, however, a more vigorous social and legal effort has been exercised, exposing what appears to be an epidemic of clandestine sexual encounters between adolescents and adults.

In this context, film versions of Vladimir Nabokov's *Lolita* (1956), an erotic exploration of an adult's obsessive desire and ultimate engagement with a young teenage girl, have been socially reconfigured as sexual perversity. The sexual ambiguity that mobilizes the novel and film's comic drama is now repudiated as a demonstration of monstrous and predatory male sexuality—Professor Humbert is not only a paedophile but the creative work itself is an apologia for the worst excesses of patriarchal ideology. Similar attacks have been made against artists like Bill Henson whose photographic exhibition in Canberra, Australia (2008) was closed down because it included a portrait of a naked teenage girl. The movie thriller, *Hard Candy* (David Slade, 2005), provides a template for adolescent vengeance against paedophiles who have escaped prosecution or punishment but whose clandestine desires have provoked considerable personal and social damage. The paradox of this film, like the broader discourse on teenage sexual prohibitions, is the vaguely latent erotica—the sense in which the taboo is suspended through a spectral and illicit visual pleasure and prurient desire.

Teachers and priests are particularly despicable, it would seem, as they are invested with power and a social trust that should not be abused. Of all crimes, the news media seems to revel in a discourse of dangerous sex in which the perpetrators of the crimes are socially reduced to the level of their animality. Significantly, too, women who have sex with under-age males are becoming increasingly vulnerable to prosecution. While in previous generations, teenage boys who had sex with older women were heroized by their peers, the regime of gender equivalence has shifted the legal emphasis somewhat, revealing that women can be as equally reprehensible in their sexual predations as men. Novels and films like *Devil in the Flesh* (Raymond Radiguet, orig. 1923) and *The Reader* (Bernhard Schlink, orig. 1995) might also be regarded now as promoting paedophilia. Certainly, the orientation of news and public forum media (talkback, chat rooms) betrays a deep social confusion about such cases, particularly in terms of the status and social power of women: on the one hand, women continue to be regarded as vulnerable, while on the other they are considered powerful sexual agents who are capable of defiling vulnerable young males. Same gender sexual transgressions appear to elicit even greater social disgust; however, the most vitriolic social hatred is directed towards adults who sexually abuse pre-pubescent children.

The paradox of this situation is that adolescents are increasingly sexualized in the media and are constantly encouraged by the pleasure economy to engage in desire that leads ultimately to sexual activity. As a compound of self-imagining, fantasy and product consumption, teenage sexuality has become a critical component of value production and economic exchange. Indeed, through the general flow of teenage discourses, product and personal prestige converge around peer sanctioned sexual activity and prowess. How a teenager looks, consumes and performs sexually (through allure and physical engagement) contributes significantly to their positioning on the peer group hierarchy.

Statistics are suggesting that people are having their first sexual experiences at younger ages than the past several generations. Surveys in the USA indicate that around a quarter of adolescents have had penetrative sex by the age of 15 and around 50 per cent by the age of 17 (Mosher et al., 2005). These percentages are even higher in European societies where many adolescents have had intercourse or oral sex as early as 13 (see Cornell and Halpern-Felsher, 2005). These figures suggest that adolescent 'age of consent' laws don't protect adolescents from early sexual activity for the sanctity of a virginal marriage. Thus, community discourses around paedophilia and teenage sexuality suggest, rather, that the laws are designed to protect teenagers from the power and sexual interest of adults, presumably because adults represent sexual danger. In a culture that actively promotes and yet seeks to suppress sexual pleasure through a vaguely articulated ideal of durable love, it is not surprising that adolescents opt for early and immediate pleasure against the confused messages of adult generations.

Thus, if the community were serious about deferring teenage sexual activity it would address the mediasphere's continued stimulation of social libido through the sexualization of adolescent bodies. In fact, the paradox is bound to an economy of pleasure that demands sexualization in order to exist. The particular imagining associated with adolescence—the overflow of innocence—provides yet another motif for libidinal stimulation and product value. Adolescent bodies, that is, become available materials in the imaging of an innocence that is surreptitiously exceeding itself in desire. Like vaginal exfoliation, which is the sexual mimicry of innocence, and styles of modulated but provocative modes of dress (cleavage, mini-skirts, hip level jeans), this overflow of innocence is constituted as acute desiring—as not quite achievable or consummatable sex. The power of sex, in this instance, is in the convergence and exchange of innocence and allure.

This is not to say that law consciously provokes a libidinal effect, but rather that it is part of a context of power that is fundamentally contradictory. The law and liberal ethics can barely constrain the economic and cultural omnipotence of mediated sexualization, and yet for teenage girls, in particular, this sexualization and the pursuit of sexual prestige brings with it the dangers of comparative failure, destabilized friendships, unwanted pregnancy, transmissible diseases, precarious sexual labelling ('ho, slut, cock-teaser'), depression and body image disorders like bulimia. As children of the infinite pleasure fantasy, teenagers also discover at a young age that sex bears its own burden of complexity and disappointment. At a young age, too, many adolescents articulate that displeasure through performance and pleasure enhancing drugs. TV series like *Skins* and films like *Thirteen* (Catherine Hardwicke, 2003) explore these complexities and the use of drugs both to inflate pleasure and defer disappointment and anxiety.

The Internet has become a key component of teenage sexuality and various modes of experimentation. Through the rise of Web 2.0 and social networking, adolescents have extended their peer-based sexualizations through wider social connections. While much of this networking is benign, some adolescents have amplified their vulnerability through connection with dangerous social and sexual pleasures. In particular, the Emo culture, which is an amalgam of punk and gothic nihilism, has been linked to teenage suicides across the world. Establishing its name from 1980's punk and its energetic '*emo*tional' style, Emo migrated onto the web where it attracted a more insidious and dark demeanour. The sexual potency of popular music seems to have provided a particular kind of focus for disturbed adolescents and their vocabulary of despair. In a world that is so focused on hierarchy and pleasure, the Emo cult seems to have generated a safe place in which adolescents can find a respite in displeasure—'where nothing is good'. Many of the Emo related suicides that have been reported over the past several years have been early teenagers. The suicide notes that have been posted on MySpace and Facebook speak tragically of the Emo friendships and the deep sadness that these young adolescents have experienced in their short lives. Many include an apology to the friends and to parents—but nearly all impugn a world that seems brutal and indifferent to the suffering of lonely people.

While the suicide of young people is not unknown in other cultures, teenage suicide is clearly linked to the lifestyle and apocalyptic crises consciousness that is propagated through the first world mediasphere. If adolescence represents an overflow of sexual and economic imaginaries, then in many respects Emo suicide is the apex of a more pervasive and spectral psycho-cultural sensibility. It is, in fact, the extreme condition of dissatisfaction and displeasure that haunts our pursuit of infinite desire. Adolescence, in this sense, is another cultural innovation that is propelled through the conditions of crisis and the surplus-driven economy; self-destruction represents the personalization of our cultural inheritance and its vision of the end.

Alternative sexualities

GLBTI (gay, lesbian, bisexual, transgender and intersex)

Many of the issues and complexities discussed above also apply to the gay, lesbian, bisexual, transgender and other alternative sexuality communities. For these communities, however, there are other quite specific issues relating to desire, subjectivity and the experience of being marginal. This is particularly true for those people who regard themselves as significantly different and whose identity is constructed around sexual practices and preferences that are often ascribed as 'alternative'. Thus, naturism, multiple partnering, cross-dressing, swinging, bondage and occasional same-gender encounters are often practised by individuals and couples who might otherwise regard themselves as entirely mainstream heterosexual. On the other hand, individuals and couples may more strongly identify with a community of shared practice which contributes significantly to their social and cultural environment, living arrangements, recreational activities, moral framework and vocational activities.

In the GLBTI communities, for example, the tensions between committed loving relationships and innovative erotica are further complicated by a more limited spatial and community context for linking and partnering. While there is clearly an increasing respect and tolerance for same-gender partnering in contemporary, advanced societies, significant parts of the 'straight' community continue to stigmatize, exclude and ridicule gays and lesbians. Along with the smaller size of the prospective partnering community, this exclusion inevitably produces a stronger sense of isolation for many gay and lesbian people. Not surprisingly, young gay men, especially, suffer significant psychological distress, particularly during the process of 'coming out'—that is, when members of the GLBTI community disclose their sexuality to friends, family and work group. There is, for example, a significantly increased incidence of suicide among young gay men during this critical phase (see Paul et al., 2002; Osborne, 2005). Not surprisingly, this process of disclosure varies enormously, with some GLBTIs openly and fully expressing their sexuality, and others taking a very long time or only partially disclosing their sexuality to a limited number of people. Equally problematic for many GLBTIs, however, is the need to hide their sexual identity from others in the straight community, leading to a complicated association of lies and disclosures through the selective presentation of self in everyday life.

Outraged by this sort of homophobia, a number of second wave, radical feminists have deployed their sexuality as a form of political expressivity designed to disrupt the categories and gendered assumptions that have been generated through patriarchal capitalism. This type of feminism, most particularly as it has attached itself to other liberational ambitions such as lesbian separationism, remains determinedly adversarial. The notion of 'difference' becomes the rallying point for the social and sexual fulfilment of women. 'Woman', in this sense, is a radical concept which ultimately seeks the erasure of *man*— not just patriarchy or 'phallocentricism'. This form of separationism is advocated by radical structuralists like Sheila Jeffreys who contends that male sexual penetration of women is generally tantamount to rape. In this broader context, woman to woman sexual engagement would replace heterosexuality, applying technological solutions to the 'problem' of reproduction. Believing that male sex hormones condemn men to dispositions of violence and control, radical separationists argue that lesbian sexuality is necessarily founded on social and sexual equality (Jeffreys, 2004, 2007; see also Haraway, 2000).

In many respects, these views run counter to other recent discussions of sexuality as a cultural construction that is oriented towards new possibilities for pleasure and open identity. Emanating from 'queer theory' (see Jagose, 1997; Patton and Sanchez-Eppler, 2000; Halle, 2004), these ideas challenge assumptions about the cultural fixity and essentialism of gender, identity and sexual orientation. Particular areas of queer theory, in fact, propose that all human sexual agents have a potential for same-sex attraction and modes of erotica that are repressed by social institutions and norms. Once liberated from these constraints, sexual agents have the opportunity to explore their sexuality, desires and pleasures through a widened lexicon of bodily imagining and deployment. Queer theory focuses on diversity in gay, lesbian and bisexual communities, eschewing the prescriptive politics of radical and separationist lesbianism, which remains predicated on an essentialist gender dualism

Plate 3.1   A Muslim family bears the rainbow flag in the 2009 Gay Pride celebrations in New York.
Photograph by Belinda Lewis.

it claims to abhor. While separationists build their identity and sexuality around this difference, queer theory reduces the dualism to an incomplete interplay of biology and culture, a space in which games can be played and pleasures unleashed. Queer politics, thereby, are formed around the release of pleasure and gender from the harsh politics of radical feminism, on the one hand, and mainstream homophobia, on the other.

Beyond sexual orientation, there is also a significant diversity of individuals and communities who move between gendered ascriptions, either temporarily or on a more permanent basis (see Plate 3.1). These transgender and intersex groups represent an even more direct challenge to mediated conventions around gender and associated assumptions about desire, sexual practice and pleasure. While these practices have been evident across innumerable cultures, the more recent exposure in the first world media further destabilizes the fabric of contemporary sexuality and its systems of gendered meaning-making. Within this context, new spaces are emerging in which erotica and performance are evolving new modes of expressivity. These transgender and intersex groups include:

- Cross-dressers and transvestites. While most of these individuals move from male to female, there are still many women who dress as men and seek to be identified as men. Certainly, there are a number of lesbians who identify as 'butch' or 'soft butch' who wear masculine clothing styles and adopt vocal and postural styles which are often associated with men. There are also degrees to which the transvestite communities adopt the alternative gender mode. For some it is an entirely private activity, while for others it is practised on a regular basis and in public. Individuals with a very strong compulsion to identify with the alternative gender may sometimes advance to the second category of transgenderism.
- Transsexuals. These are individuals who often have a very long history of cross identification, dating back in some cases to pre-puberty. Such people often report that they feel trapped within the wrong gendered body and its physical genitalia. A number of these individuals opt for hormone treatment and surgical solutions. Surgery usually involves a genital reassignment process, as well as cosmetic modifications to the chest, brow, jawline, chin, lips and throat (Adam's apple).
- Intersex. There are estimates that up to 1 per cent of babies are born of indeterminate gender. Very often, parents choose medical interventions to enable male ascription, which is more easily altered, if the child later requests reassignment.

Very clearly, the personal crises that individuals experience around these various forms of transgenderism are generated through the intensification of sexuality, masculine performativity and the centrality of feminine allure.

In one very spectacular example of the disruptive power of transgenderism, the global media spectacle of the World Athletics Championships was radically inverted in 2009 when the winner of the women's 800 metres event, Caster Semenya, was accused of being intersex. While the athlete, a South African woman, was defended by her family and national government, the media was nevertheless catatonic with prurient interest. Calls for protection of privacy were largely ignored, since the Championships, like other media products, prospers on publicity and the celebrity status of its stars—its athletes. As symbols within the exchange system, the athletes and their sexuality are absorbed into the ambit of advertising via the public's libidinal fascinations. The disruption to the normative paradigm of gender provided the media and

audiences with a stimulus for their own sexual and cognitive engagements: the expectations of the product were suddenly transformed as
sex became the primary rider of the athletic performance, rather than
the other way around. Sex, which is sublimated within other mediated
fantasies and narratives like *sport,* was suddenly exposed in the harsh
light of our own crisis consciousness. In the end, however, the central
question was not whether the athlete should retain her winning medal,
nor even whether she should be permitted to compete against other
women. The major question and its titillating possibilities was—what is
a woman?

The global mediasphere could not answer this question without
recourse to expert knowledge systems which convened their judgement
against the perturbation of sports fans and sympathizers. The spectacle of Caster Semenya's body was set against the normative presence
of gender and a cultural libido that has confounded itself within an
incandescent fantasy of excess. Caster Semenya could not be permitted
to be a woman, as the category has become essentialized in the global
mediasphere through its economic ascriptions and pursuit of infinite
pleasure.

4
Global Inequalities: Changing World Conditions

Political economy... proposes two distinct objects. First, to provide a plentiful revenue or subsistence for the people, or more properly to enable them to provide such a revenue or subsistence for themselves; and secondly, to supply the state or commonwealth with a revenue sufficient for the public services.

Adam Smith, *The Wealth of Nations* Book IV

Perhaps the last fifty years have seen more developments and more material progress than the previous five hundred years... [But] we are living in a world of fear. The life of man today is corroded and made bitter by fear. Fear of the future, fear of the hydrogen bomb, fear of ideologies. Perhaps this fear is a greater danger than the danger itself, because it is fear which drives men to act foolishly, to act thoughtlessly, to act dangerously.

Indonesian President Sukarno, Opening the Bandung Conference, 1955

According to UNICEF, 25,000 children die each day due to poverty. And they die quietly in some of the poorest villages on earth, far removed from the scrutiny and the conscience of the world. Being meek and weak in life makes these dying multitudes even more invisible in death.

Anup Shah, *Global Issues*, March 2010

Global media and local poverty: Mukhtaran Bibi

In 2009 the *New York Times* ran a story about the marriage of a Pakistani woman, Mukhtaran Bibi, who had been caught up in a village honour

131

dispute several years earlier. While there are numerous accounts of the event, it is clear that the village council was controlled by the Mastoi clan, which was richer and far more powerful than Bibi's clan, the Gujjar Tatla. The Mastoi accused Bibi's 12 year-old brother of *ziadti* (rape, sodomy or illegal sex) or *zina* (fornication or adultery) on the grounds that he had been seen walking unaccompanied with a Mastoi girl. According to the brother's testimony delivered much later to an authorized, state court, he had himself been raped and sodomized by three Mastoi men, who then invented the honour crime story in order to deflect attention from their own crime. When the Mastoi abducted the accused brother, Bibi's family offered a settlement arrangement, even though they believed the boy to be entirely innocent. In the terms of the agreement, the brother would marry the Mastoi girl he had supposedly been seen with, and Bibi would be married off to another Mastoi man.

Towards evening on the day of the supposed crime, the brother was released into the custody of the police from the township of Jatoi, about 18 kilometres from the village. Around 200 Mastoi gathered to discuss the settlement proposal, but it was clear the men wanted revenge and the restoration of their family honour. When Bibi's family came to the gathering to discuss the proposal, Mukhtaran Bibi was seized and taken at gun-point into the stable, where she was gang raped and tortured for nearly an hour. Her clothes were thrown into the dirt and she was paraded, near-naked, through the village streets. Word was sent to the police station at Jatoi that the honour crime had been settled and the brother was released.

In such circumstances, it is common for women to commit suicide following an honour-based punishment. With very low levels of education and an often ineffectual judicial system, Pakistan's civil society is severely under-resourced and underdeveloped: in these circumstances, warlords and religious militants are able to assert their own interests as 'law' and a mechanism for social control, particularly in rural areas and small villages (Lau, 2005). Women, in particular, are subject to the brutal impositions of violence and threat that are deeply rooted in patriarchy, history and culture. The notion of 'honour', in this context, is a discourse of terror which sustains the systemic control of women's bodies and reproductive capacity through a scrupulously managed system of property control and inheritance. As noted in Chapter 1, a family's honour is tantamount not only to the religious and social values that sustain a community and its moral and legal integrity—it is also an essential component of an hierarchical system of inheritance and property control, a means of protecting a family's claim to property against the claims of another familial lineage. Where survival is critically bound to the amount of land and livestock a family controls, clans are perpetually vulnerable to the threat of forced or quasi-legal appropriation by other clans. Using all the powers available, clans like the Mastoi will swoop on vulnerability; in the outreaches of a country like Pakistan, these strategies include the taint of female dishonour (Warraich, 2005).

If Mukhtaran Bibi were to suicide, therefore, she would erase her own dishonour and limit the Mastoi property claims against her family. Her death would be her restitution. Indeed, even if women like Bibi have not committed any notional 'crime', social and familial pressure is often brought to bear and suicide is generally the outcome. In Mukhtaran Bibi's case, however, the family refused to submit to this horror, choosing instead to pursue an alternative form of justice through Pakistan's secular judicial system. Pursuing her case through Pakistan's Anti-Terrorism Court and ultimately the High Court, Mukhtaran Bibi was viewed by the country's non-Islamic media as a victim of religious traditionalism which continually undermines Pakistan's economic, social and cultural development. Many in Pakistan's more secular middle classes, in fact, regarded the story as a mark of deep national shame and the abominations associated with Islamic extremism. For the secular media and their middle-class audiences Bibi's pursuit of justice was a test case for the country's modernizing institutions and 'rule of law', which are ensnared in a mortal struggle over nation, modernity and the role of religion.

These struggles immediately connected Pakistan to the global 'war on terror' and globalization processes of international economy more generally. As a nation constituted around the Muslim faith and Islam, Pakistan had become implicated in western anti-Islamic anxieties which had erupted after the al-Qa'ida attacks on America in 2001. Not surprisingly, Pakistan's allegiance to modernist ideals and rule of law were cast into question by the USA and its allies—first, because it bordered Afghanistan whose Taliban government had supported and sponsored the al-Qa'ida attacks; and second, because of Pakistan's own internal turmoils, which combined deep poverty and underdevelopment with a seething sectarian and religious disharmony.

In many respects, Bibi's story personifies these complex global matrices, connecting a dispute in a small and largely illiterate rural village to powerful, global geo-political conditions. For many people from western developed nations, their new vision of Islam became emblemized by events like the honour punishment of Mukhataran Bibi. Indeed, the alignment of western political and public opinion, which sanctioned the reprisal attacks in Afghanistan, was facilitated by images of female oppression under the Taliban. The exclusion of women from all modes of public participation, including basic education, fortified western antagonism towards the Taliban; even those western citizens who are generally opposed to extra-territorial war found it difficult to resist the need to 'liberate' Afghanistan from this violent and oppressive regime. The story of Mukhtaran Bibi, which was picked up by BBC News in 2002 (Harrison, 2002), confirmed for many western audiences that these Islamic religious fanatics were depraved and needed to be stopped: this was not just an abstract war between different politicians, their armies and ideologies—it was a deeply personal event being experienced through the body of one woman.

Within the context of the global war on terror, this convergence of personal violation and political infamy conjured an ineluctable news event for the advanced world media, particularly in the Anglophonic frontline of the Coalition of the Willing. Bibi's story seemed to arouse a particular kind of curiosity and outrage within the ascendant ideological dispositions of the west and its ensign of news values. Beyond the immediate news event, however, the narrative was also an account of social heroism and the confirmation of western values and secular modernism. Bibi's pursuit of justice through the Anti-Terrorism Court, both practically and symbolically, fortified the Anglophonic world's sense of itsef and the importance of the Fourth Estate. This was a story that defied Islamic extremism and the oppression of women, a story in which justice was the province of western cultural institutions that had been grafted to the developing world. Thus, the story became one of celebration and, inevitably, celebrity. After a series of legal struggles, Mukhtaran Bibi became more than an illiterate woman who had been the victim of a village dispute over sexuality, kinship and religious law: through the amplitude of the western mediasphere and its polis, Mukhtaran Bibi became a crusader—a leader against oppression in the great march of secular, democratic and economic modernization. In 2006 *Time Magazine* reported:

> Only a few leaders are alchemists who take the worst of human behavior and turn it into the best. Mukhtaran Bibi, a Pakistani woman raised in poverty and illiteracy, has responded to the violence and gender apartheid directed at her and other women with an insistence on justice and education.... There are perhaps thousands of such 'honor crimes' in Pakistan each year. Survivors are more likely to kill themselves or be killed by their families than turn

to a legal system that requires four male adult Muslim eyewitnesses to testify to rape—otherwise the victim can be convicted of fornication and adultery. But Bibi went to court. Her bravery attracted support from international media and women's groups, and her attackers were convicted. With the compensation money plus contributions from people who read about her struggle, she created a girls' school. Now 33, she has become a skilled organizer and trusted leader, and a magnet for other women escaping violence.... Like Nelson Mandela, another alchemist who redeemed human nature by example, she depends on ordinary supporters to keep herself and her work alive.

(Steinem, 2006)

In 2005 an international women's lifestyle and fashion magazine, *Glamour,* presented Bibi with the 'Glamour Woman of the Year Award'. *Glamour* followed up the award with an article in 2008, which described Bibi as 'the new Mother Teresa' (Power, 2008). Alongside other 'real-life heroes like Michelle Obama', Mukhtaran Bibi was featured in a magazine edition that included notable articles like '10 things he's thinking about while having sex', 'A sexy bedroom game that your boyfriend will LOVE' and 'My boyfriend went hot-tubbing with random women'. Also in 2008 Abdullah Haris, in the rapper persona *ABZ (thelyricist,)*, released a song on YouTube which described Bibi as 'No mother-fuckin' lie, but a human being' who had survived the outrage of honour crime. The video clip presented an often reflective and sensuous portrait of Bibi—including close-ups of her face and eyes, images of her work with other honour crime victims, and several motifs of Bibi leading women's protest rallies in Pakistan. This juxtaposition of affective imagery and the raw energy of *ABZ*'s lyrical protest contrasts somewhat with the more reverential tone of the European Council's North-South Prize, which was awarded to Bibi in 2007. For the Secretary General of the Council, Bibi's commitment to the education of women in Pakistan demonstrates that 'Gender equality is a human right that not only liberates women; it liberates societies as a whole, and it allows them to prosper politically, economically and socially' (Council of Europe, 2007). It was also reported by the *New York Times* that Mukhtarann Bibi's autobiography had reached no. 3 on the French best-seller list and that a Hollywood movie was being planned. Also, according to the *New York Times* report, Bibi's work among indigent Pakistani girls had attracted the praise of the French Foreign Minister and Laura Bush, the wife of then US President George W. Bush.

Bibi's iconic status for western media audiences, however, is per-haps best symbolized through her presence in online celebrity sites like Celebritywonder.com. Featured among film-stars like Angelina Jolie and socialite sex symbols like Paris Hilton, Mukhtaran Bibi has assumed a particular kind of *corpus sexualis*, the circumstances of her rape being somehow transmogrified as a kind of amorphous erotic redemption. It is as though the horror of the crime and Bibi's moral defiance have sim-ply been reappropriated and transformed by western culture's obsessive and restless libidinal volition—as though the media economy and its celebrity industry have reconstructed and integrated the atrocity into another permutation of the fantasy of infinite pleasure.

Of course, we should remember that a favoured motif of western media culture is the redemption of poverty, violence and humiliation—especially where this redemption can be sexualized within the broader heroics of nation and national power. Certainly, the *New York Times'* article, which describes Bibi's marriage to a police constable who had guarded her through the 2002 trials, betrays this same kind of cultural and sexual voyeurism. The constable, we are told, threatened to kill him-self if Bibi continued to refuse him; and worse, he threatened to divorce his first wife, as an expression of his devotion to Bibi. It was this lat-ter threat, and its inevitable insult to the first wife, which ultimately persuaded Bibi to accept the marriage. In a society where four wives are permissible and where the worst social condition of a woman is to be divorced, Mukhtaran Bibi decided she must marry the constable in order to protect the first wife. The beautiful and mysterious Mukhtaran Bibi, thereby, acceded to a sexual ensemble that confounds, as much as stirs, the western media's prurient delight.

The sexualization of poverty and violence

In this way, Mukhtaran Bibi's personal crisis became amplified through the volition of globalization, most particularly as this momentum is generated through processes associated with economy, geo-politics, the media and culture. As we have noted throughout this book, the social control of fertility and libido is a central component of human survival and economy. In agricultural communities, in particular, this process of control is exercised in the management of female sexuality and sex-ual pleasures, which have been frequently symbolized as 'dangerous' and 'natural' (see Griffin, 2000). Female gender, fertility and sexuality are often represented in political and cultural texts in terms of seasonal and meteorological variations which are so critical to human survival.

In this sense, honour killings are an extreme manifestation of innumerable ritualized social practices that are designed to control female sexuality—everything from arranged marriage to virginal sacrifice, radical genital circumcision, skeletal and other cosmetic distortions, and the burning of witches.

For western developed nations, practices like honour punishment and female genital mutilation represent a profound affront to the cultural values associated with civil secularism, modernism and the pleasure economy. The patriarchal violence and honour system represent a distinctive perversion and brutal deployment of Qu'ranic precepts and the management of female sexuality (Warraich, 2005; Chesler, 2009). In this context, there is a clear link between an historically dense patriarchal genealogy and Mukhtaran Bibi's story. While estimates vary, a newswatch organization estimated that around 179 people (138 women, 41 men) were killed in honour related punishments in Pakistan in 2008. This figure accords with numerous other estimates, including the United Nations (UNPF, 2000) which calculated that around 5000 people are murdered each year as honour punishment. Unni Wikan (2008) suggests that honour killings are embedded in a mode of masculine social violence that has its roots in deep culture. According to Wikan, many purist or 'traditional' Muslims, Sikhs and Hindus view honour and morality as a collective, family responsibility, a matter of familial heritage: rights, values and law are constructed through the family, tribe and kinship, rather than through the secular western notion of 'human rights' or 'rule of law'. Phyllis Chesler (2009) argues, in fact, that western citizens experience considerable cultural disjunction when, through immigration or travel, they encounter these traditional values and practices: westerners find it difficult to reconcile their own strong objection to violent practices perpetrated in the name of 'honour' with their own secular, modern and globalist modes of tolerance and embrace of cultural diversity.

These 'encounters' are more likely to be generated through the modern mediasphere. In this context, the moral and cultural disjunctions associated with these encounters are engendered through the narrative of primitivism, religious violence and a form of female heroism that accords with western cultural values—Bibi overcomes adversity, poverty and oppression in order to prosper socially. This image of poverty is, of course, the central motif that encourages and supports charity, as it confirms western values and precepts about 'the poor'. It allows the citizens of the economically advanced societies to experience their prosperity (and superiority) as a normative narrative that perpetually defers embarrassment or guilt. In the logics of poverty and wealth, the story of Mukhtaran Bibi accords with the liberal-democratic narrative of economic and social progress, a mediated imaginary which provides for personal advancement.

In this way, Bibi becomes a celebrity politician, 'like Nelson Mandela and Mother Teresa', a figure who is both 'more than human' and yet intensely familiar. Indeed, her presence in the western mediasphere is not simply a gesture of curiosity or newsworthiness in and of itself: Bibi exists within a particular discursive framework which says far more about western cultural politics and cultural values than it does about the plight of indigent people and their lives in developing countries like Pakistan. In a very genuine sense, in fact, Bibi exists for us—along with other global citizens of the developing world—because she performs a particular function for the advanced world mediasphere and its self-imagining.

Thus, expanding on the more usual deployment of the concept of media celebrity (Corner and Pels, 2003; Kamons, 2007), we may usefully consider Bibi, and others in the class of indigent developing world citizens who appear in our media, as a prefiguration of our own sense of self and self-ascription. They are not 'others' in the simple sense that they are an identification of what we are not; rather, they are others in that they are a mirror of ourselves as interdependent and recognizable beings in whose mediated reflection we find the amorphous illusion through which we try to stabilize and confirm our sense of self. It is, in fact, through their mediation that the recognizable similarities and differences are mobilized in terms of the illusion of knowability—that precarious process which determines a certain reshaping of the other being as comprehensible and either within the ambit of inclusion or exclusion by which politics and community coalesce.

This coalescence has been adapted by authors like Gayatri Spivak and Homi Bhabha in their analyses of postcolonial societies and global diaspora. For these theorists, the 'subaltern' individual is formed through the association of western 'colonizer' culture and non-western (de)colonized culture. The subaltern exists, that is, in the complicated web of language and culture, as well as the gaps that are created by differentials of power. Unlike other postcolonial scholars, however, both Bhabha and Spivak acknowledge that this process of interdependent cultural exchange is not simply an act of domination and exclusion, but is rather a process of interdependent and mutual exchange and change: the dominant and subaltern deliver significant changes to one another in the course of their interaction—the interplay of transculturalism.

Thus, the construction of the Mukhtaran Bibi character and narrative in the western corporate media is not mono-directional, but is rather shaped through this exchange of interests—the cultural encounter, audience engagement, knowledge systems and imaginings that surround the Bibi story inevitably change the western news media and, by filtration, the cultural context of the global mediasphere. Indeed, it is arguable that these encounters are themselves necessary for the cultural transformations of globalization that the west and non-west are currently and continually undergoing.

In particular, the existence of this otherness, generally, and the global indigent citizen, specifically, is an intrinsic condition of contemporary culture and global capitalist economy. This point does not just repeat the familiar Marxist claim that the world's rich require the cheap labour or products of the world's poor. Rather, it is to claim that the sense of otherness enables the functioning of a capitalist system and an amorphous political mediasphere to generate their fantasies of wholeness and unity—to generate, that is, their productive intelligence of purpose and destiny. We have already noted that the early forms of agricultural and capital exchange were fostered through complex narratives of desire and danger. Embedded in this fantasy, of course, is the grounding of human community and the imaginary of peace which is always the predicate of violence and power. Through the evolution of global capitalism, particularly in its current incarnation of pleasure, this community fantasy is besieged by its own alternative other—social dissension and a sense of separation that articulates itself through social hierarchies, power relationships and ultimately violence. In opposition to this formation is the imagining of human bonds, many of which are conveyed through the exchange of products, services and symbols which create a sense of mutual need and species-wide communal purpose.

The aesthetics of global poverty

A considerable number of scholars suggest that this sense of mutual destiny is propagated by a western-centric, liberal democratic and capitalist ideology, a sustaining validation for the actions of power elites like the US government and its military (see Herman and McChesney, 1997; Taylor, 2007). However, it is probably more accurate to say that this sense of community volition is borne by a more complex interaction between the fantasy of infinite pleasure and the anxieties that are associated with violence and hierarchical differentials that lead inevitably to various forms of social separation. It is not simply the conscious imposition of power differentials and modes of violence that impels our sense of shared being, but rather the interaction between the respective imaginings of pleasure and danger that drives a much broader conception of 'the global' and its disjunctive and complex engagement of knowledge systems. A volition to community—including global community—is therefore set upon the unstable geomorphic terrain of media and social libido, and their contingent imaginings of pleasure and displeasure.

The poverty of the developing world, in this sense, is conceived through the sexualization mediascope of the developed world. The mediated presence of the developing world is therefore constituted through the sublimation of differences in cultural values and practices, including the aestheticization of significant differences in wealth, security and quality of life more generally: sex and desire provide the amorphous materials that enable us to imagine and aestheticize these bonds. This aestheticization is necessary if the citizens and governments of the advanced world are to justify their own privilege, as well as reconcile the capitalist paradox between communalism and social hierarchies. That is to say, in order to create the imaginary of communalism, the advanced world governments and citizenry are required to render as defensible their own privilege and power, which is fundamentally indefensible in terms of western nations' underlying values of justice, law, freedom, equality of opportunity and rights. While these values are often interrogated in terms of the domestic citizenry and their quality of life, they are even more problematic when measured against the abject poverty and suffering of humans in the developing world.

Tourism and travel texts are especially designed to aestheticize developing world poverty in terms of a transformative global imaginary, the global mediasphere and the economy of pleasure (Lewis, 2008; Lewis and Lewis, 2009). Thus, the effects of global capitalism, including the period of European colonialism, are reconfigured in terms of a cultural and spatial 'difference' which is accessible, inexpensive and re-rendered within the aesthetic framework of developed world taste. This is precisely the same indigent imaging that has popularized slum tours in places like Mumbai and Jakarta. Local entrepreneurs now take western tourists on a guided adventure through some of the most horrendous living conditions in the world, adding to the travellers' sense of authentic cultural experience and moral outrage (see Lewis, 2008). While paying protection money to secure the tour routes, these entrepreneurs have identified a paradoxical western predilection for desire within the stench of a danger that can be safely mediated.

And indeed, even those more active and committed practitioners of international aid are not exempt of the aesthetics of poverty. Indeed, one of the paradoxes of international aid, even when it is exercised on the ground, is that it remains subject to a discursive and cultural system that can never be leavened away from its national and cultural origin.

Major aid and development agencies like USAID, the United Nations Development Programme (UNDP), the IMF and the World Bank, as well as innumerable non-government organizations (NGOs) that work on the ground, are part of this same poverty aesthetic. For all the good work that these organizations may do. they inevitably configure the crisis landscape in terms of a particular cultural and aesthetic paradigm. While I will discuss this aid and development paradox below, there is a suggestion in some development literature that a portion of aid workers and organizations are motivated as much by their own voyeuristic dispositions, as by the suffering and needs of others (Crackwell, 2000; Easterly, 2006; Lewis and Lewis, 2006a). In this way, aid-based concerts for Bangladesh, BandAid, Live Aid and Make Poverty History are not simply cultural events designed to assist disaster victims or the world's poor: they are cultural events designed to confirm the privilege of the donor within a context of the logics of global inequality and a mechanism for imagining its resolution in aesthetics. Global scale poverty and inequality is absorbed into the imaginary of its transformation through the glorious pathway of modernist culture and its economy of pleasure.

Poverty and the global landscape

In the crisis of global inequality, the world's poor are a fundamental component of the advanced economies' world imaginary: the world's poor are conceived as *our* poor. Thus, western discourses tabulate and scale their poor against their own wealth and the normative values of economic income and growth, which are the primary development indicators.

Table 4.1 provides a world ranking list by national product and quality of life standards. Clearly, most national governments and economists privilege the discourse of economic growth and performance, particularly through indicators like gross national product (GNP) per capita. For most governments and economists GNP per capita represents the primary indicator of the nation's global status and well-being. Tabulations of this kind are, above all other things, a validation of the central role of economy and surplus value within a generalized ideology of species pleasure and survival.

Table 4.1   International economic and social development index

Country	Human Development Index ranking	GNP/Capita in US$	World GNP/Capita Ranking
Norway	1	38,454	4
Australia	4	33,935	8
USA	8	39,676	2
UK	16	30,821	13
Canada	6	31,263	10
Cuba	50	4100	110
China	81	5896	89
Brazil	69	8195	64
Indonesia	108	3609	113
India	128	3139	114
Madagascar	143	857	164
Yemen	150	870	163
Niger	177	779	165
Sierra Leone	176	562	172

Source: Adapted from UNDP Human Development Report (2006).

However, while GNP is an indicator of the relative economic performance of each nation-state, the Human Development Index (HDI) seeks to mediate the primacy of economic output with other life-pleasure indicators. This index is compiled by the Human Development Report Office of the UNDP. The HDI provides a composite measure of three dimensions of human development: living a long and healthy life (measured by life expectancy), being educated (measured by adult literacy and enrolment at the primary, secondary and tertiary level), and having a decent standard of living (measured by purchasing power parity and income). While the HDI does not entirely address the question of income inequality, it does provide an indication of access to education and indirectly to health services through average life expectancy data. Indeed, according to the UNDP, the HDI provides a more complete prism for viewing human progress, freedom and the complex relationship between income and well-being.

As Table 4.1 shows, we can see that those countries with strong social welfare programmes, better income distribution, gender equality and recognized rights tend to do better on the HDI. We can also see from this sample table that HDI performance is clearly related to GNP, but this relationship is not an absolute correlative. Thus, the USA has the world's second highest GNP per capita, but it is ranked only 8th on the HDI scale. Japan at number 7 on the HDI has a GNP ranking of 18. Cuba, with its universal health system and high life expectancy is ranked at 60 on the HDI, which is generally much higher than other countries with equivalent or much higher incomes like Brazil.

Having identified these variations, however, we can also see that there is generally a strong correlation between income and HDI: wealthier countries tend to have higher life expectancy, educational levels and general states of well-being. And indeed, even while there are some variations, there is also a tendency for the wealthier countries to have better systems of public infrastructure, welfare, educational and health services. Even in the USA, which is exceptional among the advanced wealthy nations in terms of its high poverty rates and poor social health system, the broader indicators of public well-being are still much higher than those of the middle-ranking and poorer countries of the world. As noted, the communist-based Republic of Cuba is exceptional amongst developing world nations for having a highly effective public health system, well-trained medical practitioners and highly sophisticated systems of social care and welfare. Bhutan, a tiny nation located at the foot of the Himalayas, is also exceptional in that it measures its own economic and social performance against an indicator it calls the Gross National Happiness Index (GNHI); as an alternative to GNP, the GNHI was designed by King Jigme Singye Wangchuck in 1972 to take into account people's life satisfactions, non-material pleasures and spiritual contentment.

More broadly, however, some significant shifts have been occurring in the global conditions of inequality, particularly over the past two decades. As Cormac O'Grada (2009) points out, the global community is rarely faced with the level of famine that was evident in the early and middle phases of the twentieth century. While this contraction in widespread famine is partly due to recent and rapid economic development in the world's two most populous nations—India and China—it is also the result of significant advances in agricultural technology. In particular, highly systematized agricultural production techniques and the application of fertilizer, pesticide and new technologies have enabled specific parts of the planet to specialize in food production and produce marketable food surpluses. While these corporate agricultural systems and food surpluses have contributed to the excessive degradation of forests, oceans and other natural systems, they have nevertheless established a specialized supply chain that has become integrated into the global economy. Developed world national groups like the USA, European Community, Canada and Australia maintain substantial agricultural industries that are capable of sustaining highly urbanized populations. While these national groups merely supplement their food sources through imports, other developed nations like Singapore, Taiwan and South Korea are heavily dependent upon imported food. With the exception of food primary industry exporters like Australia and Canada, in fact, developed world economies have a vested interest in maintaining low prices on globally exchanged agricultural products. This is a major reason for the continued exclusion of food and agriculture from world trade agreements.

Indeed, and as many development scholars highlight (see Haslam et al., 2009: 324), agriculture remains the most distinguishing characteristic of poorer nations and their economic and cultural practices. In the world's poorest nations, in fact, the vast majority of people are engaged in subsistence farming, that is, agricultural production that produces very little or no tradable surpluses. And indeed, while the retreat of famine and emergence of new development models have focused international attention away from agriculture, it is also very clear that the world's subsistence farmers remain profoundly vulnerable to hunger, malnutrition and extreme levels of poverty (World Bank, 2010). Despite this obvious vulnerability, the percentage of Overseas Development Aid being directed towards agriculture has declined from around 17 per cent in the early 1980s to less than 8 per cent during the 2000s (Rao, 2007). Even the UN Millennium Development Goals, which have focused global attention on the plight of indebted, poor nations, have barely improved the condition of subsistence agriculture and the rural poor. In this light, the laudable goal of halving global poverty by 2015 seems to gratify the rhetorical imaginary of the west through an abstract notion of 'food security' which can distract from the specific needs of specific people.

Such abstract and largely unattainable objectives, therefore, merely confirm the causal connection between world poverty and western self-interest and affluence. Indeed, while paying little attention to the real causes of poverty—the cultural and economic imperative of hierarchy—the developed world focuses instead on questions of food security that are linked to grander issues of western primacy, the war on terror and perceived security threats associated with the economic rise of China. Indeed, along with increasing anxieties over climate change and its implications for drought and agricultural production, these broader insecurities are contributing to new fears over the prospect of severe global food shortages. After 60 years of surplus, it seems that the spectre of famine is returning, especially for the world's poorest people who are concentrated in Africa and other developing territories.

These problems are further exacerbated as energy consumption across the globe continues to escalate and first world nations seek alternatives to fossil fuels. With the prospects of increased coal and oil consumption in the emerging economies of China and India, advanced nations have sought to fulfil their Kyoto Protocol commitments through an increase in the use of non-carbon fuels for electrical production, transportation and manufacturing. Hailed as a radical environmental innovation, the use of organic materials for bio-mass fuel production has contributed to significant global changes in agricultural production. In particular, land that had been previously dedicated to subsistence or surplus-based food production is being converted to bio-mass production.

Increasing concerns and policy responses to the rising cost of oil and climatic change associated with global warming have clearly con-tributed to the rising use of food products for fuel production—maize and soybean in North America; palm oil in South East Asia; sugarcane in Brazil and Australia; jatropha, pongemia and sugar beet in India; rapeseed, sugar beet and wheat in Europe. In developing countries, like Indonesia, the lure of cash cropping through palm oil production has led to serious degradation of forests and rice production, effacing not only the livelihoods of many Indonesian small farmers but also the cul-tural and historical significance of rice farming. According to Indonesia's Agricultural Minister in 2008, Anton Apriyantono, despite strong rice harvests in 2007–2008, there was an overall increase of around 10–14 per cent in food prices, some of which was associated with an average fuel increase of around 28 per cent: 'Poor households were the most vulnerable to food insecurity' (Apriyantono, 2008: 2).

Indeed, while world food prices eased a little during 2008, the Food and Agriculture Organization (FAO) reported that prices were still 28 per cent higher than the previous year, and the cost of fertilizers and seeds were double the 2007 figure. According to the FAO, nearly 863 million people in the world are 'chronically hungry'. The vast majority of the world's undernourished people (907 million) live in developing countries, according to the 2007 data reported by the State of Food Insecurity in the World. Of these, 65 per cent live in only seven countries: India, China, the Democratic Republic of Congo, Bangladesh, Indonesia, Pakistan and Ethiopia. However, the greatest proportion of the world's population who are hungry are located in sub-Saharan Africa (236 million), which is around 30 per cent of the total. The Congo, which has been besieged by political violence and warfare, has radically increased its proportion of hungry people.

Of course, these conditions of poverty are extant within the global mediasphere, but it is largely as evidence of social exotica. As noted in Chapter 2's discussion of the Global Financial Crisis, poverty is itself a contingency of self-identification—the totem by which affluence and security assembles itself as what it is not. Images of African poverty, in this sense, are a critical component of the imaginary of the developed world and its fundamental economy of pleasure. Indeed, it is almost a prerequisite of affluence, providing a measure by which the knowledge system of economy is shaped and fortified. It is a crisis by which the affluent world secures itself in its own imagining of pleasure.

Food crisis and the west

Clearly, a good proportion of this global hunger and food crisis is related to consumption and lifestyles in developed nations, that is, to the economy of pleasure and the global mediasphere. As noted, in order to reduce carbon-based fuel emissions and their reliance on Middle East oil, the USA and other high consuming nations have established emission control legislation and subsidies that are designed to lure farmers into bio-fuel production. Other countries, like Brazil, have legislated to ensure that a certain proportion of all fuels used in automobiles is ethanol based. The underlying assumption of these emissions laws is that ethanol produces less carbon emissions than oil fuels. And while this is certainly true, questions are now being asked about the environmental damage and overall emissions that issue from fertilizers, farm machinery, transportation and production processes that are involved in ethanol and other bio-mass products.

The USA, along with other high consuming advanced nations, has established legislation that is designed to limit carbon fuel emissions; in the belief that ethanol fuels are lower emitting than fossil fuels, governments have also provided bio-fuel subsidies which have diverted many farmers from food production to energy crop production. The USA is now producing around 335 million tonnes of maize and four billion gallons of bio-fuel per year of which 90 per cent is derived from maize. While much of this crop has replaced food-based barley, it has also contributed to the doubling of maize prices since 2000. These policies, however, have an even more circuitous connection to global consumer practices and the mechanisms by which American and other first world nations manage their food surpluses. As they are often a solid voting block, the 'farmers lobby' strategically exert considerable influence over the democratically elected governments and farm policies of the USA, Japan and Europe. This powerful lobby has for decades successfully limited the inclusion of agriculture in international free trade agreements, and hence maintained artificially high domestic prices for agricultural products. Through a complex web of tariffs and local subsidies, first world agricultural producers have been protected from international competition, especially from low cost producers in the developing world.

One of the consequences of these protectionist measures has been the limitation of production to ensure market scarcity and higher prices. In particular, American producers have often destroyed crops and harvests in order to avoid flooding their own markets and putting downward pressure on prices. The US Dumping at Sea (Amendment) Act of 2004, administered by the Department of Agriculture, Fisheries and Food, is a formal recognition that food dumping is a normal practice in countries that seek to manipulate agricultural markets and trade prices. What is perhaps more resonant for this discussion, however, is the practice of 'dumping' food through the international aid system. On the surface, this action of national governments and aid organizations alleviating hunger and crisis through food donation appears to be a genuine humanitarian gesture. Beneath the surface of this system, however, there are numerous problems, the most obvious of which is the radical impact of low price or free product flooding into already stressed, indigent markets. As numerous commentators have observed, this practice of dumping food surpluses through donation practices radically distorts small agricultural economies, leaving local farmers without a market to sell their goods and a labour force that is rendered redundant by handouts (see IATP, 2004; Elliot, 2005).

Even the rising bio-fuel market may not prove a boon to the world's poorest farmers, as their own crops are either unsuitable for bio-mass fuel production or they are produced in such low volumes that they are not worth delivering through the export system. In this context, the poor farmers of the world are vulnerable to the financial power of large corporations that buy up the farmers' land for corporate bio-fuel production, leaving the farmers with a little cash but no livelihood and few prospects of employment. This is precisely the case in Indonesia and Malaysia, which now produce most of the world's palm oil for bio-fuel production. Farmers have sold their land to international palm oil companies, but have been left in a state of cultural and economic atrophy. In Indonesia and Malaysia nearly half of the increases in palm oil production have been created through the devastation of forests and consequent loss of rain forest biodiversity (Koh and Wilcove, 2008); the other half involves the removal of food-based farmers from their lands and livelihood. Thus, while the citizens of the developed world are rejoicing in the imagining of an emergent, greener economy of pleasure, they continue to transfer their displeasures to the world's indigent peoples.

Inequality redux: pirates of Somalia

As described above, the first world's vision of the world's poorest people is constituted largely around self-interest and a humanitarian communalism that assumes western primacy. The poor, that is, are not simply malnourished and living in squalid conditions; they are imagined as 'unequal' within the tabulation of western constructs of wealth and poverty. Whether by market forces or development aid, the poor, poverty and its alleviation are constructed by the developed world media in terms of an imaginary of significant Difference. This Difference can be modulated as a more contiguous and comprehensible 'difference' through the mobilization of developed world knowledge systems and discourses. That is, the radical and repugnant Difference that is attached with extreme poverty is reconceptualized through the language of targeted development programmes, aid, the market and trade. In this way, the world's poor become absorbed into the knowledge systems and desire economy through a shared culture of pleasure. This pleasure is projected into the indigent community by first world knowledge systems in their own pursuit and understanding of pleasure.

A sense of global community or even 'human species community', therefore, is conjured within a first world imaginary that has little to do with the actual living conditions of the world's poorest people, and much more to do with the purpose of wealth. News reports, documentaries, public development, charitable and NGO aid discourse are all mediated through an ideal of wealth and a materialism that prefigures the conditions and culture of those whom it imagines as 'needy'. That is to say, the purpose of wealth is to replicate itself and produce more wealth: the perspective of the wealthy nations necessarily forms the basis, authority and ideological-moral character of the global community and the encompassing progress of its poorest constituents. Humanitarianism, in this sense, is an amplification of the moral coding that drives liberal democracy and which contributes to an imaginary by which its intrinsic and hierarchical divisions are reconciled. Within an economy of pleasure, this imagined communalism is nestled across the complex displeasures, agonisms, resentment and guilt that are intrinsic to systematized global inequality.

When nations and peoples refuse to comply with this imagined communalism, they are usually regarded as renegades, failed states or simply 'hopeless'. Somalia and the small band of pirates who are working the Aden coast provide a clear case study of the ways in which the first world media approaches issues of global crisis. In many respects, Somalia is a paradigm example of a failing modern state. Created by Italian and British colonial cartographers in the late nineteenth century, Somalia produced little more than strategic military advantage for its European overlords as it lies on the Horn of Africa and the trading routes that connect Africa to Asia. The country's warrior kings defied European administration and law, until independence was finally granted in 1960. Like Afghanistan, however, Somalia immediately became the subject of intense Cold War rivalry, with the Soviets and Americans flooding the country and its nomadic communities with military hardware and munitions. While the dictator Major General Mohammed Said Barre held tight to Mogadishu from 1969 to 1991, much of the country was overrun by heavily armed warlords and their clan-based armies. After the ousting of Barre, the skirmishes became increasingly violent and chaotic as the clans fought over arable lands, ports and fisheries. Anything that might elevate Somalia into a functioning civil state has been seized or destroyed, as the clans continued to wreak havoc on the nation into the present day.

In a rare moment of clan consensus, however, two American Black Hawk helicopters were shot down in 1993 by thousands of Somalis bearing hand-held rocket grenades. The Americans were trying to protect an aid shipment of grain and arrest one of the most villainous of the warlords, Mohammed Farrah Aidid. The clans killed 18 US soldiers and carried their bodies through the streets of Mogadishu, an event which continues to rouse deep anger in the US military and political administration. During the 2000s, as the country continued to wallow in blood and political chaos, a relatively small group of Wahabbi Islamists gradually seized power in the capital and imposed a brief period of calm through *Sh'ariah* inspired order. Sitting outside the clans and the money lords, the Islamists' law was not subject to the vicissitudes and chauvinism of the clans, but threatened to unite all of Somalia's people under the banner of a single and integrated system of governance and law. By 2006 the Islamic government appeared to have brought a genuine peace, law and order to the country. Remarkably, they had even reduced the piracy and drug smuggling that had characterized much of the previous decades in Somalia. In 2006 the International Maritime Board based in London recorded only 10 acts of piracy off the Somalia coast, which was the lowest number for over a decade (Gettleman, 2009: 65).

In the post- 9/11 environment, however, Somalia came to be viewed by the US government as a distinct threat, a chaotic territory which promoted itself, like Afghanistan, as a breeding ground for Islamic terrorism. As a Muslim-dominated state that was awash with belligerence, armaments and a series of incompetent and ineffectual governments, Somalia appeared to have the same conditions that brought al-Qa'ida and the Taliban into power in Afghanistan. In this light, therefore, the Americans were particularly suspicious of the al-Shabab faction, which helped to form the Islamist government in Mogadishu; reports in the USA accused the al-Shabab of attacking and murdering women. According to Jeffrey Gettleman (2009), a journalist with experience in Iraq and Afghanistan, Somalia became the subject of intense CIA activity from 2006, as agents paid local warlords to fight against the rising influence and presence of Islamism in the region. In this same vein, America supported Christian-dominated Ethiopia in its ongoing attempts to destabilize the Islamists in Somalia. According to Gettleman, Ethiopia's military strategies included attacks on entire villages, resulting in significant civilian deaths.

Somali buccaneers

The result of all of these interventions and the rise of radical groups like al-Shabab is a return to chaos and bloodshed. According to Gettleman:

> [T]he problem with Somalia is that after 18 years of chaos, with so many people killed, with so many gun toting men rising up and then getting cut down, it is exceedingly difficult to identify who the country's real leaders are, if they exist at all. It's not just Mogadishu's wasteland of blown-up buildings that must be reconstructed: it's the entire national psyche.
>
> (Gettleman, 2009: 65)

While the US government denies any direct involvement in Somalia, it is nevertheless clear that the Ethiopian army has been funded and armed in part by the USA, as well as the African Union (Shaul, 2008). Even so, the Anglophonic media has shown little interest either in the conflict or its base causes, preferring instead to focus on the more spectacular events associated with Somali piracy and its mythical resonance of a high seas narrative. These high seas narratives are generated through much of the pinnacle literature of British and American imperialism, particularly through the adventure texts of Charles Johnson, Daniel Defoe, Robert Louis Stevenson, Joseph Conrad and Herman Melville.

The 'high seas' defines a global terrain that is both the conduit of global trade, transportation and migration—but also the violence and crime that was the predicate of European power and colonial conquest. Indeed, the complicated narrative of desire and danger that we have used as our central trope for this globalizing economy of pleasure is evoked through Melville's account of the 'Whiteness of the Whale' and the apocalyptic 'horror' of Conrad's Mister Kurtz.

In *Moby Dick* Melville specifically contrasts the 'villainy' of piracy against the nobility ('gemming') of whaling (chapter 53). Melville's ironical account of pirates, however, folds into a conception which vacillates between adventurous and lovable rogue, and a more insidious threat to the state and authorized maritime trade. It is precisely this dualism that has been adapted for popular cinema narratives like *Pirates of the Caribbean* (Gore Verbinski, 2003) and which underpins global news accounts of Somali piracy. Indeed, as it began seriously reporting on the Somali pirates in the latter 2000s, the global media seemed to move restlessly between a Johnny Depp vision of roguish miscreance and a sense in which the pirates represented a genuine lawlessness and danger to western lives, trade and authority. In either case, however, the media, not surprisingly, set its vision upon its own cultural terrain and the pleasures it projected for its home audiences. As entertainment or aggravation, the Somali pirates assumed international notoriety through the vision of enormous cargo vessels being attacked and captured by small bands of marauders, who would only release them on payment of millions of dollars in ransom.

Thus, while Somalia continued to be torn apart by civil war and external bombardment from US-sponsored Ethiopia, the media focused its attention on a piracy business that had been reinvigorated after the fall of the Islamic court government during 2006. Initially, vision of a small band of Somali pirates boarding and overtaking a massive cargo vessel in the Sea of Aden created ripples of amusement around the global mediasphere. Armed with rocket launchers, AKM rifles and semi-automatic hand guns, mostly acquired through Yemen and Mogadishu illegal arms traders, the pirates have adopted a range of strategies for excising food and cash from small and large trading vessels. Perhaps the most spectacular attacks have been on Indian, Russian and French cargo vessels, which are largely disinclined to engage the pirates in direct battle.

According to Jeff Nygaard, the ship owners are generally willing to pay the ransom, as the pirates have a good record for honouring hostage agreements and their treatment of captured crews is 'relatively humane' (BBC News, 2008). In either case, it is clear that the attacks on shipping have been as lucrative as they have been audacious, with suggestions that the returns have been as much as US$100–200 million. Even more compelling are the ways in which several investigative journalists explained the piracy as a reaction to western waste dumping and illegal fishing on the Somali coast. Conducted by major western corporations, these activities have devastated the fishing stocks and livelihoods of coastal communities in Somalia. And while the relationship between the fishermen and pirates is ambiguous, it is clear that some of the fishermen provide their seamanship and vessels to the pirate clans in return for direct payment and spending in the local community economies.

The deployment of Russian and Indian warships to the region during 2008 was also reported by the Anglophonic media in terms of ethnic stereotypes and a sense in which these vessels represented a disproportionate reaction to the tiny pirate boats and their somewhat comic escapades. Even so, this vaguely bemused reporting shifted in April 2008 when Reuters released images of French commandoes attacking pirates who had just received ransom payments from the owner of a French luxury yacht. The media images of high-tech commandoes pursuing and capturing the pirates contributed further to the ambiguity, as the pirates suddenly became the enemies of western technological superiority: the once-noble pirates became a pathetic quarry scurrying across the Somali desert in a dilapidated and barely mobile utility truck. Neither the French commandoes nor their prey seemed nobly human: they appeared rather to be the agents of a system and a technological hierarchy that stripped both their humanity and moral dignity.

In many respects, too, the French commando attack stripped away the ideological and mythological base upon which the reporting of Somalia and the Somali piracy was based. In essence, the crisis of Somalia was, momentarily at least, able to raise itself through the fissures of meaning and expose its deep fallibilities. The poverty and horror of Somali life suddenly betrayed itself in a simple narrative of human hunting. This 'gap in meaning', as I have described it here and elsewhere (Lewis, 2005; Lewis and Lewis, 2009), was seen as a considerable threat to the fabric of state authority. During 2008, in fact, the Anglophonic media began to invoke the authority of the USA against the pirates who became increasingly represented as dangerous renegades and a threat to global maritime trade. In this sense, the pirates' poverty and the calamity of state failure could no longer be used as an excuse for crime.

The romantic image of piracy was directly attacked by American state authorities, up to and including President Obama.

In April, 2009, Associated Press reported on 'a riveting high-seas drama [in which] an unarmed American crew wrested control of their U.S.-flagged cargo ship from Somali pirates.... And sent them fleeing to a lifeboat with the captain as hostage' (AP, 2009). Thus, a year after the French commando attacks, the American media syndicates told a much more forceful story about the pirates, their links to terrorism and the heroism of their own commando forces in freeing the ship's captain. The *New York Times*, for instance, reported:

> Acting with President Obama's authorization and in the belief that the hostage, Capt. Richard Phillips, was in imminent danger of being killed by captors armed with pistols and AK-47s, snipers on the fantail of the destroyer Bainbridge, which was towing the lifeboat on a 100-foot line, opened fire and picked off the three captors.
>
> (*New York Times*, April 2009)

Accompanied by a photograph of the celebrating (black and white) crew members displaying the American flag, the article presented an image of American military success over these dangerous 'brigands'. Unlike the farcical representation of the French commando attack, the *New York Times* report presented the event as a life and death struggle—a just war in which the word pirate is replaced by brigand and the act as 'criminal'. Thus, the hierarchy of power and moral authority is replenished by its relocation in the mythology of violent crime and the heroic omnipresence of the American ethos. This ethos is fortified through the image of black and white sailors raising the American flag in a gesture of powerful racial and global unity. Unlike the Europeans and other states, the Americans refused to negotiate with these criminals, preferring instead to invoke their own moral and presidential authority to blot out the lives of their enemies.

> It took only three remarkable shots—one each by snipers firing from a distance at dusk, using night-vision scopes, the officials said. Within minutes, rescuers slid down ropes from the Bainbridge, climbed aboard the lifeboat and found the three pirates dead. They then untied Captain Phillips, ending the contretemps at sea that had riveted much of the world's attention. A fourth pirate had surrendered earlier.
>
> (*New York Times*, April 2009)

The journalist's awe here is clearly marshalled through a profound conditioning about American military and moral privilege in the world. The technology and technical skills that guided the retribution is perpetually fortified through the US military's highly disciplined and elaborate information infrastructure. While the journalist's account has been clearly fed through this machinery, the US navy presented its own very particular image of Somali piracy and the need to regard it as a security threat, rather than a harmless or romantic narrative. On their in-house magazine *All Hands*, a naval commander, Nathan Shaeffer, explained the military's position on piracy in the following terms:

> Contrary to the romanticized portrayal of pirates that have populated folk tales and captured youngsters' imagination, modern-day pirates pose a clear and present threat to lives, commerce and the environment, as they lurk over shipping lanes, attacking ships and crew without regard for nationality or cargo. Piracy in the Gulf of Aden not only poses a threat to global commerce but also threatens aid delivery by the United Nations World Food Programme to victims of the ongoing civil war in Somalia. An estimated 2.4 million Somalis depend on WFP shipments, which contribute more than 30,000 tons of aid to the impoverished nation.
>
> (Shaeffer, 2009: 20)

Of course, this sort of self-validation might be expected from a naval commander, but the same tones were replicated across most of the US popular media as they focused specifically on the humanitarian and anti-terrorist mission of the USA.

And indeed, this same connection has been replicated in the reporting of Somali communities in Canada, the USA and Australia. In particular, accusations have been levelled against young men of the Somali diaspora who are believed to be working with the Islamic militant group al-Shabab, an organization that purportedly has ties with al-Qa'ida. In August of 2009 members of the Somali community in Australia were arrested on suspicion of preparing a terrorist attack on military bases in Sydney. Reports inevitably restored anxieties about insecurity and Islamicism associated with attacks in New York, Bali, Madrid and London. The revivification of these fears again prompted news media to invoke the narrative of Islamic violence, giving new context for the chaos of Somalia and the violent crimes of the Aden Sea brigands.

Africa and the ideology of debt

Somalia's problems with poverty, crime, violence and governance are replicated across many parts of Africa, particularly sub-Saharan states. And while we need to be wary of speaking generically about the 'African' problem as a condition which overrides the significant national, ethnic, religious and cultural diversity of the continent, it is nevertheless important to contrast the conditions of large parts of Africa with those of the advanced and emerging economies of the world. Indeed, Africa includes many of the poorest and most vulnerable people on Earth. As many scholars and development agencies have clearly seen, many of the nations of Africa continue to struggle under the burden of appalling social infrastructure, low education levels, crippling debt, high population growth, and a political instability which is constantly fostered through military coups, civil violence, corruption and external interventions. While the case of Somalia is perhaps the extreme, there can be little doubt that other nations of Africa—Sierra Leone, Liberia, Cote D'Ivorie, Kenya, the Sudan, Zimbabwe, Chad, Eritrea, the Congo—are among the world's most dangerous and dysfunctional states.

Clearly, many parts of Africa have not been able to shake themselves free of the ravages of economic and cultural exploitation that were imposed by European colonialism. Unlike emerging economies such as China, India, Brazil and various parts of South East Asia, many regions of Africa remain besieged by the triple jeopardy of political instability, high levels of debt and economic underdevelopment.

As we noted in Chapter 2, many of the problems associated with underdevelopment derive from the chaotic resonance of colonization which forced various ethnic and religious groups into a contiguity that they were not adequately able to manage. The exploitative practices of the colonists were replicated by multi-national corporations that extracted considerable wealth from the African states without investing in local, public infrastructure, education and training. The hierarchical structures created by colonization disrupted the old order, but left very little that was solid or sustainable when the colonists withdrew, mostly after the Second World War.

Development loans and projects, along with attempts to complete the modernization process, have been constantly frustrated by corruption, poor governance, exploitative practices, crime and inter-ethnic violence. In a series of studies from 2000 to the present, a range of United Nations agencies have recognized that the accumulating debt of African nations was fundamentally unsustainable, and that there was virtually no chance that these states could meet the Millennium Development goals set in 2000: 'The continent's debt problems and its resource requirements are inextricably linked to the capacity of African countries to generate capital accumulation and growth.... There now seems to be an emerging consensus ... that many African countries continue to suffer from a debt overhang' (UNCTAD, 2005: 1), It is now well understood that this crippling debt burden is a significant inhibitor for economic development (Plate 4.1).

As Paul Collier (2007) has noted in his study of the world's 'bottom billion', the development needs of Africa are complicated. According

Plate 4.1   Family life in the South Sudan, Africa. Photograph by Simon Richards.

to Collier and numerous other development scholars, developed world governments like the USA and the UK need to reconcile their own international security policies with genuine development strategies: a 'whole of government' approach which is formed around genuine trans-national co-operation is required for a solution to Africa's profound problems of malnutrition, disease, violence and state failure (Collier, 2007: 13). Indeed, the free trade and deregulation policies that were adopted and imposed by major lenders such as the World Bank and the IMF from the 1980s have clearly impacted both on the social growth potential of many African states as well as their ability to foster economic growth, security and capital accumulation. These loans were offered on condition that the receiving nation adopt free trade and other policies which subscribed to the lending organization's ideological alignment with free market and neo-liberal ideology. The conditions usually included structural readjustment policies such as:

1. *The dismantling of all protection and trade barriers.* This policy ensured that local manufacturers had to compete with goods produced by multi-national corporations using high-tech manufacturing equipment and employing the best trained and cheapest labour that was globally available.
2. An emphasis on trade also led to *significant changes in agricultural production.* As noted above, food crop farming was often replaced by trade-based crops. However, small farmers often found it difficult to compete with larger and more sophisticated farming techniques, leading many farmers to leave the land and migrate to urban centres where there was little opportunity for work. This pool of cheap labour enabled foreign companies, in particular, to move their manufacturing into the 'sweat shops' of the developing world. Where farmers did try to compete, the competition often led to decreasing returns on cash crops. Cocoa, for example, decreased in value from US$2604 per tonne in 1980 to around US$900 per tonne currently.
3. *Removal of all restrictions on labour.* This ensured that multi-national corporations would have direct access to cheap labour in the indebted nation. The inability to organize labour and unions ensured that factories producing products like footwear and clothing could employ cheap and abundant labour without concerns over strikes or other 'restrictive' labour practices.
4. *Deregulation of property and access to title.* This meant that multi-national corporations could buy up real estate and develop their own factories and economic infrastructure without government

interference. It also facilitated the growth of developing world tourism in various parts of the world, as foreign companies could buy up prime real estate for international first world tourism. This transformation in title and economic practices is also connected to the first world mediasphere and reconceptualization of indigent people and their cultures. Through this reimagining of poverty, poor people become reframed as accessible curiosities, performers and servants for first world pleasures (see below).

5. *Radical reductions in public spending by the indebted nation.* A free market economy was one that had minimal government intervention in the economy. Governments were not permitted to invest in public health, education, public welfare and public infrastructure. Policies of this kind contributed to social unrest and political instability.

For many nations of Africa, the financial returns for their restructured agricultural sector has proven to be less than the original loan (Haslam et al., 2009). Even with the Millennium Goals and the United Nations-directed Heavily Indebted Poor Countries (HIPC) Initiative, development in Africa remains constrained by external debt and often ineffectual aid projects (Easterly, 2006). Indeed, while emergency relief in periods of human-derived or natural disaster has stirred international interest from well-meaning NGOs and public donations , the processes of longer term development support perpetually struggles with the contradictory global dispositions of excessive indifference or excessive interference.

Global aid, power and terror

In December 2004 an earthquake on the north-west coast of Sumatra, created a massive release of oceanic energy. The resultant tsunami waves travelled in a devastating arc across the Indian Ocean, destroying the city of Bandah Aceh and innumerable villages and towns along the Indonesian coast. While over 200,000 Indonesians were killed by the event, many more tens of thousands of people were killed as the tsunami swept across the coasts of Thailand, Mauritius, India and Sri Lanka. An enormous relief effort was undertaken by governments, NGOs, aid agencies and public volunteers in both the developing and developed world. Marshalling more funds than had ever been previously donated for a disaster event, first world aid organizations moved quickly into action. In the emergency phase, relief workers provided blankets, medical treatment, clean water, food, clothing and shelter. Images of the disaster and suffering of so many poor people dominated the global news media, as citizens of the first world revelled in Christmas festivities and an elevated sense of good will and humanitarian compassion. News and magazine stories were replete with vision of misery, which seemed all the more poignant within a context of family bonding, vacation, spiritual renewal and reflection. The suffering of the tsunami victims (very few of whom were western or Christians) was absorbed into the symbology of the Christian-based festival of Christmas, stimulating a more acute sense of common humanity and care for those who had fallen victim to the vicissitudes of nature. People of the west gave generously.

As numerous development scholars have noted, natural disasters like the tsunami are usually far more devastating in developing countries than they are in wealthy countries. This is not surprising, not only because wealthy nations have much better warning and protective systems that might limit the impact of a disaster; they also have better relief, emergency treatment and public infrastructure that enables people and communities to recover from disasters (Lewis and Lewis, 2009). Six months after the disaster, this difference became starkly evident when a colleague and I conducted empirical research on community recovery in tsunami-affected south-east Sri Lanka. In this phase of the recovery, the area remained fraught by many of the often-cited difficulties associated with international aid and development, particularly through the convergence of natural disasters and local conditions of social and sectarian instability (Lewis and Lewis, 2006a).

Our research found, for example, that the presence of large numbers of international emergency relief and development workers created critical distortions in the local economy and cultural order. Many of the survivors of the disaster abandoned their usual economic activities, including farming and fishing, to engage in commercial activities that were designed purely for the demand of international aid workers who had disproportionately large disposable incomes. Moreover, the local community was quickly overwhelmed by the arrival of many thousands of Sri Lankans who had not been directly affected by the tsunami but who sought to acquire donated food, goods and survival packages. These outsiders also misappropriated aid and development investment funds for losses and hardship they didn't suffer. Indeed, even the survivors engaged in various acts of fraud, with one well-connected entrepreneur receiving (and reselling) multiple replacements of a fishing boat he never actually owned.

Perhaps the most spectacular of these donor calamities, however, was exercised by USAID, one of the world's largest and most important aid organizations. With a considerable sum of money to invest, the Sri Lankan director of the organization was instructed to rebuild the road bridge that connected the Islamic township of Pottawil to the small fishing and tourism village of Arugamby. After 6 months of aid interventions, Arugamby still had no reliable electricity, water supplies, sanitation or road infrastructure. Its school was destroyed and much of the tourist economy of the village remained in ruins. Following the catastrophe, the Indian government donated a single lane bridge which, while somewhat inconvenient, provided a useful transportation conduit for the area. When we asked the director of USAID why the organization was prioritizing a new bridge over other, far more critical infrastructure needs, he replied that the US Congress expressed its political interest 'in a very high profile project' (Lewis and Lewis, 2006a: 138). It then became clear that in a context of the global war on terror and a local area that was dominated by Muslims, the bridge represented a powerful metaphor that connected America to its Muslim friend in need. A new bridge could be photographed and delivered across the global media as evidence of America's good work in the world—Muslims were friends of the USA. Bridges were a lot more photogenic than sanitation pipes.

The reality in this area of Sri Lanka is starkly different to the Congressional imaginary of peace and harmony. While Muslims are a significant majority in this small coastal zone of Sri Lanka, they represent only a small proportion of the island's total population. The dominant island group—the Buddhist Sinhalese—have only a small representation in Arugamby, but they are nevertheless very active in the area's tourist economy. Hindu Tamils are also present in the area; until 2009, there were frequent outbreaks of sectarian violence around Arugamby associated with the ongoing secessionist activities in the north of the island. Indeed, while the tsunami created a brief moment of peace and co-operation between these ethnic groups, the arrival of the aid organizations created new tensions and competition for favours, support and investment. While we were conducting our research, a new, aid-sponsored Buddhist temple was erected in the main street of Arugamby, a public space in which there had not previously been any sectarian religious symbols. Within a week, the temple was bombed, leading to the establishment of a new Buddhist structure and an armed guard appointed by the national Sinhalese government.

For all their best intentions, the on-the-ground aid agencies contributed to the sectarian insecurity of the area. The violence that has dominated Sri Lankan domestic politics since the 1980s found a new site of conflict in the tsunami disaster and the complexion of global geo-politics. While the Americans were trying to foster an image of global compassion, the Saudi government was pouring its own aid money into the Muslim areas of Pottawil, an area that had been barely touched by the tsunami. The militants of Tamil Eelam (Tamil Tigers) were also infiltrating the area, seeking to access the enormous sums of money that first world agencies were bringing into the region. None of this, however, penetrated the veneer of first world news reports, which seemed to content themselves with the imaginary of humanitarianism and global community. Like the Mukhtaran Bibi story, the news media satisfied itself with a narrative of otherness which gratified the pleasure of charity and the superior status of the giver. This calamity of clumsy ignorance merely confirms the crisis of inequality and its perspective of wealth.

Women and sanitation

In many respects, the convergence of desire, poverty and violence is best expressed through the experience of women across the globe (UNIFEM, 2009). We began this chapter with an account of Mukhtaran Bibi, a young woman living in provincial Pakistan who was raped and vilified as punishment for an honour crime that was supposedly committed by her 12 year-old brother. The sexual assault that was perpetrated against Bibi symbolizes the oppression, poverty and brutality which many women in the developing world experience as a matter of every-day life. In their annual report on the state of women and children in the world (see UNIFEM, 2009), the United Nations describe clearly that these are the poorest and most vulnerable people on Earth, exposed not only to the ravages of poverty, malnutrition and disease, but to the most brutal excesses of warfare and institutionalized modes of social exclusion and violence.

Within a global pleasure economy, we might describe indigent women and their children as the lowest cast of the exchange spiral— the resting place of all human history and its volition of displeasure. Maggie Black and Ben Fawcett (2008) explain this problem in terms of the most basic of human needs and related diseases—sanitation. According to Black and Fawcett, there are over a billion people across the world who do not have access to a toilet of any kind. Combined with equally limited access to clean drinking water, these people are often bound to a cycle of contamination, as their waters are perpetually polluted by *E. coli* bacteria, frequently derived from human faecal wastes. During times of natural and human disasters such as wars, floods or earthquakes, these problems are even worse as common diseases like diarrhoea are further compounded by typhoid and other water-born infection. Black and Fawcett note:

> Of the over 2 million deaths a year associated with diseases of dirt and squalor, most are due to diarrhoeal diseases, and of these the vast majority are in children under five years old, almost all of them in developing countries.
>
> (Black and Fawcett, 2008: 78)

Poor women, who are engaged in primary reproductive and family care roles, are further constrained by libidinal practices and masculine modes of violence which create further dangers, even during the simple process of elimination. According to Black and Fawcett, women are forced to protect their bodies and dignity by eliminating in the hours before or after sunrise, rendering them vulnerable to a range of dangers, including and most especially sexual assault by men.

Beyond these basic dangers, women are often denied education, political participation and other rights afforded men. The United Nations and innumerable scholarly accounts of poverty recognize the connection between women, education and development. It is something of a development axiom that the pathway to improved economy involves the education of women and women's liberation from the ceaseless cycle of reproduction. In this context, women's bodies, which have borne the greatest burden of the volition of economic surplus and crisis conditions, remain constrained within a global hierarchical imaginary. As the Mukhtaran Bibi story demonstrates, women and women's bodies can be centralized within a collective imaginary of desire, while simultaneously being disgraced as agents of unseemly animality. In the crisis of inequality, women have thereby suffered the most profound outrages, despicable acts of terror and humiliation. In order to recast these bodies as worthy beings, the western mediasphere needs to place the libidinal imaginary of woman within a broader imaginary that acknowledges a woman's right to sanitation, security and dignity.

5
The Shadow and the Fawn: Sustainable Nature and Collapsing Ecologies

> The Supreme Truth exists outside and inside of all living beings, the moving and the nonmoving. Because He is subtle, He is beyond the power of the material senses to see or to know. Although far, far away, He is also near to all.
>
> The *Bhagavad Gita*, 13: 16

> Most of the luxuries, and many of the so-called comforts of life, are not only not indispensable, but positive hindrances to the elevation of mankind. With respect to luxuries and comforts, the wisest have ever lived a more simple and meagre life than the poor.
>
> Henry David Thoreau, *Walden*, 1854

The nature of nature

In a brief parable, Aesop tells the story of a fawn who asks his mother: 'You are taller and swifter than a dog; why then are you so fearful?' The mother answers: 'Yes, it is true, but I can't explain—when I hear the howl of the hounds, I feel faint and have to run away.' An explanation for the mother's insecurity appears in another of Aesop's fables. In this story a dog is carrying a piece of flesh across a bridge. The dog glances into the water and sees the reflection of another dog carrying meat that is twice the size of his own. The dog snarls and tries to attack the reflection, dropping his meat into the river. Now the dog and his shadow are left with nothing, as the flesh is swept away by the rolling eddies.

In Classical Greece, Aesop could not have imagined the extent to which his moral prescience might be realized. The hound is lured by the fantasy of plenitude, an excess, which ultimately betrays his desires.

And yet the rapacious dog is that part of our own nature which pursues its desires in the grotesque degradation of the body as flesh—that defilement which sacrifices the miracle of a life for the nourishment of its conqueror. In this context, the terror of the fawn announces the underlying paradox of nature: that innocence is unsustainable and always vulnerable to the desiring of others. A simple imagining of the innocence of nature is shattered within the hierarchy of contending needs and desires, including those of human beings. Neither human nor nonhuman nature, that is, can secure itself against the rapaciousness that is inscribed in these hierarchical systems and the power of desire.

In this light, Aesop's moral allefores, which represent human attributes in animal characters, might simply caution citizens against the damaging consequences of excessive desire. The baying hounds that terrify a fawn allegorize the excesses of greed or the abandonment of moral principles and law. These attributes of human nature, which Aesop represented in his animal characters and fables, were not uniform or monadic but were best understood in terms of these paradoxes and contending dispositions. In keeping with the prevailing ideas of the time, Aesop commended a system of reasonable balance by which the individual remained obedient to the moral structures of divine and state laws. Nature could not be parenthesized. Rather, nature must be confronted, controlled and mobilized, both as an external cosmological force and as a set of internal forces that drive our animal character but which must be controlled by law, that is, by reasoned, human culture.

Yet even through the progress of early agricultural and industrial modernism, these questions over the fundamental 'nature' of being human continue to be formed within a broader context of humans' status within, and relationship to, 'nature'. Through various aesthetic, religious, philosophical and scientific narratives these questions interrogate the essential or ontological core of the human presence in the universe and in relation to planetary life systems. For a species that has evolved a reflexive consciousness, questions about our fundamental 'being in nature' are critically linked to those broader and more apocalyptic fascinations with our own survival, future and prospects of annihilation. In the contemporary mediasphere these agonisms are circulating around a bleak and Titanic imaginary of human and ecological catastrophe—the end of the world, that is, is being powerfully rendered in the discourse of environmentalism, global warming and the complete collapse of global life systems (McGuire, 2004; Kunstler, 2006).

In this way, our collective and individual destiny is bound by a barely comprehensible natural order which both sustains and terrifies us, and to which we feel both intrinsic and alien. Within this context, humans exist uncomfortably within the violent paradox of the natural order. Where every element or being is the subject of others' survival claims, the state of 'being human' is precariously suspended between this web of animate and inanimate objects, and the counter-claim of being exceptional, that is, between our underlying animality and our claims to a culturally constituted distinction. In the volition of the Holocene agricultural cultures, in fact, this claim to exception is fortified by a spiritual or metaphysical distinction that ultimately separates us from the nature over which god and humans preside. Unlike our hunter-gatherer forbears, that is, agricultural and industrialized cultures relinquish our ancestral engagement with natural forms, preferring instead to imagine a religious hierarchy by which we serve our god against the vicissitudes of impious nature.

To this extent, we are not simply the fawn and the craven dog of nature, but we exist as the chimerical shadow, that conflux of desire and plenty that addles our corporeal self and sense of belonging in nature. In this sense, we are actually the inverse of the Aesop fabulation. In the shadow of our self we look back at our animality and the bridge from which we gaze narcissistically and ravenously at our suspected other. We lure the loss that we have deceptively desired. We exist in a suspended moment of our own desiring.

Framing the unframable

The underlying argument of this book is that a combination of ecological and human population pressures precipitated a radical change in human economy and culture around the end of the last major Glacial Phase. These changes have contributed to the formation of ongoing crisis conditions and the evolution of a crisis consciousness. A parallel combination of ecological conditions and human economic-cultural practices are converging in the current phase of climate change and other critical ecological crises. As we consider these questions of ecology more directly in this chapter, the concept of 'nature' and the human relationship to nature become critically implicated, particularly within the context of complicated and often contending knowledge systems. These knowledge systems—particularly the ways in which we conceptualize and comprehend humans, human nature and nature itself—are bound to our pleasure economy and the ways in which the contemporary media represent ecology and ecological catastrophe.

Clearly, our contemporary readings of nature are drawn from innumerable sources—including hunter-gatherer pre-history, Classical agricultural cultures, and Enlightenment visions of science and cultural apocalypse. In many respects, the clash of knowledge systems that characterizes nature narratives in modern societies resonates with the same perplexities that Aesop and other Classical thinkers had explored well before the Christian era. Even so, the scientific rationalism that was propitiated through Enlightenment scholars like Charles Darwin, Herbert Spencer, George Wallace and Thomas Huxley sought to situate humans within a natural order that was clearly designed to overwrite the propositions of the Abrahamite religions. Indeed, while debates over natural selection and divinely directed 'intelligent design' continue in various social and scholarly settings (see Ayala, 2006; Frame, 2009), Darwin's concept of evolution constitutes a primary framework for contemporary readings of nature. As we have indicated, however, these readings are not simply external to the human condition, but are embedded in our broader readings of the human and the ways in which culture is shaped and deployed.

Indeed, as Ian McCalman (2009) argues, Darwin's natural selection needs to be understood as a radical social manifesto in the same lineage as Marx's theory of communism. While meticulously avoiding reference to 'man' in *On the Origin of Species* (orig. 1859), Darwin surrendered to his deeper judgements on human evolution in his later book *The Descent of Man* (orig. 1875). In many respects, Darwin's description of natural selection as the mechanism of all species evolution confirms by another means the primacy of humans over other nature. Of course, the radical displacement of Biblical descriptions of Creation required some epistemological and ideological adjustment, particularly the idea that humans are descended from a simian lineage. Within a broader historical context, however, Darwin presented an explanation for the process of evolution that many Enlightenment thinkers in Europe had been long discussing and which was part of a broader cultural and economic volition. Through the rise of new epistemological systems associated with science, technology and economics 'nature' could no longer be satisfactorily conceptualized by standard theology or its related aesthetic incarnations. And while the human had always been the centre of these theories of nature, Darwin's *Descent of Man* provided a new ideological and epistemological framework for the anthropocentricism that had driven the agricultural transformation of human culture and planetary ecology. Without entirely extinguishing the great agricultural religions, Darwinist conceptions of nature provided a new vision of human primacy, one based on our competitive advantage as rational and technologically superior beings.

This superiority expressed itself in the Enlightenment through industrialization and the extension of the surplus value economy: modern, globalizing capitalism. Indeed, the very force of modern capitalism is ideologically emblazoned through the social adaptation of Darwinist theories of nature, particularly through the rise of social disciplines like anthropology, eugenics, economics and demography. Darwin's theory of natural selection provided for many social scientists a more 'objective' and scientific explanation for human differentiations, both within nations and across the globe. Herbert Spencer's (in)famous conception of 'survival of the fittest'[1] was adapted to explain class and cultural differentiations, providing the moral framework for the colonial conquest and administration of 'inferior' peoples and their culture. More dramatically, however, the Darwin conceptualization was applied by both Left and Right political institutions to explain the world and the economic processes that divided human groups. Eugenics, which emerged as an explanation for these *natural* human physical and cultural divisions, was easily invoked to justify the most heinous of human crimes, including genocide.

Nature, in this sense, binds humans to a set of inviolable laws, including the laws governing human superiority over other species and hierarchical divisions between humans themselves. Marshalled through the various permutations of capitalist economy, these same laws might seem to have justified the radical degradation of those non-human elements of nature, particularly the 'other' species upon which we depend but over which we are superior. That is, our anthropocentricism ennobles the transformative and destructive dimensions of our creative economy since this is a natural, even universal, alignment with irrevocable law.

As we have noted, however, this conception of nature as 'natural laws' is only one discourse in the phalanx of our knowledge systems. Modernism and modernity have not erased theological or aesthetic conceptions of nature, nor indeed have the laws that were interpreted by Darwin, Spencer and others remained sacrosanct. Rather, our readings of nature, and the relationship between the natural and the human, are the subject of evolving discursive and ideological contentions—ongoing and emerging knowledge systems which challenge the ways in which the relationship between the human and nature might be assumed or described. This is particularly the case for a cultural politics of nature in which nature is regarded as either 'natural resources' and subject to human use and value, or an aesthetic, spiritual and material system which has an integrity that humans must celebrate, protect and confirm.

Within this dualism there are a range of conceptions that emphasize either the creative power of human culture and economy and the danger of destructive nature, or the beauty and value of nature in its own terms or for the sustainability of planetary life. Alongside the pragmatic vision of nature and its availability, human exploitation through agriculture, industry and commerce is another vision of nature as transcendent and mystical—a sense in which nature is a perfection of itself or God's divine creativity. Between both zones is a sense of danger, an apocalyptic vision that has permeated all cultural imaginings through the transformative crises of the Holocene.

Indeed, our attempts to frame the concept of nature throughout the Holocene period have always been compromised by our power of knowing which immediately distances us from the other, non-human components of nature. The comfort of this distance or the otherness of nature, however, is itself undermined by the constant reassertion of our own intrinsic nature—our animality—which forces our knowing into a state of misrecognition as we are forced to look at ourselves in the mirror of the nature we presumed to be 'other'. This oscillation between distance and misrecognition becomes more acute as humans have sought to adapt to the conditions of Holocene ecological change, and the volition of their own cultural and economic innovations. In attempting to reconcile our intrinsic knowing (culture) and non-knowing (animality), these anxieties about extrinsic nature become even more perplexing, filtering our knowledge systems through a perpetually emerging crisis consciousness.

That is, through this convergence of crisis conditions associated with the progression of global warming and agricultural-industrial economic adaptations, our knowledge systems have become inevitably reconfigured in terms of a progressive crisis consciousness, an apocalyptic vision that imagines the end of humankind and the assemblage system we project as 'the world'. As noted in Chapter 1, the hunter-gatherer communities that emerged during the Pleistocene period had no conception of 'the world' in the sense of an entity that was distinct from a human-nature continuity. The world that was imagined by the Holocene agricultural societies, however, was constituted in terms of a hierarchical, cosmological order by which divine beings imposed their will over a mortal world where humans battled with nature and each other. Thus, while the divine realm was infinite, the human as material nature was distinctly finite. Unlike the hunter-gatherer animistic continuities, the world of the agricultural societies was vulnerable to destruction by both nature and god.

In this sense, the nature that Darwin describes in terms of the laws of natural selection appears somewhat deceptive, as natural systems continue to overwhelm us by their chimerical character and capacity to impose themselves—both as greater power and crumbling ecology. In this sense, the most frightening thing about nature is not simply its ubiquitous and indifferent malevolence, but rather its resistance to our knowing and our desires, including our desire to revive and marshal its power. Nature, therefore, exists at the centre of our crisis of knowing—our knowing of ourselves, our intrinsic animality and our cultural projections of a collective self. By this human-nature dualism, we seek perpetually to reveal the complexity of a sense of being that is both part of nature and apart from nature Our incapacity to resolve this aporia has led us again into the most profound anxiety about the future and the ways in which we might restore the embattled life systems—the nature—upon which our existence depends.

From nature to ecology

As Alexander Wilson (1991) so deftly described, there is nothing natural about nature; and indeed, the cultural conception of nature is definitively implicated in all human knowledge systems, and vice versa (Goodman et al., 2003). These knowledge systems, particularly as they are filtered through a crisis consciousness and the contemporary mediasphere, create a range of cultural imaginings about nature. These imaginings seek inevitably to establish an ideological discourse that resolves the human-nature aporia and enable humans to 'recognize' the true nature of nature. Indeed, it is precisely this aporia and the unframable nature of nature which continues to perplex our multiplying knowledge systems. Indeed, while many commentators identify the Cartesian division of body and mind as the core of modernism and its epistemological volition, this dualism in many respects is simply an extension—a modern incarnation—of the Holocene aporia. The rattling and unsteady oscillation between distance and misrecognition of nature continues to drive our pursuit of pleasure and the spectral prospect of complete annihilation.

The human-nature dualism, therefore, is a primary driver in the contemporary framings of nature. Through the evolution of an economy of pleasure, nature has become imagined through a range of knowledge systems and discourses, particularly around a cultural politics of 'ecology'. Significant social fractures, in fact, have emerged around the meaning and political deployment of ecology, most notably in various conceptions of pleasure and the transferral of displeasure to others. In this sense, ecology becomes a rubric for an almost infinite range of perspectives, experiences and knowledge systems, which define nature in terms of complex cultural, political and economic contentions.

The primary driver and context for these contentions, of course, is the global mediasphere. Indeed, as the human-nature aporia is mobilized through the multiplying conceptions of ecology, nature is becoming increasingly lost (or misrecognized) in the social debates about pleasure and the vision of annihilation. Nature, then, is that amorphous omnipresence that lurks behind a conception of ecology and the ways in which first world citizens, in particular, know and articulate their desires and anxieties about the possible confrontation of consumption and ecological catastrophe. These anxieties, that is, circulate around the conception of nature as 'natural resource' which is available for human economic exploitation, and nature as a distinctive zone that is not only necessary as a life sustaining system but a source of spiritual replenishment.

Indeed, the nature that first world citizens most frequently encounter in the mediasphere is constituted around the pleasure imaginings of cultivated gardens, nature parks, domesticated pets, tourism and wildlife documentaries. Through the security of these pleasures, however, the spectre of crisis reveals itself in the narratives of over-consumption, environmental destruction, global warming, extreme weather events and the loss of animal habitat. These stories and images agitate those deeper, cultural anxieties about humans' own destructive animality and the hierarchies by which displeasures express themselves in violence, sexual frustration, injury, disease and ultimately death. In the discussions that follow, these crisis anxieties will be examined in terms of contentions over nature and ecology, specifically as they are borne out in the contemporary mediasphere.

Ecological disaster, excess and motion

The imagining of nature as 'ecology' is perhaps the most formidable zone of the current crisis consciousness. Over the past decade, cultural and social commentary has become increasingly focused on ecological disaster and the threats posed to human and planetary survival. Indeed, while the essential argument of this book is that the current incarnation of crisis has deep roots in human and geological history, this most recent incarnation of ecological crisis is now dominating global, public and political interest. As Kim Humphery (2010) has noted, issues of global warming and environmentalism are intricately woven through the practices and politics of everyday consumption. More broadly, the news, information and entertainment media are replete with stories and references to greenhouse gases, carbon footprint, environmental protection and the aesthetics of ecology. Barely a day passes without a news story about new energy saving devices, sustainability, or references to extreme weather and melting ice.

And while a counter discourse is emerging, particularly through the rising tide of climate change scepticism, these environmental narratives are largely embedded in imaginings of some amorphous apocalypse and a vision of 'the end'. While rarely explicated, these environmental narratives, along with their spectral occlusion, are themselves bound to the conditions of pleasure, excess and the agitated imagining of human progress. Driven by the imperatives of perpetual innovation and economic-population growth, this volition has expressed itself in terms of mass industrialization, urbanization and the broad transformation of ecological systems across the planet. As many commentators have noted, this process of transformation, borne by the ideology of progress, has accelerated at exponential rates over the period of the Holocene (Gleick, 2000).

As noted in previous chapters, this volition is often imagined as a creative and generative force—the destructive dimensions are discursively prefigured as development, growth, progress and 'the modern'. Yet the shadow of the hungry dog has never been annulled: the brighter the light of our human ascent and civility, the more ferocious the destructive capacity. These are not 'unintended consequences' as Beck imagines, but the calculated devastation that necessarily accompanies human recreation of ecological systems. Progress, in this sense, necessarily implicates destruction and transformation.

For the resistant politics of environmentalism, this progression has exceeded itself, passing through the 'tipping point' of sustainability to ecological catastrophe. The media, particularly the more open spaces of the Internet, abound with doomsday predictions and images of ecological collapse through the impact of—greenhouse gases, polluted waterways, crumbling ice sheets, flooded island territories, the destruction of coral reefs, droughts, famine, and the proliferation of extreme weather events like hurricanes, blizzards and record high temperatures.

In this sense, the prefiguration of progress is imagined as a condition of regress, a retreat from biodiversity to a singular and catastrophic volition to disaster. While we will discuss these resistant politics in more detail later in the chapter, we need to address the cultural conditions within which progress is imagined and the means by which ecology has been marshalled through this accelerating economy of desire.

Mobility as progress

The convergence of a sense of human progress and civilizational advance is often imagined in relation to human mobility. Indeed, the capacity of humans to move cognitively and physically across space has been a central component of economic and social change, particularly in relation to the modern globalization. Over recent decades, in fact, social commentary has often characterized the increasing dependence on innovation and mobility in terms of 'the acceleration of just about everything' (Gleick, 2000, 2003), an idea derived from cultural theories of postmodernity (Jameson, 1991), post-industrial society (Bell, 1973) and hyperreality (Baudrillard, 1984). Indeed, while conceding that environmental change is the mainstay of planetary ecology, J. R. McNeil (2000) argues that the twentieth century was marked by a radical acceleration in ecological transformation:

> In environmental history, the twentieth century qualifies as a peculiar century because of the screeching acceleration of so many processes that bring ecological change.... The scale and intensity of changes were so great that matters that were for millennia local concerns became global. One example is air pollution. Since people first harnessed fire nearly half a million years ago they have polluted air locally.... But lately air pollution has grown so comprehensive and large-scale that it affects the fundamentals of global atmospheric chemistry.
>
> (McNeill, 2000: 435)

Thus, it is the combination of an exponential increase in human populations across the planet, and the accelerating mobility and intensity of particular economic and technological practices that has wrought such widespread environmental effects. This is particularly the case for economically advanced, industrial societies whose mobile populations and economic practices are clearly responsible for the extremes of energy consumption and the production of global greenhouse gases. The acceleration of everything—urbanization, travel, communications, Internet downloads, transportation—is largely centred around the economically advanced nations and cities. In these high-desiring, high-consuming global terrains, individuals and organizations are engaged in unremitting and intensely competitive economic and leisure practices that are constituted around the increasingly erratic rhythms of production, consumption and disposal.

Among many others, Fredric Jameson (1991) explained the acceleration associated with a new cultural epoch of postmodernity in terms of the compression of time and space. Through the development and deployment of elaborate transportation and communications systems, humans have been able to move across space at increasingly rapid speeds. Within the global mediasphere, in fact, time and space have become so densely concentrated that symbols, narratives and information can be transferred across the globe almost instantaneously. Mass transportation systems that developed during the twentieth century also allow individuals to travel to exotic parts of the globe that *appear* to be culturally, politically and physically very different to their home. These 'contiguities' and appearances contribute to an extraordinary sense of temporal and spatial compression—as they confirm the ideology of progress and cultural mobility that is a dominant ethos of modernizing globality.

The paradoxical notion of 'progression as compression' has contributed to a particular kind of epistemological effect—the formation of a knowledge framework that compounds the precarious and contradictory disposition towards perpetual motion and stasis. While mobility was a characteristic of early human cultures, the rise of agriculture created a new imperative for population growth, technological innovation and the expansion of economy and territorial control; this competition-driven progression was accompanied by the establishment of property and land management systems that required a high degree of social stasis. Of course there were specialists who travelled—traders, military forces, explorers, missionaries—but the majority of people lived their lives in fixed locales doing relatively sedentary agricultural work. Thus, the imaginary of progression and mobility is woven across an otherwise static social environment. This conflux of mobility and inertia is represented in pre-industrial cartography: divinity maps present an image of the cosmos that is largely hierarchical with the gods and heaven set at the apex, humans, animals and the earth as the centre zone, and hell as the lowest dominion. In pre-industrial travellers' maps the land is presented as flat relief with trails being identified by fixed and recognizable landmarks such as monuments or distinctive land-features and buildings; the maps also tended to radiate out from the king's court which was the epicentre of civilization (Anderson, 1991).

The evolution of the mediasphere and the economy of pleasure has intensified this conflux of motion and inertia to such an extent that the demands of mobility have evolved into a system of what Jean Baudrillard calls 'appearances'. As noted in earlier chapters, the world has become increasingly rendered through these appearances within the mediasphere and its capacity to form knowledge through the compression and exchange of symbols and mediation. Thus, the speed of motion over stasis has created an imaginary of mobility that is designed to substantiate the cognitive conception of advancement and social progress. Of course, humans still move themselves and their products across space; the argument here is that these modes of mobility are fostered around an appearance of motion that encases a more static condition of human stasis. This conception of progress is necessary, I would suggest, for an economy that is constituted around an ideology of progress that is fostered through fantasies of infinite pleasure.

Thus, the movement of humans across space is frequently mediated through a complex convergence of the appearance of motion over the inertia of the body. Indeed, much of the perpetual motion that supposedly characterizes contemporary cultures is shaped through the appearances that are facilitated by communications systems and a process of globalization that is deftly double-coded as cultural difference. Just as Aesop's hungry hound imagines a difference in the waters of the river, in communications-based globalization the difference is rarely substantial as it merely elicits a fantasy of infinite pleasure in the desiring of the social agent. As we have also noted in earlier chapters, the difference which the contemporary individual imagines in places, people and products is often just a propagation of the economy of pleasure. When we travel 'vast distances' to exotic locations, we are very often pursuing a variation in ourselves and our home cultures—an appearance of difference rather than a distinctive and potentially threatening Difference.

In this way, humans in advanced societies might be accelerating in some respects, but this velocity is returning upon itself, as first world citizens become increasingly contained within the sitting space of their screens and the inertia that enables de-corporealized communication. As they become increasingly inert, first world humans are getting bigger and fatter, as labour and recreation are conjoined around the static activities of viewing, eating and listening. Even the pluralism and community diversity that interactive communications systems appear to deliver are becoming increasingly standardized so that the imagined difference of others is filtered through the pleasure economy and its meticulously designed conflux of consumable variety. The pleasure economy, to this extent, deconstructs the dualism of homogeneity versus heterogeneity: rather, everything is mixed through the designer industry as consumable diversity.

Cities, hotels and shopping malls are all formed in the template of a 'Macdonaldization', as George Ritzer so cannily describes it. Even in Mumbai, the MacDonald's restaurant has assumed a certain bourgeois commonality by which the American hamburger has become localized in toasted vegetarian and curry sandwiches. This constrained pluralism is not evidence of human mobility and acceleration, but a standardization of space and culture that recreates distance as contiguity. Our acceleration, that is, is also a deceleration, at least inasmuch as the cultural distance that separated spaces across the globe are now being compressed into a new form of cognitive and cultural contiguity and hence inertia. Whether by aeroplane or media text, our sense of the world is thereby concentrated through consumption and a mediated economy of pleasure that radically reduces diversity—including biodiversity—into a common cognitive sphere.

Similarly, the mobile devices we once called cell phones are frequently celebrated by techno-utopians as liberational tools that enable us to foster our social connections while increasing our geo-spatial and cultural mobility (Agar, 2004; Goggin and Hjorth, 2008). These 'digitopians' (Lewis, 2000, 2008) rejoice in a de-corporealized communicational community that has the appearance of perpetual motion and connectivity, but which remains strangely transfixed in the static conditions of solipsistic, first world screen life and standardized frames of difference—the critical components of consumable culture in a pleasure economy.

In bodies that barely move but which are rather transported by various technological and communicational machinery, we might then accept that much of the sense of motion that we experience in contemporary culture is an appearance that is set in rather isometric conditions. Our sense of motion, therefore, is largely an action of desire, that same agitated and restless desire that drives our pleasure economy and its ideology of progress. This isometric volition is, therefore, largely cognitive, a sense of motion that stimulates us to produce, consume or recreate within the broader context of our personal and collective pursuit of pleasure. Fragile as it is, this common cognitive sphere enables the first world to pursue its pleasures without regard to the value of diversity, including the diversity that is manifest in the non-human world. In our discussions on inequality (Chapter 4), we understood this first world disposition in the absorption of 'the poor' into the hierarchical system of the economy of pleasure and the global mediasphere. In a similar isometrics of progress, first world citizens have subdued the non-human conditions of ecology and nature, transforming them into a common cognitive space that facilitates an astonishing degree of brutality, indifference and anthropocentricism. Where they are not destroyed, these non-human systems and creatures (again like 'the poor') are domesticated and absorbed into the first world mediasphere for the pleasure of the citizenry and their imaginings of pleasure. This too, is a confirmation of progress as regression, as the natural world represents some vaguely constituted past that the miracle of the modern media somehow restores or conserves. The standardization of the world, that is, remains fixed upon a conception of progress that enables the transfer of displeasure through the reimagining of other creatures, alternative aesthetics and the claims of natural diversity.

Population as global destruction

Most cultural studies scholars acknowledge that history is written from the perspective of victors and other social elites (see de Certeau, 1988). Those who win the battles, control the money and the media are most able to explain the world in terms of their own ideological, cultural and economic interests. Writers like Charles Taylor, Edward Herman and Henry Giroux argue, further, that the world and its complex of knowledge systems are shaped by historically structured ideologies which replicate themselves through the alignment of economic elites, first world governments and a compliant corporate media. Thus, the environmental damage associated with over-consumption is due in large part to elites who impose their controlling ideologies over the citizenry, leading them into attitudes and practices for which they are not entirely responsible. These elites fortify their interests and pleasures through the transfer of displeasure to other social groups—particularly the poor, and even more particularly the poor in the developing world. Multi-national corporations, in particular, are responsible for much of the appalling environmental degradation associated with developing world economic development projects.

In ecological terms, the same pattern of pleasure transferral is further exercised through the treatment of non-human species, landforms and ecological systems. That is, in the promulgation of their own economic and political interests, these elite groups marshal the media in support of their corporate and commercial interests, transferring damage and displeasure to less powerful human groups and to the environment itself. Through their management of public and media affairs, such corporations seek perpetually to generate a sense of corporate and ecological responsibility, aligning their activities and public image with discourses of 'sustainability', environmental management and civic citizenship.

And while there is clear evidence that corporate powers are implicated in the economy of ecological destruction, this anti-corporate perspective of our environmental history tends to parenthesize the role and responsibility of all other historical and contemporary agents whose practices have contributed significantly to the crisis of planetary life systems. Indeed, while we might readily acknowledge that the pursuit of pleasure and transferral of displeasure is a primary political practice in agricultural and advanced cultures, social hierarchies are not simply dualistic, as this structural model implies. It is not simply a matter of government, corporate and media elites pursuing their interests over a brainwashed other: it is rather that power and pleasure are embedded in the hierarchical and intensely competitive practices of creative-destructive economy. Through the various imaginings of nature, ecological systems have become a war zone in contemporary cultural politics, particularly in light of global warming, deforestation and the radical degradation of oceanic environments.

Indeed, at the core of much of this creative destruction is the simple fact of Holocene human desiring, a desiring that is replicated through the proliferation of the species itself. This proliferation has been driven, from the very beginning of the agricultural period into the present, by a formidable pursuit of economic surplus, labour, markets and military security. As it has evolved, the surplus economy has depended critically on human population proliferation; specifically, the proliferation of desiring, labouring and consuming human bodies. It is not simply that humans are the dupes of elite interests—but rather most of the six billion plus people on the Earth today are implicated in the global pursuit of surplus and the globally evolving economy of pleasure.

To this end, human planetary mobility, the imagining of progress and exponential population growth are directly responsible for the creative-destructive transformation of ecological systems and nature. While it is fairly clear that human migration and population expansion were taking place from around 40–100,000 years BP, the really significant population growth and radical disruption to ecological systems is an accelerating trend, particularly during the period of industrial and communicational modernization. Critical innovations in health, sanitation, building construction, transportation and communications have facilitated both the broadening of human settlements and concomitant concentrations of populations in urban centres like the sky-scraper city. The following table gives a sense of how rapidly the human species has grown over the past two millennia.

Year	Population (millions)
0	200
1000	275
1500	450
1900	1600
1960	3000
1970	3700
1980	4500
1990	5300
2000	6100
2010	6800

Source: Adapted from United Nations Population Division, (2010).

As this table indicates, human population growth has accelerated at exponential rates over the past 2000 years. While it took nearly 250,000 years for the population of modern humans to reach 200 million, this figure was doubled in only 1500 years and doubled again in 250 years. On a much higher base, world population doubled from 1960 to 2000 when the figure reached six billion.

Population and the destruction of ecosystems

Of themselves, these figures say very little. However, as we examine the impact of populations as agents of mobile progressivism, then we see that humans are responsible for the radical transformation of natural landforms and ecosystems through the expansion of human economy, settlement, consumption practices and culture. Clearly, the sheer mass of human population and the hierarchical practices associated with population pressure are clearly implicated in the radical disruption of natural ecosystems. Thus, the complex interchange of elements, energy, genes and survival practices that are balanced through symbiotic and competitive survival activities in a given ecosystem are vulnerable to any form of disruption: the more significant the human intervention in an ecosystem, the more precarious its sustainability.

However, it is not simply the size of the human population that distinguishes the level of disruption: it is also determined by the technological, economic and cultural practices of the specific human group that is exploiting the ecosystem. Within an ideology of progress, these interventions are conceived as evidence of human advancement and civilization. James Williams (2008) of the Franklin Institute parenthesizes the whole idea of ecological damage, arguing, in fact, that human progress should be measured in terms of the capacity of humans to transform nature into more useful economic forms:

> The widespread belief that energy and civilization are inextricably linked certainly has historical foundation. Throughout history, humans have focused on controlling the energy stores and flows that are part of nature. For tens of thousands of years, people relied solely on the chemical (caloric) energy gained from food that produced the mechanical (kinetic) energy of working muscles.
>
> (Williams, 2008)

Similarly, the use of tools as a measure of human advancement leads technological historians like Vaclav Smil to rejoice in human intellect, which expands our power and overcomes the physical limits of 'nature' by 'using tools and harnessing the energies outside their own bodies' (Smil, 1994: 3).

Within a first world mediasphere, then, the knowledge systems that regard nature and ecology in terms of 'natural resources' are fostered through a civilizational progressivism that is fostered broadly through the social hierarchy and the first world mediasphere. The collapse of ecosystems is deferred through an ideology of mobility that propagates imaginings of cultural success and the transferral of displeasure on to others. This deferral process is, however, finite, and alternative discourses are achieving greater cultural traction in the mediasphere, particularly through the volition of crisis narratives and the crisis consciousness. Thus, the discourses of nature as economic resource are encountering increasingly voluble alternative discourses which conceive of nature in terms of diversity, aesthetics and dignified other. In the raillery of these language wars, nature is imagined as a compelling cultural force that challenges the ideology of progression and civilization.

Radical environmentalism

Radical Environmentalism is among the most powerful of these alternative discourses. The roots of this form of Radical Environmentalism might usefully be traced to Romantic reactions to the emergence of

European industrialism and mass urbanization. Romantic artists and philosophers like Rousseau, Blake, Swinburne and Thoreau felt overwhelmed by the calamities of rapid industrialism and social change which, they believed, was destroying the human spirit: nature was conceived as the restorative and transcendent power that could reconcile humans with their true essence as natural beings.

It could be argued, in fact, that the origins of modern environmentalism or the 'green movement' can be traced to books like Henry Thoreau's *Walden* (orig. 1854) which advocated a simple lifestyle that was in harmony with nature. Certainly, the American hippie movement of the 1960s and 1970s frequently invoked *Walden* as a template for resistance to rampant consumerism and the ongoing devastation of nature and provincial lifestyles (seeaynard, 2004). Popular music and movies at this period transformed the alternative lifestyle ideal into a green ideology which reinvigorated the Romantic poetry of the early nineteenth century. The paradox of middle-class youth rejecting the volition of economic growth while transforming it into a new zone of popular cultural consumption contributed, perhaps, to the ephemera of the mass movement. Even so, the lineage of resistance continued beyond the burst of popularity, as the hippie movement evolved into alternative lifestyle and green resistance (Forsyth, 2003).

Thus, the message of peace, love and simple living became diverged from its San Francisco imaginary into a more strident and politically hardened resistance movement through the course of the 1980s and 1990s. Within the green political movement that emerged during this period was a collective of organizations which have been labelled Radical Environmentalism (RE). While these organizations have their own distinctive history, practices, focus and personnel, RE shares a political view which centralizes the environment above all other issues (Manes, 1990; Wall, 1999; de Steiguer, 2006). There is also agreement that the collective is characterized by a form of political thought and activism that challenges the fabric and maintenance of the global capitalist economic system. This is not simply a mode of resistance to over-consumption or the excesses of corporatism and greed, but a direct challenge to the assumptions which underscore liberal capitalism, western anthropocentricism and contemporary cultural values and priorities (Humphery, 2010).

RE-based organizations like Greenpeace, Earth First, Earth Liberation Army and the Animal Liberation Front, while different in emphasis, strategy and focus, share a common belief in the overriding supremacy of nature and the need to return *Homo sapiens sapiens* to a more compatible natural order. For these organizations, global capitalism and western culture have condemned innumerable ecosystems and life forms to extinction, and threatened the viability of the whole Earth. Unlike other, more temperate environmental organizations such as the Worldwide Fund for Nature, Radical Environmentalists tend to impugn and implicate all humans who benefit from the destruction of nature; developed world governments and corporate practitioners, in particular, are seen as brutish, self-interested and ethically egregious, deserving of the highest condemnation of nature itself. Particular militant sub-groups within the RE movement seek redress for nature through violence and the destruction of corporate property.

Many of these organizations, in fact, seek to overthrow what is regarded as the despotism of governments and citizens who prosper on the pain of animals and ecosystems. This would mean an end to the slaughter of animals, the destruction of forests and the degradation of water and atmospheric systems. While governments, economists and other environmentalists may offer a sanguine notion of 'sustainability' or a 'low carbon economy', the RE-style groups demand the complete overthrow of an economic system that is predicated upon product consumption, growth and the destruction of other species. This is not simply a mechanism for the salvation of the human species, but rather the salvation of all species. Indeed, invoking ideas like the Gaia hypothesis (see Lovelock, 1965), RE supporters proclaim the primacy of nature, the Earth and the universe over humans who have proved such a violent, selfish and destructive species. Through the popular imagining of Gaia, Radical Environmentalists argue that the Earth and its progenitive life systems will recover and continue beyond the extinction of humans and their self-destructive practices and instincts.

Groups like animal liberationists, specifically, demand an end to economic and development practices that have led to one of the planet's most devastating periods of animal extinction. Indeed, the Holocene extinctions parallel the last great phase of mass extinction which occurred during the late Jurassic when a meteor cloud appears to have destroyed nearly half the world's life forms—including the dinosaurs which had dominated the planet for nearly a hundred million years. While the Holocene extinctions first emerged with global warming and the rise of human agriculture, the speed and breadth of these losses have extended during the past 300 years. Industrialism and industrial agriculture, massive accelerations in human population, urbanization and the consumerist practices associated with global pleasure economies have all contributed to the destruction of species and species habitat.

Within the human pleasure economy, this destruction of habitat may be viewed as a necessary consequence of development and human land use, either directly or as an effect of aquatic, atmospheric or soil pollution. For animal liberationists, in particular, practices like animal experimentation for human health and cosmetics, industrial food production like fisheries and food-lots, and the incarceration of pets and zoo menageries are not only morally egregious but criminal acts of cruelty (see Dawkins and Bonney, 2008). According to many Radical Environmentalists, animal species are subjected to a brutal system of torture and death that is thoroughly integrated into a globalized human pleasure economy.

Indeed, it is the global reach of this human assault on non-human nature that has prompted many of the RE groups to assume their own global mode of political activism. Thus, the focus, support networks, activities and ideological framework of organizations like Greenpeace have a distinctively global orientation. Greenpeace's activities and focus have often been directed towards first world national and trans-national corporations and governments that are exploiting globally significant natural resources—Japanese whaling in the Antarctic, French nuclear testing in the Pacific, American logging in the Amazon rain forest. Along with their global focus, Greenpeace also established tactics of direct confrontation that were designed to disrupt the activities of their opponents and attract global media attention. Through the creation of a combat spectacle, this strategy seeks to realign public opinion in the developed world and put pressure on governments and corporations. This strategy has been spectacularly successful in activities like whaling where public opinion in most of the advanced world has swung strongly against whaling and whaling countries like Japan and Greenland.

Beginning in 1972, Greenpeace also waged a campaign against the French government which was conducting nuclear tests on Moruroa Atoll in the Pacific. When French secret agents sabotaged the Greenpeace protest vessel and killed an onboard photographer, world headlines were vitriolic in their criticism of the French. These headlines prompted a severe diplomatic crisis and the global boycott of French products, leading to the accelerated conclusion of the nuclear tests. The event has led subsequently to the production of an opera, popular songs and a major international movie—all of which have contributed to the popularization of the Greenpeace mission.

Greenpeace's use of a dramatic conflict and spectacle for global media consumption has considerable parallels with contemporary terrorist strategy. While Greenpeace is opposed to violence, the communication strategy, nevertheless, creates considerable drama and cultural impact.

An even more confrontational approach to activism has been adopted by organizations like Earth First and the Earth Liberation Front. The Earth Liberation Front, in particular, became notorious in the USA when it sabotaged a range of corporate installations which it regarded as symbols of environmental destruction; these included a ski resort in Colorado in 1998 and a SUV dealership in Oregon in 1999. Members of a related organization, the Earth Liberation Army, were tried and convicted of setting fire to the Vail resort in Washington DC, an act that contributed to the FBI's conception of a new kind of social threat, eco-terrorism. Following the 9/11 attacks on New York and Washington, James Jarboe, Chief of the FBI's counter-terrorism unit, testified to the House of Representatives that RE organizations like the Animal Liberation Front, Earth Liberation Front and Earth Liberation Army posed as much of a security threat to America as any of the external international organizations, like al-Qa'ida. According to Jarboe's testimony, these special interest terrorists have become increasingly active and dangerous during the period up to 9/11:

> In recent years, the Animal Liberation Front (ALF) has become one of the most active extremist elements in the United States.... Estimates of damage and destruction in the United States claimed by the ALF during the past ten years, as compiled by national organizations such as the Fur Commission and the National Association for Biomedical Research (NABR), put the fur industry and medical research losses at more than 45 million dollars. The ALF is considered a terrorist group, whose purpose is to bring about social and political change through the use of force and violence.... The most destructive practice of the ALF/ELF [Animal Liberation Front/Earth Liberation Front is arson. The ALF/ELF members consistently use improvised incendiary devices equipped with crude but effective timing mechanisms. These incendiary devices are often constructed based upon instructions found on the ALF/ELF websites. The ALF/ELF criminal incidents often involve pre-activity surveillance and well-planned operations. Members are believed to engage in significant intelligence gathering against potential targets, including the review of industry/trade publications, photographic/video surveillance of potential targets, and posting details about potential targets on the internet.
>
> (Jarboe, 2002)

The FBI's views of these radical organizations are not surprising, given that the philosophy and rhetoric of groups like the ALF and the ELF is decidedly anti-capitalist and anti-western consumerist. In tones that are not dissimilar to Islamic militant organizations, such groups seek to overthrow the brutish violence and oppression of the American-dominated world capitalist system.

Moreover, Jarboe's reference to the Internet acknowledges that the global communications system has been critical to the force and activities of these organizations. While applying highly sophisticated mechanisms of surveillance, the FBI and other law enforcement agencies have nevertheless found it difficult to monitor and control radical organizations like the ALF and the ELF, More broadly, and as I have outlined elsewhere (Lewis, 2008), radical green protest attacks are also perpetrated through the Internet and networked systems more generally. Motivated by environmental and anti-corporate politicism, a range of chameleon organizations disrupt and sometimes seriously damage the communications systems of large corporations. These tactical attacks include hacking, virus attack, data disruption and email bombing. In a game of security chasey, the hack warriors often penetrate the system and deliver political messages to the corporate enemy, insisting they change policies and practices or face the consequences (Vanderheiden, 2005; Dartnell, 2006; Lewis, 2008).

As a new terrain of global language wars, the Internet provides for economic progressivists and Radical Environmentalists a significant facility for generating their messages and distributing them to the citizens of the global mediasphere. For organizations like Greenpeace, which have less funds and resources than their corporate opponents, the Internet is an essential tool for mobilizing support and cracking the shell of dominant economic and ecological knowledge systems. Stimulating crisis anxieties and alternative conceptions of pleasure, environmentalists are attempting to constrain the volition of capitalist economy, urging a vision of nature that is both Romantic and intensely political—a vision that releases preconceptions about the use and value of nature that is often inscribed in more standardized knowledge systems and media texts.

The media, global warming and extreme weather events

In the most general terms, the media is both the captive and progenitor of crisis consciousness and the complex knowledge systems that comprise contemporary culture. A great deal has been written about the deficiencies of the mainstream, corporate media and its reporting of environmental issues, particularly around the media's fascination with personality politics and drama, and notorious incapacity to deal with complexity and science-based information (see Cottle, 2009).

By 'media', most of these criticisms refer to the agglomerate of corporate news outlets, an easy target for those who have become disillusioned by the putative contraction of the Fourth Estate and its promise of an objective information system that supports democracy and effective civil institutions.

While these criticisms have some validity within their own referential sphere, I have argued in this book and elsewhere (Lewis, 2005, 2008) that the media also needs to be understood more expansively as a set of processes that implicate the entire polity in meaning and media making. This is particularly the case for an understanding of the mediasphere and the proliferating pursuits within a pleasure economy. I have suggested above that a structural, ideology-based analysis of ecology tends to over-emphasize power elites and under-emphasize the responsibility and implications of all other members of the polity or mediasphere including those many citizens who act against the excess of destructive economic practices.

This is clearly also the case when we consider the ways in which the media itself is involved in the representation of ecology and nature, and specifically the ways in which ecological crisis is being fostered. This is not simply an exercise in fallible reporting of environmental issues by news agencies; it is an issue about the ways in which the environment is implicated in particular kinds of knowledge formation and how that knowledge is aligned and generated through political decisions and actions.

To this end, the discourses of consumer capitalism and resistance are generated around a polyphony of varying perspectives over the human-nature relationship. There is no simple divide between the supporters and antagonists of 'nature'. However, nature and ecology are becoming increasingly marshalled through a crisis consciousness that ranges from a discourse of sustainability through to the apocalyptic consternations that imagine complete human annihilation. Thus, Al Gore *An Inconvenient Truth* (2005) extends the disquieting tradition of apocalyptic films like *The Day After Tomorrow* (Roland Emmerich, 2004) by which climate change achieves a certain social and political respectability—at least inasmuch as the social elites are taking seriously the problems associated with critical human interventions in the global biosphere. Indeed, the same message of doom and climate anxiety has become the chorus climax of Discovery TV whereby virtually every narrative about natural life systems concludes with a vision of despair, extinction or species death. Images of collapsing icebergs, Caribbean hurricanes, sub-Saharan droughts and Australian firestorms have become a mainstay of television and print news stories, particularly through major political events like climate change conferences, carbon trading scheme debates or energy shortages.

What is significant about the popularization of these issues and especially the broad mediation of apocalypse narratives is the activation of popular imaginings around nature and ecology. Witnessing the devastation of old growth forests, the slaughter of whales and the wretched struggles of an oil-soaked penguin, media audiences are confronted by a disjunction of their own desires and anxieties—a fracturing of economic and ecological knowledge systems by which the world has previously been ordered and rendered comprehensible. In this sense, members of the communicational global sphere, whether in the first or developing worlds, are being confronted by their own culpabilities, at least in terms of the ways in which economic systems and practices have contributed to serious environmental damage. Through this prevailing sense of ecological crisis social agents and their belief systems are being forced by these newer narratives and informational discourses to confront their older assumptions about the relationship between economy and ecology. That is, these older knowledge systems are being penetrated and disrupted by new knowledge which connects human pleasure to the devastation caused by climate change and extreme weather events. The transferral of displeasures associated with environmental damage, in this context, is reaching saturation, creating fissures in older understandings and systems of knowing.

In this context, the volubility of ecological claims and counter-claims, particularly by economists, industrialists, political leaders and scientists, represents an attempt to close the ideological fissures that have emerged in our knowledge systems. As with other crises, the ecological crisis constitutes a semiotic rupture by which the media and mediated discourses flood into the knowledge systems in order to re-set political alignment, meanings and public understanding. It is not surprising, therefore, that climate change remains a very significant issue for many people, even through the consideration of their own economic and ecological practices and the discretion of their political choices.

Climate change believers and sceptics

Science-based ecologists frequently complain that political action on climate change is too slow and that this procrastination is further exacerbating the dangers associated with anthropogenic economic and industrial activities. In public debates around climate change and adaptation, strategies such as carbon reduction targets and Emissions Trading Schemes (ETS) elicit particularly intense contention. Publicly funded scientific organizations are often engaged in vehement debate with private enterprise and neo-liberal economists who see environmental regulation as an unnecessary constraint to free market commerce.

However, because the climate change science and carbon reduction schemes like the ETS are framed within specialized language and knowledge systems, they are often difficult for journalists, public officials and citizens to understand and translate. While this may be a limitation of the specialist scientists who are often constrained by institutional cultures that seek to shield their knowledge from non-specialists, it is more broadly associated with the media industry itself which is predicated upon particular informational and entertainment parcels. These parcels—narratives and narrative structures—are often very inflexible as they are fostered around market-based typologies and highly formulated genres. In either case, the disjunction between the knowledge systems and media audiences provides considerable space for the invasion of cultural politics and their appropriation by particular interest groups and ideologies. As noted in our earlier discussion on the standardization of cultural knowledge, these understandings of ecology and environmental crisis are not simply propagated by the interests of corporations, governments and other elites—they are also generated by media audiences themselves, people who are consumers and active participants in the economy of desire and its fantasy of infinite pleasure. Within this context of standardized and culturally constituted pleasure, the interpellation of climate change science and the ETS is often attached to public perceptions of science more generally, as an alien and overly lobical discourse for nerds.

According to Boykoff and Rajan (2007), the news media's reluctance to report and analyse climate change stories has largely issued from the topic's scientific and political complexity. This reluctance by the media to engage with such a significant global 'crisis' confounds Boykoff and Rajan, who can only explain it in terms of cultural disposition:

> Although a greater appreciation of the environment has evolved over the past 50 years in both the USA and UK, historically entrenched cultural preoccupations with the markets and economic growth—along with the concomitant politics of interest groups—has also caused an attitude of denial that has strengthened scepticism of scientific

claims about environmental decline and more specific anthropogenic climate change.

(Boykoff and Rajan, 2007: 208)

While the authors concede that these difficulties are exacerbated by the differences in public and scientific language use (Boykoff and Rajan, 2007: 209), a more compelling problem for the media is the ethics of 'balanced reporting' which, in Boykoff and Rajan's view, usurps the more important responsibility of journalists to crack the code of scientific validity. The idea of presenting both sides of the story merely distracts from the imperatives and importance of truth.

Jennifer Good (2008) confirms this view, arguing that climate change remains constrained within the comfort zones, interests and knowledge sphere of mainstream media. According to Good, climate change can only exist within the mainstream media as long as it doesn't contravene the interests of corporate media themselves.

The analysis here highlights the story that climate change *is* being told (even within the United States, albeit somewhat less frequently), and that there is debate, criticism, and dissent. When the frames move into potentially more threatening territory, however, such as the linking of climate change with extreme weather events or decreasing/different energy, the story frequency plummets.

(Good, 2008: 248)

This view of the media and its reluctance to report on climate change frequently point to the presidency of George W. Bush (2001–2009) as a source of greenhouse gas scepticism. Bush, himself a dynastical oil magnate from Texas, refused to sign the Kyoto Protocol, which required developed world countries to reduce the level of their carbon dioxide emissions. As one of the world's highest per capita and aggregate carbon emitter, the USA has barely engaged in climate change issues, particularly in comparison to Europe and other parts of the developed world (Pawa and Jrass, 2006; Nisbet and Myers, 2007). Opinion polling in the USA, for example, suggests that most Americans continue to believe that the scientific evidence on climate change is 'in dispute', whereas the vast majority of advanced world scientific opinion is unequivocal, accepting that anthropogenic global warming is underway and threatens the entire planetary system (Pawa and Krass, 2006; Nelson-Gammon, 2007; Dunlop and McCright, 2008; Enting, 2009). While the presidency of Barack Obama has changed the thrust of US climate change policy, opinion polling continues to lag the aspirations of the Obama administration.

The emergence of climate change sceptics has accompanied the rising tide of climate change debate and governmental actions around the advanced world. While few ecologists actually doubt the climate change science, a number of other specialists have sought to undermine what they regard as a new scientific and media-generated climate change orthodoxy. Ian Plimer (2009), for example, has pointed out that this pattern of global warming and cooling has been occurring throughout the history of the planet, and that the recent warming phase is not exceptional by the standards of geological planetary history. In particular, the Earth's climate has warmed and cooled many times during the Holocene period (12,000 BP-Present), and in most cases humans have prospered during the warmer phases. Plimer, in fact, accuses the media and a range of scientific communities of promoting their own interests and careers through the propagation of a climate change crisis. For Plimer, the mass media has been far too supportive of the climate change lobby and the false science it perpetrates.

Plimer, a mining geologist with a strong affiliation with corporate economics, has been savagely criticized for his ideas (see Enting, 2009). The Intergovernmental Panel on Climate Change, in particular, criticized the actual science that Plimer applied to his study and, specifically, the tendency to parenthesize human interventions as a cause of climate change. Even so, Plimer's scientific reading of climate change offers considerable comfort to those political and public sceptics who believe that the environmentalists have found yet another route for their destructive critique of market capitalism and the rights of the individual to prosper. For conservative politicians, media professionals, corporatists and members of the public who oppose any compromise to their personal prosperity and lifestyle—climate change scepticism provides a reassuring basis for the maintenance of the status quo and the unrelenting fantasy of infinite pleasure.

Sustainability and carbon trading schemes

The battle over nature and its meanings are most succinctly expressed in the notions of 'sustainability' and 'sustainable development'. On the surface, this concept appears to be an exhortation to sustaining economic progress through a manageable system of growth: the term was established by corporations and governments in order to bridge the growing opposition between ecology and economy. As a bridge between economy and ecology, the concept of sustainability addresses two overriding problems associated with human interventions in the ecosystem—first, sustainability acknowledges the need to manage natural resources carefully in order to limit over-exploitation and hence their economic value; and second, sustainability acknowledges that economic development causes ecological degradation such as atmospheric pollution, destruction of forests, loss of habitat and species extinction.

Emerging in the 1990s, the sustainability discourse registers an alternative to the more strident and RE which advocates reduced economic growth and an absolute protection of ecological systems (Lemons et al., 1998; Trosper, 2009). Advocates of a sustainability politics challenge the more revolutionary perspectives of RE that promote social panic and an apocalyptic vision of planetary futures. In many respects, the sustainability discourse sits behind the anxiety of everyday consumers who might, on the surface, be prepared to compromise the extremes of their purchasing and consumerist practices, but who fundamentally resile from any radical disruption to their affluence, privilege and pleasures. To this end, a sustainable development discourse entreats the switch to green energy, halogen light bulbs, efficient car engines, and the use of recyclable packaging, toilet paper and shopping bags. It resists, however, the radical reduction in energy use, the social destruction of the flat screen, digital TV or the adoption of a vegetarian diet (Edwards and Orr, 2006).

In fact, much of the public debate and discussion on greenhouse gas emissions and climate change has been conveyed through similar contentions between radical and apocalyptic subversion, and a more measured discourse of sustainable development. In this context, sustainability has conjured a formal framework for the social, cultural and technological 'adaptation' to climate change, as well as a more direct strategy of 'mitigation' which would confront the sources of greenhouse gas causes. This approach to ecological catastrophe seeks to mobilize the economy of pleasure through the reformulation of opportunities and knowledge systems that maintain hierarchy within a cultural politics of sustainable development. Governments and corporations seek to mobilize public support for the emerging 'greener economy', offering a scheme that accords with the consumer imaginary of the first world mediasphere.

Through the Kyoto Protocol (1997–) and the Copenhagen Accord (2009–) advanced world governments, specifically, are adopting a range of strategies which are designed to reduce the total load of their emissions. The most contentious and complex of these strategies has been the ETS (also called Carbon Cap and Trade Schemes) which many countries have adopted as a mechanism for engaging polluters in a market-driven carbon reduction system.

In most ETS systems, governments issue carbon producing organizations with a permit to generate a certain amount of carbon-based emissions; the organization is also required to hold an equivalent number of carbon credits (or 'allowances'). The cap on emissions can only be exceeded through the purchase of credits from another, presumably less-polluting organization or company. Thus, there is an incentive to not only limit the production of carbon gases, but to reduce emissions through the adoption of alternative energy sources and technologies. The trading of these carbon credits mobilizes the profit motive in order to restructure economies and their fuel technologies without excessive government, public, economic or cultural disruption.

Schemes of this kind have been adopted through the European Union Emission Trading Scheme, and the more recent American Green Energy and Security Act (2009). Critics of the carbon trading scheme have argued that it is a system that is overly consolatory for large polluting organizations like energy producers. According to this criticism, providing big polluters with a large emission permit merely entrenches their bad practices and expands their opportunity for profit making. It is argued that these big polluters will simply go on generating carbon emissions, offsetting their energy business with other commercial activities, such as forestry, which generate carbon credits. This issue of offsetting is even more contentious when major first world emitters invest in forestry in the developing world—an inexpensive strategy for establishing carbon credits that involves no significant reduction in carbon outputs in the home nation. However, supporters of the ETS argue that it doesn't really matter where the carbon offsets are achieved, so long as the overall global impact on climate change is positive.

In Australia a proposed ETS excludes the agricultural sector, even though many American agriculturalists have used the US nitrogen oxide trading scheme as a means to generate new income through various technological adaptations and initiatives such as forestry (Reed, 2009). Nearly a half of all greenhouse gases are produced by livestock stomach exhalations (belching), and so many critics argue that exempting agriculture renders the whole scheme ineffectual. Indeed, the greatest criticism of the European Union system is the large subsidies and exemptions that have been made to major polluters like energy companies. For these major polluters, the European scheme has provided a financial boon. In the view of many environmentalists, an ETS is worthless unless it is based on uniform standards and is constituted through extremely high reductions in carbon gases. Radical Environmentalists are even more hostile, arguing that all these systems of climate 'adaptation' are merely propaganda and generally ineffective. They represent the power of capitalism to recreate itself in different ways that simply delay the destruction of the Earth and nature, rather than mitigate against it.

Michael Sendel (2009a, 2009b) has argued that the real problem with the ETS is that it merely sustains the sort of market triumphalism and neo-liberalist ideologes that have created the damage in the first place. For Sendel, market economics have no place in issues of collective public benefit. Rather, the problems of environmental damage and climate change are ethical and civil issues that require collaboratively derived strategies and solutions. The 2009 Copenhagen Climate Change Conference certainly bears out Sendel's prescience, as negotiations for a shared responsibility collapsed under the pressure of national self-interest. Emerging economies like China and India refused to set carbon reduction targets which might hinder their programme of rapid economic growth. Poor countries in Africa, which are suffering most from the effects of climate change and extreme weather events, produce very little greenhouse gases per capita; these countries argued that it is the responsibility of the rich, industrialized nations to reduce their outputs since global pollution has been largely generated through first world prosperity and pleasure.

For their part, the world's wealthiest and most polluting nations would not accede to the wishes of the world's poorest. Absorbed by domestic financial strains and wars in the Middle East, countries like the USA and the UK refused to assume sole responsibility for global climate change and mandatory greenhouse gas reductions. In the end, there was no universal emissions reduction protocol, and the global mediasphere rattled with disappointment, repudiation and even relief. The sceptics and heavy polluters had won a glorious battle, as though the solution to the human-nature aporia was delivered in the weakness of international governance. Government, that is, could not resist the power of the people's pleasure and the economy that propelled itself on infinite desire. Nature had been set back into its subjugant role: the crisis anxieties were set adrift. But through the baying of the rapacious hound, Aesop's fawn can only tremble. The Erath trembles. Nature continues to disintegrate.

6
Fear and Trembling: The Vicissitudes of Global Terror

> [Abraham] spent seventy years in getting a son of his old age...but that is not the task—he is tried.... Who can bear it?...Finally he gets a son. That took long enough. Now he wants to sacrifice him. So is he not mad?
>
> Sören Kierkegaard, *Fear and Trembling*

> But when the forbidden months are past, then fight and slay the pagans wherever ye find them, and seize them, beleaguer them, and lie in wait for them in every stratagem (of war); but if they repent, and establish regular prayers and practice regular charity, then open the way for them: for God is Oft-forgiving, Most Merciful.
>
> *The Qu'ran*, 9: 5

> Terrorism has long been a tactic, but modern technology allows a few small men with outsized rage to murder innocents on a horrific scale.... We must begin by acknowledging the hard truth that we will not eradicate violent conflict in our lifetimes. There will be times when nations—acting individually or in concert—will find the use of force not only necessary but morally justified.
>
> Barack Obama, Acceptance Speech, Nobel Peace Prize, 2009

Terrorisme

The word 'terrorism' first appears in English as a rubric for British opposition to the French Jacobin Revolution and its 'Reign of Terror' (Laqueur, 1987, 2003; Lewis, 2005). While the Revolutionary People's Republic believed that the purges known as the Reign of Terror (June 1783–July

1794) would liberate the people and subdue iniquitous power, many British thinkers and public officials saw the purges as a tyranny of violence and mob rule. Through this same conception of malevolence, Joseph Conrad describes the principal antagonists of *The Secret Agent* (orig. 1907) as 'the old terrorist':

> On the other side of the fireplace...Karl Yundt, giggled grimly with a faint black grimace of a toothless mouth. The terrorist, as he called himself, was old and bald, with a narrow, snow-white wisp of a goatee hanging limply from his chin. An extraordinary expression of underhand malevolence survived in his extinguished eyes.
>
> (Conrad, 2005: 56)

Conrad's fictional account of the decrepit and malevolent anarchist established a rhetorical diction that was ultimately absorbed into the language wars of modern political violence.

Thus, the concept of 'terrorism' has become a general descriptor for illegitimate political violence that is perpetrated against noncombatants. US law defines terrorism as 'premeditated, politically motivated violence against noncombatant targets by sub-national groups or clandestine agents' (USC, 22- 2656 [d]). This definition privileges 'the state', which is legitimized by the citizenry and rule of law, and which is protected by military and paramilitary agents who conduct 'policing' and 'war' in order to maintain order. The US Department of Defense expands the definition, suggesting that this 'calculated use of violence or threat of violence against individuals or property' is an act of terrorism when it is designed 'to inculcate fear, intended to coerce or intimidate government or societies in the pursuit of goals that are political, ideological or religious' (DOD, 1986: 15).

In *Language Wars* (2005) I argued that these definitions constitute an apologia for the state and state power. Other definitions recognize that state agencies have themselves frequently deployed terrorist tactics, specifically through assaults on ordinary citizens or 'non-combatants'. To this end, the concepts of 'terrorism' and 'terrorist' are politically charged, as they are often deployed by warring parties in order to impugn their enemies' behaviour as excessive, illegal and inhuman. In this presiding crisis of political violence, therefore, the concepts and language of contention emerge as the critical components of a significant global rupture. That is, the cultural and social contiguities associated with globalization and the expansion of the pleasure economy have produced new zones of doubt and a radical disjunction in knowledge spheres. Like the other crises we have investigated in this book, these new forms of political violence—especially as they are exercised through concepts like terrorism—are shaped by the volition of pleasure and displeasure and its volatile hierarchies of cultural power.

Indeed, as much recent scholarship has recognized, the tactics associated with political violence and terrorism are motivated principally by a desire to communicate an idea, emotional condition, ideology or cultural perspective (Schmid, 1983; Laqueur, 1987, 2003; Nacos, 2002; Lewis, 2005). Since the al-Qa'ida attacks on America, commentators have increasingly defined terrorism in terms of its communicational and cultural power. The emotions of hatred and vengeance are amplified as persuasive acts of political terror:

> Terrorist acts are often deliberately spectacular, designed to rattle and influence a wide audience, beyond the victims of the violence itself. The point is to use the psychological impact of the violence or of the threat of violence to effect political change. As the terrorism expert Brian Jenkins bluntly put it in 1974, 'Terrorism is theater'.
>
> (Chitty, 2003: x)

In a contribution to *The New Yorker*, novelist and eyewitness John Updike (2001) notes that 'the destruction of the World Trade Center twin towers had the false intimacy of television, on a day of perfect reception.... [T]here persisted the notion, as on television, this was not quite real' (Updike, 2001: 28).

Thus, as a communicational event, the terrorist spectacle brings together complex historical, cultural, political and psycho-emotional threads into a moment of consummate horror. The communicational motives of present-day terrorism are folded into the broader context of the mediasphere. Perpetrators of this kind of violence, whether by state or sub-state agents, are certainly aware of this context and their role within the complex of contemporary language wars. The crisis of political violence, therefore, needs to be understood in terms of specific communicational motives and the following characteristics:

1. *The desire to terrify* and hence alter the perspective of an enemy government, military forces or citizenry: that is, they are designed to shift the balance of a given social hierarchy and the mechanisms by which communities may be 'excluded' or oppressed from power nodes like 'the west'. This enemy may be foreign (as for the al-Qa'ida attacks in America) or domestic (as for the Islamic militant attacks

in London and Tamil Tiger attacks in Colombo). Many domestic attacks are associated with violent disputes over sovereignty and territory (as for the IRA attacks in the UK and the Palestinian attacks in Israel). Some domestic attacks are designed to change the nature of state and law through a form of highly targeted violence (as for Islamic militant attacks in Indonesia). There are also attacks that are directly associated with organized crime such as drugs trading (Mafioso in Italy and the Medellin Cartel in Colombia). Others are part of a generalized civil conflict associated with ethnic, religious, economic and ideological dispute (as for civil wars in Rawanda, the Congo, Solomon Islands, Fiji).

2. *The desire to solidify causes and attract recruits.* A terrorist act is frequently glorified by perpetrators in order to both terrorize targeted nations and peoples, as well as attract sympathizers and recruits. It is now clear that al-Qa'ida was struggling to survive, and that the attacks on New York and Washington represented a final 'great job', which might restore the organization and its faltering status and finances (Gunaratna, 2003). The notional success of the attacks attracted more converts to the cause, and was a primary inspiration for Jemaah Islamiyah-related attacks on Bali in 2002 and 2005 (Lewis and Lewis, 2009).

3. *The conversion and sacrifice of a particular kind of warrior class, the suicide bomber.* The spectacle of a terrorist act and its powerful cultural resonance appears to have a particular significance for the suicide bomber, that class of killer who deliberately sacrifices his or her own life for the cause. To this end, the purpose of the terrorist act brings to bear a peculiar conflux of military, political and personal, psycho-emotional factors that seem to defy our fundamental logics of survival. The purpose of the act, that is, gives expression to this complex of conditions, drawing together individual and socio-cultural knowledge and belief systems through the action of self-annihilation. Unlike other kinds of suicide, this convolution of personal and social knowledge systems is generally wrought through a higher purpose and a sense of historical, political or spiritual transcendence. Whether motivated by secular or religious politics, the suicide bomber is directed as much by a collective sensibility as by personal glorification and immortality. This particular act of terror, therefore, creates a very particular response for the perpetrators' enemies and followers (Hafez, 2007; Horgan, 2008).

4. *The terrorist act is not simply political, but existential and cultural.* It is an act which is designed to communicate an important message about

the truth of the human condition, and our ultimate destiny. While the deployment of self-endangering warriors is a critical component of all warfare, politically motivated violence involving deliberate self-destruction for a higher purpose is an essential characteristic of the contemporary terrorist spectacle. The act of deliberate self-sacrifice creates an entirely different class of warrior, one who cannot be set within the normal boundaries of warfare and its purposes. In a sense, the death of the suicide bomber is prefigured and stands outside the agreed dimensions of normality—the standards of violent conflict that clearly identify victors and vanquished and which result in particular kinds of territorial advantages and losses.

While this issue is discussed in greater detail below, it is important to note that the symbolism of the suicide warrior and a given suicide attack has effectively exceeded the purpose of the violence. Because the symbols of suicide killing are not easily constrained, they often escape the underlying motive of the perpetrators. The symbolic dimension of the act—the thing that creates its spectacle—thereby overwhelms its specific political purposes, very often becoming something more horrible than was originally intended. The symbol escapes its creators to become a free cultural agent within a mediasphere that is constituted around complex global secretions and communicational threads. Thus, it is not simply 'madness' as is often conceived in the minds and representations of the first world media—it is the flatness of death, an empty apocalypse that has no purpose beyond the collapse of the biological integrity of the perpetrator and the victims. It is the horror, that is, of meaninglessness.

5. *Islam and the 9/11 wars.* While secular violence continues across the globe, the 9/11 attacks in America have focused the attention of western world governments, citizens and the media on the political violence associated with Islamic militantism. To this end, the American-led 'war on terror' becomes a rubric for much longer term tensions and a recalibrated east-west divide. While conservative commentators like Samuel Huntington (1993) have famously imagined these tensions in terms of a 'clash of civilizations' thesis, such perspectives pervert the complexity of territorialism and human violence associated with populations, economy and the cultural contiguities associated with globalization. Thus, even as much of this chapter focuses on tensions between modern western states and Islamic militants, this focus is set within a broader context of a history of human violence that reaches back to the beginnings of the Holocene and the broad field of crises we have discussed in this

book. That is, the crisis consciousness that is emerging around terrorism and contemporary modes of political violence are understood within the indices of ongoing human brutality that is promulgated through surplus economics, desire and displeasure.

Twin Towers and the violence of a pleasure economy

The crisis of terrorism and political violence, therefore, is formed through a globally constituted mediasphere. In this sense, the terrorists' use of the media might be understood as a response to their enemies' communicational power—most particularly the capacity of hegemonic social groups—like western governments, the military and multi-national corporations—to generate and broadly disseminate their own interests, pleasures, perspectives and ideologies.

This engagement with modern language wars might in some ways appear paradoxical, as many Islamic militant organizations frequently invoke a sense of tradition and deep history as the basis of their ideo-religious project. That is, militant Islamic organizations like al-Qa'ida, Hazbolah, Shabab and Jemaah Islamiyah promote a form of theological politicism which promotes religious purity and *Sh'ariah* law that is entirely anathema to democracy and global capitalism. Such organizations align themselves with a brand of purist Islamic theology which recognizes only the authority of God and His religious teachings laid out by Mohammed in the Qu'ran and interpreted through the framework of the Hadith. In this context, these radical Islamic militants reject all forms of western political secularism and the somatic pleasures that are associated with consumerism and the modes of free sexual expressions discussed in Chapter 3.

However, while proclaiming their allegiance to tradition, these organizations deploy modern weaponry, organizational systems and communications technologies and networks as they seek to establish their own reign of terror across the globe. In particular, many of the radical Islamist groups who invoke the glory of tradition are thoroughly versed in many of the western-based knowledge systems that constitute the mediasphere, and are particularly skilled in the deployment of modern communicational warfare. In this respect, at least, the Islamists are similar to their western enemies, who also invoke a sense of the deep past in order to justify themselves and their actions (Lewis, 2002, 2005).

To this end, and as I also discussed at length elsewhere (Lewis, 2005; Lewis and Lewis, 2009), organizations like al-Qa'ida have engaged in a radical mode of language and corporeal warfare that is constituted around a primary dispute of meaning. The World Trade Center Twin Towers represents a key symbolic terrain in this war. Following the 9/11 attacks on New York, Jean Baudrillard (2002) argued that American domination of the overly mediated or 'hyperreal global system' was of itself the essence or 'spirit' of terrorism. This global domination manifests itself through the hyperreal of media communications, but is also critically linked to American military and economic primacy—which is the essence of what Baudrillard regards as economic globalization. This is not simply to acknowledge that American foreign policy contributed to the antagonistic politics that motivated the 9/11 attacks, as Henry Giroux (2006), Noam Chomsky (2001) and Susan Sontag (2001, 2004) have claimed. It is rather to suggest that the actual existence of a single and unitary global superpower stimulates its own predicate of violent resistance. For Baudrillard, it is the sheer singularity and mass of this power which cannot of itself be directly and genuinely opposed, altered or exchanged. The terrorism which assaults the unitary power of US global domination is merely reactive, an inevitable response to singularity itself.

> To a system whose very excess of power poses an insoluble challenge, the terrorists respond with a definitive act which is also not susceptible of exchange. Terrorism is the act which restores an irreducible singularity to the heart of a system of generalized exchange. All the singularities (species, individuals and cultures) that have paid with their deaths for the installation of a global circulation governed by a single power are taking their revenge today through this terroristic situational transfer.
>
> (Baudrillard, 2002: 9)

In other words, terrorism is a reaction to the singularity of a formidable power that presides over economic globalization and what Baudrillard calls the 'circulatory system' or hyperreality. In Baudrillard's terms, this power is not simply the exercise of American militarism and foreign policy as it is conceived by political critics like Noam Chomsky: it is rather the whole symbolic vestment of American-dominated western *culture* that has imposed itself through the circulatory system, including world economic and security conditions.

In this sense it is 'terror against terror' though without the density of an integrated and identifiable ideology. For Baudrillard, these cultural conditions are far more amorphous than many political commentators seem to appreciate. In a hyperreal cultural environment, therefore, the triumph of globalization leads inevitably to a battle against itself. This Fourth World War, as Baudrillard defines the current agonisms, is not a battle of ideologies or a clash of civilizations, but rather it is the world battling against the inevitable flows of globalization. In other words, it is a world system in which power is both feeding on itself and attacking itself—'if Islam dominated the world, terrorism would rise against Islam' (Baudrillard, 2002: 12).

The spirit of terrorism, therefore, is to be found in its momentous and inclusive progression. While other commentators concern themselves with the details of political or military conflict, Baudrillard's more ontological enquiry seeks to expose the force that lies behind US globalization and its propagated cultural authority. In this sense, Baudrillard's speculations confront the vision of 'America' as the divinely determined pinnacle of human history by which the good or the 'Chosen' (Nairn, 2002) must overwhelm all human evil. In many respects, this is precisely the problem that Giorgio Agamben (2005) addresses when he considers America in terms of the 'state of exception'—that unique status that allows America to determine all world history. Baudrillard's own Gnostic disposition leads him to question this state of exception, and indeed any notion that prefigures the conquest of good over evil. Baudrillard argues that good and evil work simultaneously towards the same political ends:

> We believe naively that the progress of Good, its advance in all fields (the sciences, technology, democracy, human rights), corresponds to a defeat of Evil. No-one seems to have understood that Good and Evil advance together, as part of the same movement. The triumph of the one does not eclipse the other... Good does not conquer Evil, nor indeed does the reverse happen: they are at once both irreducible to each other and inextricably interrelated.
>
> (Baudrillard, 2002: 13)

Baudrillard (2002) suggests, further, that it is the 'parallelism' of the World Trade Center buildings that made them so vulnerable to attack. Their presence in the New York and global skyline as 'twins' represents an ironical inversion—a reference to capitalism's fundamental drive to singularity, ultimate power and *monopoly*. The replication of the sign— a favoured theme in Baudrillard's earlier studies—indicates that they had already over-reached their believability. For Baurdrillard, capitalism's compulsion to monopoly is accentuated by the repetition of the sign of singularity: paradoxically, the doubling of the sign, truly puts an end to what it distinguishes (Baudrillard, 2002). The meaning of the towers as the pinnacle of capitalism, Baudrillard explains, is bereft, even before the attacks and their destruction—a destruction that was predetermined by the excess of their claim. To extend this idea, the spectacle of destruction and the gaping hole that still marks the Manhattan skyline reflect this symbolic kernel by which capitalism has become the global shell; by the aegis of this shell nothing is real but the absence of what is real. In Baudrillard's terms, that means the vacuous media and its conditions of appearance and hyperreality.

Even if we resist Baudrillard's apocalyptic hyperbole, we need to take seriously the significance of the towers within the global mediasphere and its disjunctive knowledge systems. In a very important sense, the towers were the symbolic core of American global economic primacy and a trading system within which it had become the central node. The duplication that Baudrillard identifies, therefore, is not simply a statement of monopoly and its reflexive singularity: it is also a statement about the overflow of the surplus economy as an excess of symbolic value and the uneven distribution of global wealth. In terms of the analytical framework of this book, the towers are an ideal representation of surplus, where 'one more' constitutes the primary driver of desire and duplication. Completed in 1971 at the apex of what many commentators regard as the triumph of American capitalism, the Twin Towers represented the capacity of these symbols to replicate themselves in an imaginary of infinite pleasure.

Thus, the surplus economy, and its current incarnation as an economy of pleasure, was marked by the formidable presence in the New York skyline of perfect 'replication'. The preposterous proportions of this particular design feature even eclipsed the brashness of the Empire State Building, which was for 40 years the world's tallest building. In this sense, the symbol of replication marks the capacity of the spatial icon to generate and regenerate itself through the elements and processes of symbolic trade—a trade which we characterized in Chapter 1 as fundamentally the communication of symbolic value. The World Trade Center, in this sense, becomes emblemized as twin transmitters and receptors within the complex imaginary and history of trade. As vectors of symbolic exchange, therefore, the towers also represented the convolution of power and communication, not merely for the acolytes of global capitalism, but for those whom it inevitably excludes or reduces. Thus, the power and violence that are inscribed in the primacy of America and its symbolic superstructures were absorbed into an aesthetic, architectural motif which imposed itself on the imagining and knowledge systems whose interests it served. For those who had suffered from the history of violence that this power represents, the meanings of the buildings were far less convivial. That is, in an economy that is predicated on the transferral of pleasure and displeasure, the symbolic inscriptions of the Twin Towers represent the exchange of misery, as much as the exchange of wealth (Plate 6.1).

Packed within the meanings of the Twin Towers, therefore, is a profound violence and a system of global privilege which the incendiary of 9/11 sought to expose. And indeed. even within the resonance of these effects, as tourists swarm across the site of the attacks and imagine its horror (or its glory), the deep agonisms that are conjured in the spectre of the Twin Towers' absence elicits a profound insecurity about the past and the future. With continuing attacks and violence in Iraq, Israel, Afghanistan, Pakistan and a range of African states, the sense of a civilizational divide continues to undermine an imagining of global peace and species unity. Having already been the focus of a terrorist attack in 1993, the towers were destroyed in 2001 by those who challenged the authority of the western cultural pre-eminence and sense of inviolable global authority. For the perpetrators of the attacks, the people who were killed in the towers were emblems of an iniquitous and impious system that continues to oppress Muslims in the Middle

Plate 6.1   Mediating Ground Zero—now a major tourist attraction in New York. Photograph by Belinda Lewis.

East, including Palestine. In the conception of al-Qa'ida, therefore, the victims of the attack were not 'innocent', but were the well-rewarded servants of a vile master—an evil which terrorized and oppressed Muslims across the planet.

The pleasure attacks in Bali

Thus, the tradition which is invoked by radical and militant Islam is formed within a particular political discourse that is mobilized against the volition of surplus economic systems. As we have noted, however, this is not a question of traditionalism versus modernism since both sides of the 9/11 wars invoke history, including religious history, to justify their belligerence. The violence is rather an expression of different competitive and hierarchical frames and the means by which different social groups and individuals seek to establish themselves, their modes of power, their territorial claims and their organizational-cultural systems.

It is certainly true that most contemporary modes of political violence are related in some ways to poverty and political oppression. However, the issue of poverty provides only a circuitous explanation for the recourse of particular social groups to violence and militancy very clearly: not all poor people in the world are terrorists, and indeed not all terrorists are poor. What is clearer is that a recourse to terrorist tactics in political disputes is evinced through critical competition over territory, resources and modes of governance. Social groups that are deprived through these competitive conditions might inevitably fight for their survival, congregating over their sense of injustice or exclusion. While this congregation is clearly imbued through shared cultural systems like language, ethnicity, territory, history and religion, a recourse to violence requires a more powerful synthesis of political aspirations and a shared faith in military strategies. Indeed, there may be many Muslims who align themselves with a purist form of Islam, or object to the oppression of Palestinians or the imposition of secular governments in their home country—but, only a very small minority of these people support violence in the redress of these grievances. Moreover, the use of terrorist tactics, which involves the targeting and slaughter of noncombatants, is an option exercised by minority groups who are fighting a more powerful foe, specifically in conditions that are generally called asymmetrical warfare.

The 9/11 attacks on America, as much as anything else, were shaped by a crisis of contiguity (Lewis and Lewis, 2004). Globalization has created new combinations of interaction and proximity by which an overwhelming economic system, or alliance of systems, is overwhelming all cultural, physical and geo-political spaces of the globe. In a contemporary setting, this means that those who have an advantage will seek to continue or enhance their interests, while those who are at a disadvantage will seek to redress the hierarchical asymmetry. This has less to do with 'poverty' as an aggregate condition, and more to do with the perceived state of relative advantage and differentials in power. The more disjunctive the differential, the more likely the recourse to radical ideological systems and violent contention. Through the evolution of the agricultural systems, these contentions have been waged through increasingly expanded zones of contiguity and related competition over territory and resources. In a contemporary setting of advanced globalization, these contiguities have been forged not only through increasing spatial mobilities, but also through the networked communications systems and modes of symbolic, economic exchange.

These new forms of spatial and cultural contiguity have contributed to the rise in Islamic militancy in South East Asia, including attacks by organizations like Jemaah Islamiyah in the Philippines and Indonesia. In particular, the 2002 and 2005 suicide bombings on the tourist island of Bali were designed to attack the symbolic centre of western incursions in the largely Muslim territory of Indonesia. As numerous commentators have noted (see Barton, 2004; Lewis and Lewis, 2009), these attacks were perpetrated by militant groups associated with Jemaah Islamiyah (JI), a militant Islamic organization which seeks to destroy the democratic Republic of Indonesia and replace it with a regional Islamic state. Along with its various splinter groups, JI believes that the best way to destablize the Indonesian state and establish *Sh'ariah* law and Islamic theocracy is to attack its economic sub-structure, especially through its interconnections with global capitalism. International tourism in Bali represented for JI a vulnerable and symbolically significant target, particularly through the hedonism and sexual licentiousness that purist Muslims identified with Balinese beaches and nightclubs. For the Islamist militants, in fact, Bali represents the worst of all possible worlds: not only is it a Hindu residue that has for centuries resisted conversion to Islam, it is also the centre of Indonesia's tourist economy which is the country's second highest income earner. Since the 1960s, Bali's per annum international arrivals have increased from a few thousand to over two million in 2010. Along with this dramatic increase in tourist numbers has been a radical change in the Balinese landscape, environment and cultural conditions (Lewis and Lewis, 2009). In the Badung district, in particular, Bali has become a playground for many western tourists, whose cultural practices and values are anathema to the Islamic purists and the Ulema of the surrounding regions (Hitchock and Putra, 2007; Lewis and Lewis, 2009).

Not surprisingly, therefore, the sites that were attacked by the Islamic militants in 2002 and 2005 were emblems of western hedonism— nightclubs, shopping strips, the beach and restaurants. At their most obvious level, the bombing attacks were designed to rupture the cultural and economic contiguities that had been forged through global capitalism and by which Indonesians, both symbolically and literally, were serving the interests of their indulgent and morally contaminated western 'guests'. In the minds of the militants, these guests were simply invading the Muslim lands with their illicit practices—dancing, drinking alcohol, female exposure on the beaches, drug-taking and immoral sexual practices.

Thus, just as al-Qa'ida targeted the World Trade Center as the symbolic core of American dominated capitalism, the JI operatives attacked the Kuta Beach area of Bali as a symbol of western hedonism—a feverish epicentre of a pleasure ideology that mobilizes western desires, economic imperialism and the oppression of Muslims. While the suicide bombers sought to strike fear into the citizenry of western nations and deter them from entering a Muslim land, there is a sense in which the apocalyptic vision that incited the attacks forms a circuitous but significant alignment with the pleasure grazing of the enemy. Such a view, of course, contrasts significantly with the conventional perspective of civilizational clash, or traditionalism versus modernism. However, the pleasures of the victims of the attack—that broader symbolic constituency of 'the west'—aligns in distinctive ways with the pleasures of the perpetrators, at least inasmuch as they are forged in the shadow of despair (Lewis and Lewis, 2011).

This apocalyptic imagining of despair, that is, is the spectral other that is inevitably generated out of the fatuous pursuit of infinite pleasure. As I have consistently argued in this book, the fantasy of infinite pleasure necessarily generates a condition of displeasure and threat, the most spectacular expression of which is the historical rendering and persistence of despair and apocalypse. The hedonism and induced euphoria that are inscribed in contemporary sexual practices, drug and alcohol culture, nightclubbing and beach recreation are fundamentally inverted by the fallibility of *jouissance* or excess. Apocalypse, as the historical other of this fantasy of infinite bliss, reasserts itself in the dissatisfaction, doubts and anxieties that often drive, as they undermine, this phantasmagoria.

And to a significant extent, it is precisely this same fantasy of eternal bliss which motivates Islamic militants, and indeed many of the world's citizens who have been the recipients of the transfer of economic displeasure. Mesmerized by the affluence of western lifestyles, the Bali bombers might well have reconceived their own pursuit of bliss in terms of a religious transcendence—a particular kind of euphoria that is motivated as much by apocalypse, as by Messianic imaginings. According to David Cook (2003, 2005), who has studied Islamic apocalypse in detail, this propensity for purist Muslims to adopt an apocalyptic posture is inscribed by compelling Qu'ranic motifs relating directly to the prospects of a complete annihilation and redemption. Thus the bombers, like their victims, have experienced the same apocalypse by which the pleasure and displeasure of the global economy converge into a single experience of horror and death. Whether by pursuit of an infinite bodily pleasure or an infinite spiritual transcendence, the bomber and the victim become entangled in the same bloody morass of flesh and fire—the same devastating imaginary by which the antithesis of their symbolic imaginings collapsed in the rubble of the nightclub walls.

The Bali bombings memorial

In a sense, both the targets and the perpetrators of the bombing attacks are variants of the same crisis of political violence, and the same clash of oscillating knowledge systems—the same crisis consciousness. This convergence of sensibilities is even more strangely evident in the resonance of the attacks and the establishment of a memorial at the site of one of the nightclubs that was bombed in 2002 (see Lewis, 2006; Lewis and Lewis, 2011). While designed as a solemn tribute to the victims of the attack, the memorial has now also become a popular totem for the congregation of local Balinese drug dealers and pimps, as well as an increasing number of Indonesian and other South East Asian tourists. As the only public space in Kuta, other than the beach, the memorial site has become a favoured meeting place and tourist icon. As such, many of the visitors to the island—particularly Muslim Javanese—signify their visit to Bali with family photographs taken beneath the memorial's list of bombing victims. People of many nationalities mingle at the site, laughing and chattering, while looking over the Kuta street life and enjoying the cosmopolitan energy of the site. These pleasures that are generated through the site would, no doubt, offend the spiritual sensibilities of the bombers and their spiritual leaders.

Nevertheless, it may be that the militants have achieved their primary objectives, at least inasmuch as the Muslim Javanese represent a significant religio-national group among the tourist populations in Bali, particularly during domestic holiday periods (Lewis and Lewis, 2009; Lewis et al., forthcoming). At these times, the prevalence of head-scarfs and Qu'ranic prayer rituals generates a strong sense of cosmopolitanism and an engagement in the tourist economy which was once the preserve of colonists, westerners and local elites. Ironically, perhaps, the popularity of Bali for local tourists is due in part to the strong domestic marketing campaigns which followed the brief collapse in international tourist numbers after each of the bombings. The hedonism, night-life and beach pleasures that caused so much offence for JI and other purist Islamic groups is now being enjoyed by many of Indonesia's rising middle classes, particularly Muslim Javanese. And indeed, while Australian, American and British tourists approach the Kuta memorial with a sense of anxious and sometimes outraged reverence, the domestic tourists are far less severe, using the public facility as an extension of their play and immersion in the global pleasure economy.

Terrorism as desire

With substantial advances in the Irish sovereignty issue over the past decade, and the military recapture of Tamil held areas of northern Sri Lanka in 2009, two major sources of terrorist violence have been effectively quelled. However, significant terror-based violence continues to occur through the Muslim world, particularly in Palestine, Somalia, Afghanistan, Iraq, Pakistan, Yemen, India and Indonesia. The arrest in 2009 of Umar Farouk Abdulmutalib, a Nigerian born al-Qa'ida operative, who had been radicalized in Yemen, resonated through the western mediasphere, reminding governments and the public that political violence, like trade, has been de-bordered by global contiguities. Indeed, while there have been relatively few acts of terror actually perpetrated in western nations, these cultural and economic contiguities have fostered a profound sense of threat. Within the evolving crisis consciousness and a media that thrives on the imagining of desire and conflict, countries like the US, the UK and Australia feel besieged by the imagined propinquity of Islamic danger. While each of these nations has experienced a terror-based assault on their citizens over the past decade, the actual number of victims is very low compared to the developing world trouble-spots listed above.

However, it is the nature of these targeted attacks on westerners, in territories which were regarded as secure western havens, that has stirred much of the anxiety. Suicide bombing attacks in New York, Bali, Madrid and London have precipitated the greatest anxiety, as they are so antithetical to the primary values of life and pleasure which underpin western culture and lifestyles. In a sense, the common epithets that are used to describe these attacks—'inhuman', 'animal', 'Satanic'—imbue the crime with a sense of cultural deviance that might seem to exceed human comprehension (Lewis, 2005). The conscious act of destroying one's body in order to win what is commonly viewed as an asymmetrical battle offends the deepest and most divinely constituted cultural logic.

Not surprisingly, the suicide attacks that are being perpetrated against western targets are not only regarded as criminal and perverse, but they are frequently represented within a cosmological imaginary of Good versus Evil. Within a context of declining global violence (Human Security Centre, 2005), suicide bombing has become a more acute form of threat for the western imaginary. In his historical survey of terrorism-based attacks, Robert Pape (2005) claims that secular-based violence has declined significantly over the past three decades, while suicide and religious-based violence has increased dramatically:

> At the same time that terrorist incidents of all types are declining from a peak of 666 in 1987 to 348 in 2001, suicide terrorism has grown, and the trend is continuing. Suicide terrorist attacks have risen from an average of three per year in the 1980s to about ten per year in the 1990s to more than forty each year in 2001 and 2002, and nearly fifty in 2003. These include continuing campaigns by Palestinian groups against Israel and by al-Qaeda and Taliban-related forces in Saudi Arabia and Afghanistan, as well as about twenty attacks in Iraq against US troops, the United Nations, and Iraqis collaborating with the American occupation.
>
> (Pape, 2005: 6)

Pape's appraisal of this shift from secular to religious terrorism is supported by Scott Atran (2006) who found that there has been a distinct decline in suicide bombings by non-Islamic groups and a dramatic increase in the number of Islamic-based attacks since 2003—that is, since the American-led invasions of Iraq and Afghanistan. According to Atran, there were around 400 suicide attacks and 2000 deaths associated with suicide bombings in Iraq during 2004 (Atran, 2006: 131). According to reports in the *Guardian*, the increasing activity of the Taliban and al-Qa'ida in Afghanistan over the past several years is also leading to an increase of suicide bombers; in a single roadside attack 89 were killed, contributing to an overall suicide bomber death toll for 2008 of several hundreds (Sameem, 2008). According to Amir Mir (2008) the epicentre of suicide bombings, in fact, is shifting from Iraq to Afghanistan and Pakistan. In Pakistan in 2008 there were 28 suicide attacks leading to 471 mostly civilian deaths. During a similar period in Iraq there were 463 deaths, while in Afghanistan there were around 436 people killed by suicide bombers in 2008 (Plate 6.2).

While there are considerable debates about the profile of the suicide bomber (Khosrokhavar, 2005a; Hafez, 2007; Horgan, 2008), it is very clear that the sorts of Islamic attacks that are occurring in volatile areas represent a complex weave of politicism, religious apocalypse and personal-psychological attributes and circumstances. To this end, poverty, a sense of political oppression and various forms of religious aspiration are demonstrably implicated in the 'pathways' that lead to radicalization and beyond to militancy and 'martyrdom' (Horgan, 2008). Indeed, while some analysts focus on the political circumstances in which suicide attacks take place, others focus on the psycho-cultural 'career' of the suicide bomber and the pathways that lead to the act

Plate 6.2   Armaments gathered as a grave monument in Afghanistan, 2009.
Photograph by Simon Richards.

of self-annihilation and violence. In most cases, for example, suicide bombers are male, though in certain organizations, such as the Chechan rebels, Kurdistan Workers Party (PKK) and Tamil Tigers, female suicide bombers are common, if not predominant (Skaine, 2006); moreover, during 2010 there have been increasing reports of Palestinian and Afghani female suicide bombers. In some cases, bombers' families receive significant financial compensation for the loss of the family member (for example, Hazbolah, JI), while for many assailants the rewards are in the prestige and martyrdom attached to the attack. Forensic studies of Afghanistan suicide bombers have suggested that many of these holy warriors are suffering some form of disability, including mental illness; in these cases, it is suggested that the disability limits the economic productivity of a family member who then seeks financial dispensation through his suicide attack (Kruger and Maleckova, 2003).

In any event, the overriding attribute of the holy warriors is their diversity. Indeed, and as I've intimated above, even the very idea of a 'holy warrior' is problematized through the peculiar and somewhat reflexive alignment of many of these militants with the culture and people they are attacking—particularly westerners. Thus, while the differences between Islamic militants and their western targets is clear enough, there are also some distinctive continuities, particularly through their respective engagement in historical conceptions of apocalypse, and the competitive conditions over which territory and economic surplus are acquired and exploited. Within and through their respective cultural claims, sexuality and the control of pleasure remain central to the territorial battles and their expression in culturally woven language wars. In this re-emergent east-west divide the battles are not simply over territory and resources like oil: the battles are also being waged over women's bodies and control of female sexuality. In this sense, and as we have intimated in our discussion of the Bali attacks, the 9/11 wars are being waged over sexual pleasure and desire.

Indeed, if we are to invoke Freud's conception of 'death wish' and Lacan's more generalized idea of *jouissance* we might see that the very act of self-destruction and its accompanying apocalyptic vision are themselves inscribed with a peculiar sexual and bodily intensity. In this sense, the Bali bombers' passionate disavowal of western *Eros* may simply be a reversal or expression of their own sexual apocalypse, the vision of desire that leads ultimately to self-annihilation. At a more direct level, this disavowal of illicit cultural practices is further inverted by the participation of many *jihadist* organizations in organized crime and criminal activities, including drugs trafficking, theft, smuggling, arms trading, money laundering and fraud (Dishman, 2001; Ridley, 2008). According to John Rollins and colleagues in the Congressional Research Service (2010), many international terrorist organizations, including al-Qa'ida and the Taliban, are now almost entirely dependent on criminal activities to support their political activities. This view is supported by Michael Jacobson.

> The cell that executed the devastating 2004 Madrid train bombing plot, which killed almost 200 people, partially financed the attack by selling hashish. The terrorists who carried out the July 7, 2005, attacks on the transportation system in London were also self-financed, in part through credit card fraud. In Southeast Asia, the Al Qaeda-affiliated Jemaah Islamiyah financed the 2002 Bali bombings, in part, through jewellery store robberies.
>
> (Jacobson, 2010)

Worth nearly $325 billion per annum, the most lucrative of these criminal activities, of course is the illegal drugs trade. The American-based Drug Enforcement Administration claims that as many as 60 per cent of terror organizations are suspected of having some ties with the illegal narcotics trade. Organizations like the Taliban in Afghanistan, the Revolutionary Armed Forces of Colombia (FARC) and Hezbollah in Lebanon are all active participants in the global trade of narcotics, especially heroin and cocaine.

The networking, commercial and economic value of illicit drugs has been recognized by the criminal underworld in Indonesia, including the clandestine networks of regional and global *jihadists*. Organizations like al-Qa'ida have engaged directly in narcotics trading, operating through various parts of Afghanistan and into Burma and South East Asia (Chalk, 2004). Working with local *jihadist* organizations, al-Qa'ida has also been able to operate through the clandestine communications and commercial networks that have been established by organized crime (Lewis and Lewis, 2011). These networks have facilitated the movement of commercial substances like drugs and laundered money, as well as equipment and ballistics used in suicide bombings and other attacks. This has been especially important in Indonesia where *jihadists* have mounted attacks in the outlying areas of Ambon, Aceh and Bali. Peter Chalk (2004) has demonstrated how drugs and terrorist organizations have exploited this clandestine system of financial trade and money laundering called the *hawala* (see also Levitt, 2008). Operating throughout South East Asia, the *hawala* uses a complex system of trust and coded messages to facilitate the bulk transmission and trade of very large sums of illegal finances in a very short period of time. Chalk locates the co-extensive relationship between terrorism and the drugs trade in terms of a broader, post-Cold War security context:

> One specific threat that has assumed greater prominence on South East Asia's broadened security agenda ... has been transnational organised crime. The increased salience of this particular issue stems, in many ways, from the region's overriding predilection with financial power and influence. Combined with the existence of severe and widespread disparities in economic wealth, situations have increasingly arisen where people have been motivated more by the need to possess dollars and less by considerations of the means used to acquire them. The net result has been the gradual evolution of a parallel underground economy, which is currently being powered by syndicates dealing in everything from humans to drugs, gems, timber and weapons.
>
> (Chalk, 2004: 256)

This is particularly disturbing, as it is clear that some members of the Indonesian political elite—including members of the military and law enforcement agencies—are directly involved in the drugs trade. This has been evidenced not only in the Anti-Corruption Commission hearings but in those drugs cases involving members of the Indonesian elite against whom charges have been dropped or sentences have been pitifully light (Berman, 2003; Lewis and Lewis, 2009).

These same struggles are amplified in the volatile war zones of Afghanistan and Pakistan. According to the United Nations, Afghanistan produces around 90 per cent of the world's opium, an essential ingredient for both morphine (legal) and heroin (illegal) narcotics production. The political instability that has reigned in Afghanistan since the Cold War and the Soviet invasion in the 1990s has evolved into a desperate conflict over religion, culture and territory. The Taliban, which may once have been a purist and relatively devout theocratic organization, has more recently evolved into a violent and criminal organization that is seeking to maintain its military threat and status through an engagement in the illegal production and sale of opium. With strong links to al-Qa'ida, the Taliban forces have established strong commercial networks with local farmers and the global narcotics industry. According to Gretchan Peters (2009), the Taliban are no longer satisfied with taxing drugs syndicates that operate in their control zones;

along with corrupt officials in the Karzai government, police and military, the Taliban have now established their own labs, trading networks and shipments that move out of the country through Pakistan and on to the world market. Peters argues that the Taliban and al-Qa'ida are also involved in gun smuggling, human trafficking, and the illegal trade of gemstones and antiquities, many of which have been pillaged from Afghanistan and Iraq.

Paradoxically, American, British and Australian soldiers who are deployed in Afghanistan are fighting against an enemy whose armaments are funded, at least in part, by the illegal drugs trade—the primary market of which is the first world. Thus, the death and injury of the NATO troops are bound to the economy of pleasure and hedonistic lifestyles these soldiers are deployed to protect. To this end, it may not be entirely appropriate to describe Usama bin Laden as a drug lord, but it is patently clear that many senior Taliban and al-Qa'ida officials, along with their allies in the public service, are making significant personal gains out of the illegal narcotics industry. The Taliban's involvement in bank robberies, human trafficking and drugs has clearly compromised their moral authority in Afghanistan, transforming their holy war into another field of cultural agonism. Like FARC, the Tamil Tigers and Hazbollah, the Taliban are pursuing a form of moral, religious and political revolution through the contaminated condition of the pleasure economy. The convolution of *Sh'ariah* Islamic law and the rabid pursuit of profit thorough illegal pleasure industries is clearly compromising the organization's social status and moral authority in Afghanistan. For many devout Msulims in Afghanistan, the Taliban are identified as gangsters (*gundai*) which places them at a very low social position within the Qu'ranic vista.

Ethnicity and mobility: global violence and local terror

While the al-Qa'ida attacks on America were largely perpetrated by foreigners, and the attacks in Bali took place on foreign soils, the attacks in London in 2005 were qualitatively different. These attacks were planned and perpetrated principally by British citizens who had become radicalized by global events and a cultural propinquity with trans-national Islamist organizations. Three of the four killers were the British-born offspring of Pakistani immigrants who had come to the UK in order to seek a better life and opportunities for themselves and their families. Each of the suicide bombers was male and relatively young—Mohammed Sidique Kahn, a 30 year-old husband and father, who lived in Dewsbury and was a teacher's aid at a local primary school; Shehzad Tanweer, 22, a cricket fan and notable sportsman, who lived in Leeds with his parents and worked on occasions in their fish-n-chip shop; Germane Lindsay (Abdullah Shaheed Jamal), 19, a Jamaican-born, former drug-dealer and convert to Islam, who lived in Aylesbury with his pregnant wife; and Hasib Mir Hussain,18, who lived in Leeds with his brother and sister-in-law. All four bombers had converted to Islamic purism in a very short period; each of the ethnic Pakistani bombers were second generation migrants who had visited radical Imams in Pakistan within a few years of the attacks. Lindsay, the Jamaican-born immigrant, converted to Islam through a particularly vehement anti-white and anti-western disposition, blaming white-western culture for his descent into alienation and drugs. Fifty people were killed and around 700 were injured in the four relatively simultaneous bomb attacks, three of which occurred in the London subway and one in a London bus.

The interspersion of political and cultural conditions that produces events like the London bombings draws us again back to the state of the economy of pleasure and the ways in which it deploys various forms of human mobility. In this case, the perpetrators of the London bombings are the offspring of a migrant group that sought to satisfy their own desires in the pursuit of economic and social gratification and security. At the same time, of course, these migrants are supporting a system that derives its energy and growth from the volition of population increase. With the decline in fertility in the western world—itself related to the fantasy of infinite pleasure and increasing female autonomy—most developed world nations now rely on migration to supplement their economic volition, particularly through the provision of labour and expanding domestic markets.

As we noted in the previous chapter, however, this imaginary of perpetual motion brings with it significant dangers. While celebrating the cultural transformations associated with social diversity, the growth system and pleasure economy propel themselves along an extremely precarious linguistic and material knife edge: on the one side is a celebratory multiculturalism which is grounded on secular institutional structures and which promotes diversity; on the other is a secondary code of assimilation which is relentlessly, even oppressively, secular and which demands a form of social likeness even through the discursive camouflage of tolerance and multiplicity of forms. Indeed, the transformation of countries like the UK and Australia has been undertaken with very little domestic consultation: policies around economic growth have perpetually overridden the anxieties of longer term citizens about the presence of significant numbers of new migrant groups in their social milieu. Thus, while promoting tolerance and diversity, a second coding of 'assimilation' continues to be generated by many of the longer term residents of western nations. That is, even when it is presented as a system of openness and plurality, the culture of western primacy and its economy of pleasure continues to assert itself over the prospects of radical Difference. As noted in earlier chapters, this economy is constituted around the mobilization of minor variations (difference) which can be absorbed into the promulgation of standardized and hierarchical modes of pleasure. Migration into the developed world nations is an exercise of pleasure standardization or assimilation, rather than a celebration of genuine diversity. When radical Difference presents itself against this standardization—that is, when it can't be economized—then the system becomes strained by displeasure, violence and codes of political subversion or criminality.

Very clearly, the young men who perpetrated the London bombings had themselves been radicalized through their sense of alienation and encounters with disjunctive knowledge systems. As second generation migrants, these young men absorbed and confronted the double coding of a system that had lured their parents but not fulfilled the promise of equality, tolerance and democratic justice. Rather, the second coding of a brutish and intolerant hierarchy imposed itself on life experiences by which the identity of radical Muslim was more compelling than the sense of alienated, English outcast. In this flux of culture and identity, the young murderers may have been dazzled by a lifestyle and desires that were never quite their own. In this way, and to again invoke Lacan, there emerges in these killings a sexual condition which expresses itself as masculine power and a repression of the very desires that stimulate both sexual-material allure and its offensiveness. That is, the young bombers rejected western, secular materialism as an economy of pleasure, crushing it in themselves and in the lives of those people who personified its power (see Khosrokhovar, 2005a, 2005b; NATO, 2008).

Within the context of the global war on terror and the presence of significant numbers of first and second generation migrants in the west, this precarious coding is threatening the fabric of secular pluralism. While it is very clear that the vast majority of Muslims have settled into western cultures and are living relatively comfortable and peaceful lives, the *sh'ariah* movement remains potent. The recourse to Salafism and other purist modes of Islam has emerged as a significant source of cultural threat to the integrity of 'westernism' and democratic, secular pluralism, in particular. Anxieties around the Muslim head-dress (*hijab*) and full body and face cover (*chador* or *burqa*) have provoked significant controversies in a number of countries in Western Europe, including France and the UK—the cradle of modern democratic secularism. In the UK, for example, senior Labour government Minister, Jack Straw, formally requested that visitors to his office remove their veils, explaining that he found it difficult to communicate with a woman who was masked. In France there is now a complete ban on the wearing of religious iconography in public schools, including head-scarfs and veils; and in 2009 President Nicolas Sarkozy stated publicly that the *burqa* 'is not welcome in France'. For many western cultures that have experienced sexual and gender revolutions, these religious symbols that apply only to women are signifiers of patriarchal constraint on the free expression of femininity, including feminine sexuality. In an economy that relies on sexual allure and its integration into product exchange and value, this sort of sexual repression is both morally and commercially offensive to western secularism and its standardized precepts of pleasure.

Similarly, the continuation of particular religious and cultural practices, particularly around female body modifications like genital circumcision, is deeply offensive to the ideological, moral and legal sensibilities of western nations. While the compulsory adornment of religious iconography and body coverage may be legal in many western cultures, female mutilation and punishment for putative sexual crimes transgress the legal framework of the west: that is, they constitute a form of Difference that cannot be tolerated. This ascription of difference as crime also applies to the emergence of pro- and anti-Muslim street violence that has also emerged in western states, especially during the course of the 9/11 wars. This sort of street violence is not widespread and is often located within particular ethnic groups—Pakistanis in the UK, Lebanese in Australia and Moroccans in France. Nor indeed are these youth gangs systematically organized or necessarily the instigators of violence. There is, nevertheless, a sense of growing anxiety in western states about the presence of radical and militant Muslim groups in their communities, a sense in which the high ideals of pluralism and tolerance are disintegrating under the weight of international warfare, and domestic street violence and community insecurity. While lacking any forceful political or organizational coherence, these street-based disturbances have nevertheless publicized a ferment of tension which is not focused specifically on militant or even purist modes of Islam, but is rather dispersed through a more generalized state of discontent and social disharmony (see Ahmed an-Na'im, 2008). In 2009 in the UK, for example, groups claiming to be opponents of Islamic extremism and militancy were attacked by members of the Harrow Central Mosque. Police, who intervened to protect the protestors, were also attacked by the thousand-strong crowd.

While this event, like many others in Europe and the west might be dismissed as a clash of extremisms—right wing Islamophobes versus Salafy purists—it is nevertheless symptomatic of a more fundamental social tension. Protestors at Harrow claimed that they had the right to object to mosques and Muslims because their community members perpetrate attacks like the London bombings. Muslims feel unfairly impugned and alienated, and hence they rally in defence of their religion, culture and homes within the west. This is particularly the case, as we noted above, with those second generation Muslim immigrants whose sense of identity and cultural legitimacy appears suspended between the parents' homeland and their adopted country and its dominant cultural norms. As many commentators have noted, this is certainly the message that emerges from the video recording left by London suicide bomber Mohammed Sidique Khan. Khan, who describes himself as a scholar and soldier, directly addresses his fellow British citizens as 'the enemy':

> Our words are dead until we give them life with our blood.... I'm sure by now the media has painted a suitable picture of me. This predictable propaganda machine naturally will try to put a spin on things to suit the government and scare the masses into conforming to their power and wealth-obsessed agenda. Your democratically elected governments continuously perpetrate atrocities against my people all over the world. And your support of them makes you directly responsible, just as I am responsible for protecting and avenging my Muslim brothers and sisters. Until we feel security, you will be our targets.... We are at war, and I am a soldier.
>
> (YouTube)

This deep sense of identity fracture and alienation might seem to confirm the studies of Fahrad Khosrokhovar (2005a, 2005b) and Gilles Kepel (2004), who have examined the reasons for the radicalization of young second generation Muslims in Western Europe (see also NATO, 2008). For Kepel, in particular, the most optimistic vision of Muslim migration to the west conceives of the second generation as a vibrant enhancement to the progression of modernism, Europe's newest citizens. A more pessimistic vision, however, suggests that issues of social and cultural disjuncture are exacerbated through widespread unemployment, low education levels and the global conditions of anti-Islamicism. For Kepel this rejection of secular values and re-Islamicization of second generation Muslims in the west is also associated with a critical fracturing within Islam itself. According to Kepel, this fracturing is evident within the processes of change, modernization and global dispersal. Referring to this threat of fragmentation as the *fita*, Kepel claims that migrant Muslim communities in Europe, especially, are facing the real prospect of significant religious and cultural transformation: the fracturing of identity, which is a common migrant experience, is more significant for Islamic groups that have a deep historical antagonism to Christianity and for whom apostasy is a mortal sin. The alternative to this cultural disintegration, therefore, is a more robust adhesion to Islamic principles and *jihad*—which in broad terms represents a war against a distant enemy.

While media imaginings might contribute to a sense that the adoption of Salafism and Islamist militancy are on the rise in western states, most academic research contends that radicalism is not widespread in western Muslim communities. The crisis consciousness that is generated through the media and public discourse focuses, inevitably, on dramatic and violent events, but the vast majority of Muslims living in the west are relatively well settled and peaceful. Indeed, Jørgen Stauen (2009) suggests that the radicalization of young Muslims living in the west is essentially an expression of 'securitization', rather than religious fanaticism. Thus, it is through the language of war and politics that *jihadism* draws its primary inspiration and mechanisms for self-validation. While this point has been well argued in terms of western discourses about Islam and terrorism (see Lewis, 2005), Stauen's argument points to a more worrying effect of political violence and the recourse to various modes of terror. That is, the political violence that is being perpetrated by western and western-affiliated nations in Iraq, Afghanistan and Palestine cannot be bordered within a specific, democratic political discourse; rather, these violent interventions overflow into other political discourses and knowledge systems which work against the authority of the democratic and liberal ideals. The moral and ideological justification for military intervention, that is, becomes contaminated by the evidence of injustice and brutality that necessarily issues from such violent incursions. Thus, the integrity of democracy, secularism and the pleasure economy are radically inverted, creating pathways to resistant and even militant opposition. Across these pathways, the whole concept of 'the west' and its traditions of civil order surrender their moral and historical authority—particularly for those who sit outside or beneath the sanctity of its cultural and economic hierarchies. In the collapse of its authority, the west becomes a source of alternative meanings, cultural proclivities and political pathways. For those radicals who read a different history, one that dignifies violence and self-destruction as divine retribution, the west is the source of an apocalyptic battle to the death.

Of course, the same is true for all sides of this war. The material and economic disputes that drive the violence are set within more complex and incomplete cultural agonisms that mobilize disjunctive knowledge systems and conditions of faith—and doubt. In this sense, the pursuit of pleasure, which is conceived in different ways by the warring parties, is underwritten by a sense of apocalypse that is itself an irradiation of global crisis consciousness. In their brief and disturbed life journeys, the young British Muslims who perpetrated the London bombings uncovered this crisis in the very weave of the west's cultural coding and its fantasy of infinite pleasure. They discovered that they were not complete beings, but existed in the various agonisms of a global mediasphere: that is, they discovered that the truth of the Muslim presence in the UK and the west more generally demands an obedience to the sovereignty of hierarchy, violence, hedonism and social exclusion. As in the contorted logic of a dream, militants understand these contradictions and seek—again like their enemies—to resolve their doubts and establish a system of order through the most calamitous and disorderly of means: that is, through blind faith and an ennobled imaginary of violent death.

Conclusion: Visions of the Beginning

Fortinbras: This quarry cries on havoc. O proud Death, What feast is toward in thine eternal cell That thou so many princes at a shot So bloodily has struck?

William Shakespeare, *Hamlet*

The courage to be is the ethical act in which man affirms his own being in spite of those elements of his existence which conflict with his essential self-affirmation . . . it is the affirmation of one's essential nature.

Paul Tillich, *The Courage to Be* (pp.3–4)

This book has argued that the contending human dispositions of desire and fear have become more intensely contingent through the rise of agricultural economies and cultures. In particular, the emergence of institutionalized modes of surplus exchange, social hierarchy and an unceasing drive to innovation has propelled human history into conditions of crisis that are amplified through the multiplication of complex communicational and knowledge systems. The prevalence of a crisis consciousness in the developed world, thereby, is directly connected to the evolution of the mediasphere—the space in which these agonistic conditions are formed in language, mediation and the irradiating cultural politics that dominate all knowledge systems.

This book has argued, further, that of itself crisis is neither good nor bad, since the presence of crisis may generate various kinds of cultural and social transformations. In a sense, this conception of crisis accords with Vedic and Gnostic principles which define good and evil as mutually contingent modes of cosmological and human progression: it is only possible to distinguish these contending powers through the impact of their presence in the living world (see Lewis and Lewis, 2007, 2009). Thus, while the essence of crisis may be difficult to disaggregate from the aporia of its contending dispositions, it is nevertheless clear that the presence of crisis in the living world is directly associated with considerable human suffering. Indeed, as this book has sought to demonstrate, the crises that humans themselves have generated in relation to their phenomenal world has not only created deep pain for themselves, it is also responsible for the suffering of innumerable other species and the planetary life system as a whole.

Thus, while crisis may be simply 'evental', as Alain Badiou (2001, 2005, 2005a) describes it, the human actions and innovations that surround the crisis are profoundly cultural and thereby steeped in humanly constituted conditions of hierarchy, power and politics that are infused with various organizational modes of exclusion, violence and control. As the various studies in this book indicate, crisis events might simply be viewed as the fulcrum upon which human groups battle for survival, pleasure and power. At the high point of these battles, individuals and groups seek to impose their displeasures on other, less powerful groups, shifting the conditions of crisis into a new state of imbalance.

Even so, the deficiencies of these organizational processes and systems have been obvious to many scholars and public commentators. The brutality, injustice and waste that has been amplified through human terror is enshrined in the apocalyptic vision that characterizes most of the Holocene agricultural religions. Beyond these shadowy and often inconsistent texts, however, the more 'rational' philosophical canon has also sought to resolve the aporia of human pleasure and displeasure. As sources of historical reflection, these texts often seek to realign the grotesque and vicious actions of human warfare and power struggles with problems of human governance, order, peace and morality. In this context, W. G. Runsiman (2010) argues that the most incisive commentary in Plato's *Republic* should actually be attributed to one of Socrates' rhetorical adversaries, Thrasymachus. While the Platonic method is to present Socrates' rhetorical adversaries as the straw men of a losing logic, Runsiman suggests that Thrasymachus actually offers a compelling argument against Socrates' plea for a rational and wise city-state. Indeed, looking again at Plato's utopia, and in the light of overwhelming historical evidence, we might be convinced by Thrasymachus' claim that 'justice is the advantage of the stronger' (Plato, Book I: 35).

According to Runsiman (2010), Thrasymachus presents for us the inescapable reality of the human condition and the problem of power, a reality that persists into present political conditions. Against the pragmatics of this unjust power, however, Runsiman invokes an equally potent imperative towards collectivism and human community. Elinor Ostrom (1990, 2006), winner of the 2009 Nobel Prize for economics, substantiates Runsiman's invocation, arguing that knowledge itself is constituted around a collective necessity which defies the absolute sovereignty of individualism and hierarchical social structures. Ostrom's economics, thereby, represent a panegyric for collectivism over the more commonly celebrated economics of pure liberalism and the drives of self-interest.

This same theoretical convergence of 'realism' and idealism is evident in many accounts of crisis which commend a new mode of global governance and trans-national cosmopolitanism (Zolo, 1997; Beck, 1999, 2008; Patomäki, 2008). According to Heikki Patomäki (2008), for example, the emergence of global-scale human problems is only resolvable through the evolution of nation-states into more composite governmental systems, systems that acknowledge pluralism and the rights of less powerful nations and peoples. Such views might accord with Slavoj Zizek's (2006) case for a pluralist revolution; in Zizek's schema human groups are drawn together through a genuine communal bond that is constituted around mutual contingency, rather than a puerile essentialism that falsifies ethnic, national or other forms of grounded identity.

For many scholars, too, the media represents a system of political calumny, a force that no longer supports democracy or its informational and public responsibilities (Cottle, 2009). For these critics, the media contributes to disinformation and a more pervasive atrophy in public debate, political performance and social erudition. With its focus on affective modes of entertainment, the corporate media, in particular, is actually perverting the democratic ideal and the aspiration of civic duty, freedom of speech and social justice.

Within the context of this atrophied Fourth Estate, supporters of this democratic ideal are urging a new politicism that fosters human rights as a universal panacea to human crisis. This discourse of universal human rights is appended to the sorts of social ethics—the 'good life'—that Aristotle proposes and which is now the predicate of a true global citizenship. Thus, ethical philosophers like Michael Sendel (2009) and Peter Singer (2010) commend a notion of responsible humanism that extends the rights of the human species to all planetary life forms. Sendel, in particular, seeks a system of collaborative ethics which would liberate us from the ideological rhythms of neo-liberalism and its monotone of consumer-based, individual choice.

To some extent, this scholarly interest in the ethics of collectivism, social justice and responsibility is a reaction against a reinvigorated utilitarian politics which claims that public good is simply the assembly of individual gratifications. Sendel, Singer, Patomäki and others remain either contemptuous or indifferent to the considerable social force of desire and pleasure, regarding these personal dispositions as impediments to a more elevated state of collective consciousness and ethical citizenship. As in Plato's *Republic*, the prescribed collective ethics and global governance seems to have little space for dangerous and disruptive desires nor their expression in narrative or image-based aesthetics. Even so, the rise of DIY, self-improvement, spiritual revivalism, new age philosophy and Internet-based social networking frequently commend an elevation of a collective consciousness through personal pleasure. In this light, postmodern theory, art and architecture, which reached their critical zenith in the 1990s, might be understood as a manifestation of an equally profound yearning for the rendering of a human-scale aesthetics and humanist sensibility that would challenge the persistent horror of socially created crisis (see Jencks, 2006; Lewis, 2008). Indeed, while many political theorists remain contemptuous of the postmodern twitch and its lack of realistic solutions, a gulf clearly separates the higher ideals of a Platonic utopia from the experiential conditions of everyday life, imagining and pleasure.

One of the aims of this book has been to bridge that divide—to investigate crisis across the plane of personal, community and global-scale conditions within the broader imaginings of the mediasphere. In many respects, this is the primary point of Shakespeare's tragic drama, *Hamlet*, a play in which good and evil become confounded within the moral and political complexity of the crisis. Shakespeare challenges our ethical reference through the intricate complexion of his characters' desires and their pursuit of power and personal pleasure. This moral complexity is rendered through the fantasy of an infinite pleasure that leads ultimately to the implosion of the political genealogy and its regal structure. When young Prince Fortinbras encounters the horror, he invokes the nobility of fallen princes and a barely nameable ethics of courage. These ethics are not constituted around a simple legalistic structure nor the unabridged potency of self-preservation, which can only ever be itself. Rather Fortinbras imagines and calls upon a courage that is self-sacrificing and self-denying because it is constituted around the preservation of others. In this sense, the aesthetic and ethics of this courage implicates a fantasy of grace that is as potent and powerful as the slaughter to which Fortinbras is witness.

In the face of contemporary crisis, we have no simple solutions. There can be no restoration of a hunter-gatherer or provincial idyll; nor is there a nirvana, a magical Republic, that will open like the Basilica of St Peter to the demands of our will. And indeed, if we are hurtling towards some terrible and premature annihilation, then it is simply our own doing, the exercise of our imaginings of pleasure and dread. Thus, while our desires may be deeply inscribed in the essence of our being, the choices and actions we take are not. In this sense, we must constrain our displeasures through the management of our actions and not simply by passing them away to other human groups and life forms. We can invoke an ethics of courage and a fantasy of grace that can direct our innovative capacity against the bumbling horrors of these displeasures. Here is the fount of our freedom.

Notes

1 Imagining the End: Crisis Culture and the Pleasure Economy

1. *Homo sapiens sapiens* (lit. wise wise man) is the subspecies of *Homo sapiens* who evolved around 200,000 years Before Present (BP). This group of anatomically modern human can be distinguished from more archaic humans who appear around 500,000 years ago. This chapter refers specifically to the anatomically modern human. Thus, when the term 'modern' is the qualifier attached to 'human', I am referring to *Homo sapiens sapiens*. In other contexts, I will use the term 'modern' as a social and historical descriptor, referring to the period from around the early seventeenth century into the present. This descriptor will also apply to particular cultural characteristics often associated with the Enlightenment and 'modernization'—the state of being culturally modern.

2. It is worth noting that Baudrillard dispensed with the term 'symbolic exchange' because he believed that it was ultimately ambiguous. He nevertheless maintained his interest in the idea of libidinal transferral, believing that the capitalist economy was largely driven through the exchange of simulacra (meaningless signs) and desires that could never be satisfied.

3. Immanuel Kant referred to noumenal reality as that which is tangible but not perceivable, as it is not available to the human senses. It is that 'objective' reality that Kant identifies as the fullness of objects in all their essence and complexity. Martin Heidegger takes up these questions in his study of phenomena. In his essay 'The age of the world picture' (1977) Heidegger expresses his anxieties about the new media of photography and cinema which present an oscillating image that appears to be real, but which perpetually retreats from our sensate and cognitive grasp.

3 Reckless Desire: Love, Sexuality and Infinite Bliss

1. I am aware that a number of authors distinguish between the concepts of 'sex', 'gender' and 'sexuality'. Frequently these distinctions centre on the need to disaggregate the sexual engagement of actual bodies from the textual representation of these activities. In accordance with my general approach to culture, I will be assuming a complete continuity between the phenomenal, material or biological condition of sex, the psycho-emotional experience of sex and sexual desire, and the cultural-epistemological representation of sex. At times, I will use the term 'sexuality' to emphasize this continuity,

particularly in terms of the ways in which sex and desire permeate the broad gamut of human life and culture.

5   The Shadow and the Fawn: Sustainable Nature and Collapsing Ecologies

1. Spencer developed the term after reading *On the Origin of Species*. However, Darwin himself used the term in the fifth edition of *Origin*.

Bibliography

Acocella, J. (2005) 'The end of the world: interpreting the plague', *The New Yorker*, 21 March.

Agamben, G. (2004) *The Open. Man and Animal*, trans. Kevin Attel, Stanford University Press, Stanford, CA.

—— (2005) *State of Exception*, University of Chicago Press, Chicago, IL.

Agar, J. (2004) *Constant Touch: A Global History of the Mobile Phone*, Totem Books, New York.

Ahmed an-Na'im, A. (2008) *Islam and the Secular State: Negotiating the Future of Shari'a*, Harvard University Press, Boston, MA.

Amato, P. and Previti, D. (2003) 'People's reasons for divorcing', *Journal of Family Issues*, 24 (5).

Anderson, B. (1991) *Imagined Communities: Reflections on the Origins and Spread of Nationalism*, Revised Edition, Verso, London.

Angle, S. and Svenson, M. (eds) (2001) *The Chinese Human Rights Reader*, East Gate Books, New York.

AP (2009) U.S. crew retakes ship from pirates off Somalia', Associated Press, April. Accessed September 2010. http://www.msnbc.msn.com/id/30103371/.

Applewhite, A. (1997) *Cutting Loose—Why Women Who End Their Marriages Do So Well*, Harper Perennial, New York.

Apriyantono, A. (2008) 'Indonesia's response to food-fuel-financial crisis: with a perspective of the second green revolution', Paper presented at UN ESCAP Conference, Bali, 9–10 December.

ASPE (2007) 'The effects of marriage on health: a synthesis of recent research evidence', US Government Department of Health. Accessed May 2010, http://aspe.hhs.gov/hsp/07/marriageonhealth/rb.htm.

Atkinson, M. (2002) 'Pretty in ink: conformity, resistance and negotiation in women's tattooing', *Sex Roles: A Journal of Research*, 47 (5–6), September.

Atran, S. (2006) 'The moral logic and growth of suicide terrorism', *The Washington Quarterly*, 29 (2).

Ayala, F. J. (2006) *Darwin and Intelligent Design*, Fortress Press, Philadelphia, PA.

Badiou, A. (2001) *Ethics: An essay on the Understanding of Evil*, trans. P. Hallward, Verso, London.

—— (2005) *Being and Event*, trans. O. Feltham, Continuum, London.

—— (2005a) *Handbook of Inaesthetics*, trans. A. Toscano, Stanford University Press, Stanford, CA.

Baghati, J. (2004) *In Defense of Globalization*, Oxford University Press, New York.

Baker, R. (1999) *Sex in the Future: The Reproductive Revolution and How it Will Change Us*, Diane Publishing, London.

Barton, G. (2004) *Indonesia's struggle Jemmaah Islamiyah and the soul of Islam*, UNSW Press, Sydney.

Baudrillard, J. (1998) *The Consumer Society: Myths and Structures*, trans. C. Turner, Sage, London.

—— (1984) *Simulations*, trans. P. Foss, Semiotext(e), New York.

—— (1990a) *Cool Memories (1980–1985)*, Verso, New York.

—— (1990c) *Seduction*, trans. B. Singer, St Martin's Press, New York.

—— (1990b) *Fatal Strategies*, Pluto Books, London.

—— (1993) *Symbolic Exchange and Death*, Sage, Thousand Oaks, CA.

—— (2002) *The Spirit of Terrorism and Requiem for the Twin Towers*, trans. C. Turner, Verso, London.

Bauman, Z. (2000) *Liquid Modernity*, Polity, Cambridge.

—— (2003) *Liquid Love: On the Frailty of Human Bonds*, Polity, London.

BBC News (2008) 'Pirate says *Sirius* crew safe', November 24. Accessed Spetember 2010. http://news.bbc.co.uk/2/hi/7746345.stm.

Beck, U. (1992) *Risk Society: Towards a New Modernity*, Sagem, New Delhi.

—— (1999) *World Risk Society*, Polity, Cambridge.

—— (2000) 'Foreword' in B. Adam, S. Allan and C. Carter, eds, *Environmental Risk and the Media*, Routledge, London.

—— (2008) *World at Risk*, Polity, Cambridge.

Bell, D. (1973) *The Coming of Post Industrial Society*, Basic Books, New York.

Bellwood, P. (2004) *First Farmers: The Origins of Agricultural Societies*, Wiley-Blackwell, London.

Benson, J. (1994) *The Rise of Consumer Society in Britain 1850–1980*, Longman, London.

Berman, L. (2003) 'Drug addiction in Indonesia: from junkies to jihad', *Inside Indonesia*, July–September.

Bernstein, W. J. (2008) *A Splendid Exchange: How Trade Shaped the World*, Atlantic Monthly Press, New York.

Best, S. and Nocella, A. (2006) *Igniting a Revolution: Voices in Defense of the Earth*, AK Press, New York.

Black, M. and Fawcett, B. (2008) *The Last Taboo: Opening the Door on the Global Sanitation Crisis*, Earthscan, London.

Bourdieu, P. (1987) *Distinction: A Social Critique of the Judgement of Taste*, Harvard University Press, Boston, MA.

Boykoff, M. and Rajan, R. (2007) 'Signals and noise: media coverage of climate change in the USA and the UK', *European Molecular Biology Organization Reports*, 8 (3).

Brackett, M., Mayer, J. and Warner, R. (2003) 'Emotional intelligence and its relation to everyday life', *Personalty and Individual Differences*, 36 (6).

Braun, V. (2005) 'In search of (better) sexual pleasure: female genital "cosmetic" surgery', *Sexualities*, 8 (4).

Brown, L. (2001) *Sex Slaves: The Trafficking of Women in Asia*, Virago, London.

Brulotte, G. and Phillips, J. (eds) (2006) *Encyclopedia of Erotic Literature*, Routledge, New York.

Bush, G. W. (2002) Speech delivered to the Inter-American Development Bank, 14 March, Washington, DC.

Carmody, P. (2005) 'Transforming globalization and security: Africa and America post 9/11', *Africa Today*, 52 (1).

Chalk, P. (2004) 'The politics of the South-east Asian heroin trade' in D. M. Jones, ed., *Globalisation and the New Terror: The Asia Pacific Dimension*, Edward Elgar, Cheltenham, UK.

Chesler, P. (2009) 'Are honor killings simply domestic violence?', *Middle East Quarterly*, XVI (2).

Chester, J. (2008) *Digital Democracy: New Media and the Future of Democracy*, New Press, New York.

Chitty, N. (2003) 'Introduction: subjects of terrorism and media' in N. Chitty, R. Rush and M. Semeti, eds, *Studies in Terrorism: Media Scholarship and the Enigma of Terror*, Southbound, Penang.

Chomsky, N. (2001) *September 11*, Unwin, Crows Nest, NSW, Australia.

CIA (2010) CIA 'country comparisons: GDP real growth rate', *World Factbook*. Accessed May 2010, https://www.cia.gov/library/publications/the-world-factbook/rankorder/2003rank.html.

Collier, P. (2007) *The Bottom Billion*, Oxford University Press, Oxford.

Conrad, J. (1969) *Heart of Darkness*, Bantam Books, London.

—— (2005) *The Secret Agent*, Collector's Library, London.

Cook, D. (2003) *Studies in Muslim Apocalyptic (Studies in Late Antiquity and Early Islam)*, Darwin Press, Princeton, NJ.

—— (2005) *Contemporary Muslim Apocalyptic Literature*, Syracuse University Press, Syracuse.

Cooper, C. (2004) 'Swing it baby!', *Journal of Bisexuality*, 3 (3).

Cornell, J. and Halpern-Felsher, B. (2005) 'Adolescents tell us why teens have oral sex', *Journal of Adolescent Health*, 38 (3).

Corner, J. and Pels, D. (eds) (2003) *Media and the Restyling of Politics: Consumerism, Celebrity and Cynicism*, Sage, London.

Cottle, S. (2006) *Mediatized Conflict: Developments in Media and Conflict Studies*, Open University Press, London.

—— (2009) *Global Crisis Reporting: Journalism in the Global Age*, Open University Press, London.

Council of Europe (2007) 'Award ceremony of the North-South Prize of the Council of Europe', Council of Europe, Lisbon, 19 March.

Crackwell, B. (2000) *Evaluating Development Aid: Issues, Problems and Solutions*, Sage, London.

Crossley, N. (2005) 'Mapping reflexive body techniques: on body modification', *Body and Society*, 11 (1).

Currat, M. and Excoffier, L. (2004) 'Modern humans did not admix with Neanderthals during their range expansion into Europe', *Public Library of Science Biology*, 2 (12).

Curtis, G. (2006) *The Cave Painters: Probing the Mysteries of the World's First Artists*, Knopf, New York.

Darda, M. (2008) 'Credit markets and the real economy', *Wall Street Journal*, 29 September. Accessed 2 June 2009, http://online.wsj.com/article/SB122265297211884365.html.

Dartnell, M. (2006) *Insurgency Online: Web Activism and Global Conflict*, University of Toronto Press, Toronto.

David, B., Barker, B. and McNiven, I. (2006) *The Social Archaeology of Australian Indigenous Societies*, Australian Studies Press, Sydney.

Dawkins, M. and Bonney, R. (eds) (2008) *The Future of Animal Farming: Renewing the Ancient Contract*, Wiley and Blackwell, New York.

Day, P. (2008) *A New History of Social Welfare*, Allyn & Bacon, Harrow.

de Certeau, M. (1988) *The Writing of History*, Columbia University Press, New York.

de Steiguer, J. E. (2006) *The Origins of Modern Environmental Thought*, University of Arizona Press, Tucson, AZ.

Delate, T., Simmons, V. and Motheral, B. (2004) 'Patterns of use of Sildenafil among commercially insured adults in the United States: 1998–2002', *International Journal of Impotence Research*, 16, 19 February.

DiGeorgia, J. (2005) *The Global War for Oil*, 21st Century Investor Publishing, New York.

DiNitto, D. and Cummins , L. (2007) *Social Welfare: Politics and Public Policy*, Allyn & Bacon, Harrow.

Dishman C. (2001) 'Terrorism, crime, and transformation', *Studies in Conflict and Terrorism*, 24 (1).

DOD (1986) 'Protection of DOD resources against terrorist acts', United States Department of Defense Directive, 2000.12, 16 June.

Dudink, S., Hagemann, K. and Tosh, J. (2004) *Masculinities in Politics and War: Gendering Modern History*, Macmillan, New York.

Dunlop, R. and McCright, A. (2008) 'A widening gap: Republican and Democratic views on climate change', *Environment*, 50 (5).

Easterly, W. (2006) *The White Man's Burden: Why the West's Efforts to Aid the Rest Have Done So Much Ill and So Little Good*, Penguin, Hammondsworth.

Edwards, A. and Orr, D. (2006) *The Sustainability Revolution: Portrait of a Paradigm*, New Society Books, New York.

Ehrenreich, B. (2004) 'Feminism and Abu Ghraib', *Sunday LA Times*, 17 May.

Ehrenreich, N. (2002) 'Masculinity and American militarism', *Tikkun*, 17 (6).

Elewa, A. (ed.) (2008) *Mass Extinctions*, Springer, Berlin.

Elliot, L. (2005) 'West accused of concealing farm subsidies', *Guardian*, 15 June.

Engels, F. (1902) *The Origins of the Family, Private Property and the State,* trans. E. Untermann, C.H. Kerr and Co., London.

Enting, I. (2009) 'Ian Plimer's "Heaven + Earth"—checking the claims', *ARC Centre for Excellence*. Accessed May 2010, http://bravenewclimate.com/2009/04/23/ian-plimer-heaven-and-earth/.

Essén B. and Johnsdotter, S. (2004) 'Female genital mutilation in the West: traditional circumcision versus genital cosmetic surgery', *Acta Obstetricia et Gynecologica Scandinavica*, 83 (7).

Fine, M. and Harvey, J. (2006) *Handbook of Divorce and Relationship Dissolution*, Routledge, London.

Fisher, W. R. (1984) 'Narration as a human communication paradigm: the case of public moral argument', *Communication Monographs*, 52.

——— (1987) *Human communication as a Narration: Toward a Philosophy of Reason, Value, and Action*, University of South Carolina Press, Columbia, SC.

Flanagan, R. (2006) *Globalization and Labor Conditions: Working Conditions and Worker Rights in a Global Economy*. Oxford University Press, New York.

Flood, J. (2004) *The Archaeology of the Dreamtime: The Story of Prehistoric Australia and its People*, JB Publications, Sydney.

Food and Agriculture Organization (2008) *Food Insecurity in the World*. Accessed May 2010, http://www.fao.org/docrep/011/i0291e/i0291e00.htm.

Forbes, S. (2005) *A Natural History of Families*, Princeton University Press, Boston, MA.

Forbes.com (2009) 'The world's best selling pharmaceuticals'. Accessed Spetember 2010. http://www.cuttingedgeinfo.com/reinventing-salesforces/?type=GoogleAdWordsSearch&gclid=CPXGr9ek8qMCFQZBbgodR2O-3Q

Forsyth, T. (2003) *Critical Political Ecology: The Politics of Environmental Science*, Routledge, New York.

Foucault, M. (1981) *A History of Sexuality: Volume 1*, Penguin, Hammondsworth.

Fougere, M., Merette, M., Harvey, S. and Poitras, F. (2004) 'Ageing population and immigration in Canada: an analysis with a regional CGE overlapping generations model', *Canadian Journal of Regional Science*, 22 June.

Fox, R. (1983) *Kinship and Marriage: An Anthropological Perspective*, Cambridge University Press, Cambridge.

Frame, T. (2009) *Evolution in the Antipodes: Charles Darwin and Australia*, UNSW Press, Sydney.

Friedman, M. (1982) *Capitalism and Freedom*, University of Chicago Press, Chicago, IL.

Fukuyama, F. (1993) *The End of History and the Last Man*, Harper, New York.

—— (2005) 'Identity, immigration, and liberal democracy', *Journal of Democracy*, 17 (2).

—— (2006) 'After neoconservatism', *New York Times Online*. Accessed May 2010, http://www.nytimes.com/2006/02/19/magazine/neo.html?pagewanted=print.

Gennaro, S. (2007) '*Sex in the City*: perpetual adolescence gendered feminine?', *Nebula*, 4 (1).

Gettleman, J. (2009) 'The most dangerous place in the world', *Foreign Policy*, March/April.

Giddens, A. (1990) *Consequences of Modernity*, Polity Press, Cambridge.

—— (1992) *The Transformation of Intimacy: Sexuality, Love and Eroticism in Modern Societies*, Polity, Cambridge.

—— (1994) *Beyond Left and Right: The Failure of Radical Politics*, Polity, Cambridge.

—— (1999) 'Risk and responsibility', *Modern Law Review*, 62 (1).

Gill, P. (2008) 'A political psychology analysis of suicide bomber radicalization', Paper presented at the annual meeting of the ISPP 31st Annual Scientific Meeting, Sciences Po, Paris, France. Accessed March 2010, http://www.allacademic.com/meta/p241154_index.html.

Giroux, H. (2006) *Beyond the Spectacle of Terrorism: Global Uncertainty and the Challenge of the New Media*, Paradigm Publishers, New York.

—— (2008) *Agianst the Terror of Neoliberalism*, Paradigm Publishers, Boulder, CO.

Giroux, H. and Szeman, I. (2001) 'Ikea boy fights back: *Fight Club*, consumerism, and the political limits of nineties cinema' in J. Lewis, ed., *The End of Cinema As We Know It: American Film in the Nineties*, New York University Press, New York.

Gleick, J. (2000) *Faster: The Acceleration of Just About Everything*, Vintage, New York.

—— (2003) *What Just Happened: A Chronicle from the Information Frontier*, Vintage, New York.

Goggin, G. and Hjorth, L. (eds) (2008) *Mobile Technologies from Telecommunications to Media*, Routledge, London.

Goldstein, J. (2008) *War and Gender: How Gender Shapes the War System and Vice-a-Versa*, Cambridge University Press, Cambridge.

Gonick, M. (2006) 'Between "girl power" and "reviving Ophelia": constituting the neoliberal girl subject', *National Women's Studies Association Journal*, 18 (2).

Good, J. (2008) 'The framing of climate change in Canadian, American and inter-national newspapers: a media propaganda model analysis', *Canadian Journal of Communication*, 33 (2).

Goodman, A., Heath, D. and Lindee, S. (eds) (2003) *Genetic Nature/Culture: Anthropology and Science Beyond the Two-culture Divide*, University of California Press, Berkeley, CA.

Gore, A. (2006) *An Inconvenient Truth: The Planetary Emergency of Global Warming and What We Can Do About It*, Rodale Books, New York.

Gould, T. (2000) *The Lifestyle: A Look at the Erotic Rites of Swingers*, Firefly Books, New York.

Gray, C. H. (2004) *Terror or Peace: Information, Globalization and Power*, Routledge, New York.

———— (2003) 'Posthuman soldiers in postmodern war', *Body and Society*, 9 (4).

Gray, J. (1992) *Men are from Mars, Women are from Venus*, Harper Collins, New York.

Greenwald, A. (2003) *Nothing Feels Good: Punk Rock, Teenagers and Emo*, St Martin's Griffin, New York.

Greer, G. (2000) *The Whole Woman*, Anchor Books, London.

Genschel, P. (2004) 'Globalization and the welfare state: a retrospective', *Journal of European Public Policy*, 1, (4).

Griffin, S. (2000) *Women and Nature: The Roaming Within*, Club Books, New York.

Gunaratna, R. (2003) *Inside Al Qaeda: Global Network of Terror*, Berkley Trade, New York.

Hafez, M. (2007) *Suicide Bombers in Iraq: The Strategy and Ideology of Martyrdom*, United States Institute of Peace, Washington, DC.

Halle, R. (2004) *Queer Social Theory: Critical Readings from Kant to Adorno*, University of Illinois Press, Champaign, IL.

Hallward, P. (2003) *Badiou: A Subject to Truth*, University of Minnesota Press, Minneapolis, MN.

Haraway, C. (2000) 'A cyborg manifesto: science, technology and socialist-feminism in the late twentieth century' in D. Bell and B. Kennedy, eds, *The Cyberculture Reader*, Routledge, London.

Harrison, F. (2002) 'Pakistan woman tells of rape ordeal', BBC News, 3 August, http://news.bbc.co.uk/2/hi/south_asia/2170586.stm.

Hartwich, O. (2009a) *Neoliberalism: The Genesis of a Political Swearword*, Centre for Independent Studies, Sydney.

———— (2009b) 'The great neoliberal misunderstanding', Centre for Independent Studies, *Executive Highlights*, 829. Accessed May 2010, http://www.cis.org.au/executive_highlights/EH2009/eh82909.html.

Haslam, P., Schafer, S. and Beaudet, P. (2009) *Introduction to International Development: Approaches, Actors and Issues*, Oxford University Press, Toronto.

Heidegger, M. (1977) 'The age of the world picture' in trans. W. Lovitt, *The Question Concerning Technology and Other Essays*, Harper & Row, New York.

Held, D. and McGrew, A. (2007) *Globalization/Anti-Globalization: Beyond the Great Divide*, 2nd Edition, Polity, London.

Herman, E. and McChesney, R. (1997) *The Global Media: The New Missionaries of Corporate Capitalism*, Cassell, London.

Herzog, D. (2008) *Sex in Crisis: The New Sexual Revolution and the Future of American Politics*, Basic Books, New York.

Hesse, B. (2005) 'Celebrate or hold supper? Bill Clinton and George W. Bush in Africa', *Journal of African Studies*, 25 (3).

Heyd, T. and Clegg, J. (eds) (2005) *Aesthetics and Rock Art*, Ashgate Publishing, Aldershot.

Hills, T. and Todd, P. (2008) 'Population heterogeneity and individual differences in an assortative agent-based marriage and divorce model (MADAM) using search with relaxing expectations', *Journal of Artificial Societies and Social Simulation*, 11 (4).

Hirst, P. and Thompson, G. (1999) *Globalization in Question*, Polity, Cambridge.

Hitchcock, M. and Putra, I N. D. (2007) *Tourism, Development and Terrorism in Bali*, Ashgate Publishing, Aldershot, UK.

Hite, S. (2000) *The New Hite Report: The Revolutionary Report on Female Sexuality Updated*, Hamlyn, New York.

——— (2006) *Oedipus Revisited: Sexual Behaviour in the Human Male Today*, Arcadia Books, New York.

Hopfl, H. (2003) 'Becoming a (virile) member: women and the military body', *Body and Society*, 9 (4).

Horgan, J (2008) 'From profiles to pathways and roots to routes: perspectives from psychology on radicalization into terrorism', *The Annals of the American Academy of Political and Social Science*, 618 (1).

Human Security Centre (2005) *Human Security Report: War and Peace in the 21st Century*, Human Security Centre, University of British Columbia, Canada.

Humphery, K. (2010) *Excess*, Polity, Cambridge.

Huntington, S. (1993) 'The Clash of Civilizations', *Foreign Affairs*, Summer.

IATP (Institute for Agriculture and Trade Policy) (2004) 'United States dumping on world agricultural markets', April.

IMF (International Monetary Fund) (2009) *World Economic Outlook Update*, 29 January.

ITB (2010) *ITB World Travel Report (2009/2010)*. Accessed May 2010, http://www.itb-berlin.com.library

Jacobson, M. (2010) 'Terrorist dropouts: learning from those who have left', *Policy Focus*, No. 101, January, Online journal. Accessed May 2010, http://www.pvtr.org/pdf/ICPVTRinNews/TerroristDropouts.pdf.

Jagose, A. (1997) *Queer Theory*, NYU Press, New York.

Jameson, F. (1991) *Postmodernism, or, The Cultural Logic of Late Capitalism*, Duke University Press, Durham, NC.

Jarboe, J. (2002) 'The threat of eco-terrorism', Congressional Testimony, Federal Bureau of Investigations. Accessed May 2010, http://www.fbi.gov/congress/congress02/jarboe021202.htm.

Jeffreys, S. (2004) *Unpacking Queer Politics: A Lesbian Feminist Perspective*, Polity, Cambridge.

——— (2007) *Beauty and Misogyny: Harmful Cultural Practices in the West*, Routledge, London.

Jencks, C. (2006) *Theories and Manifestoes of Contemporary Architecture*, Academy Press, London.

John Kelly (2005) *The Great Mortality: An Intimate History of the Black Death, the Most Devastating Plague of All Time*, Harper Collins, New York.

Johnson, C. (ed.) (1948) *Registrum Hamonis Hethe diocesis Roffensis 1319–1352*, Canterbury and York Society, Canterbury.

Johnson, C. (2005) *The Sorrows of Empire: Militarism, Secrecy, and the End of the Republic*, Macmillan, London.

Kaldor, M. Karl, T. and Said, Y. (2007) *Oil Wars*, Pluto Books, London.

Kamons, A. (2007) 'Of note: celebrity and politics', *SAIS Review*, 27 (1), Winter–Spring.

Kellner, D. (1995) *Media Culture: Cultural Studies, Identity, and Politics between the Modern and the Postmodern*, Routledge, London.

Kennett, D., Kennett, J., Kennett et al. (2009). 'Nanodiamonds in the Younger Dryas Boundary sediment layer', *Science*, 323.

Kepel, Gilles (2004) *The War for Muslim Minds, Islam and the West*, trans. P. Ghazaleh, The Belknap Press of Harvard University, Cambridge, MA.

Kerbaj, R. (2009) 'Thousands of girls mutilated in Britain', *The Times*, 16 March. Accessed March 2010, http://www.timesonline.co.uk/tol/life_and_style/health/article5913979.ece.

Khosrokhavar, F. (2005a) *Suicide Bombers: Allah's New Martyrs*, trans. D. Macey, Pluto, London.

Khosrokhovar, F. (2005b), 'Terrorism in Europe' in Daniel Hamilton (ed.) *Terrorism and International Relations*, Centre for Transatlantic Relations, Johns Hopkins University Press, Washington, DC.

Kim, L. and Ward, M. (2004) 'Pleasure reading: associations between young women's sexual attitudes and their reading of contemporary women's magazines', *Psychology of Women Quarterly*, 28, (1).

Kippen, R. (2009) 'A note on ageing, immigration and the birthrate', *People and Place*, 7, (2).

Kirby, Aidan (2007) 'The London bombers as "self-starters": a case study in indigenous radicalization and the emergence of autonomous cliques', *Studies in Conflict and Terrorism*, 30 (5), 415–428.

Koh, L. P. and Wilcove, D. (2008) 'Is oil palm production really destroying tropical biodiversity?', *Conservation Letters*, 1, March.

Kristeva, J. (1980) *Desire and Language: A Semiotic Approach to Literature and Art*, trans. T. Gora, Coumbia University Press, New York.

Kruger, A. and Meleckova, J. (2003) 'Educations, poverty and terrorism: is there a causal link?', *Journal of Economic Perspectives*, 17 (4).

Kuhn, T. (1962) *The Structure of Scientific Revolutions*, University of Chicago Press, Chicago, IL.

Kunstler, J. (2006) *The Long Emergency: Surviving the End of Oil, Climate Change, and Other Converging Catastrophes of the Twenty-first Century*, Grove Press, New York.

Lacan, J. (1977) *Ecris: A Selection*, Tavislock, London.

——— (1998) *The Four Fundamental Concepts of Psychoanalysis*. W. W. Norton, New York.

Langer, G. (2004) 'American Sex Survey', ABC News Online. Accessed May 2010, http://abcnews.go.com/Primetime/PollVault/story?id=156921&page=1.

Laqueur, W. (1987) *The Age of Terrorism*, George Weidenfeld and Nicolson, London.

——— (2003) *No End to War: Terrorism in the Twenty First Century*, Continuum, New York.

Lash, S. and Urry, J. (1987) *The End of Organized Capital*, Polity, Cambridge.

Lau, M. (2005) *Role of Islam in the Legal System of Pakistan*, Martinus Nijhoff, London.

Legrain, P. (2007) 'The case for immigration', *The Global Economy*, Summer, 21 (3).

Lemons, B., Westra, L. and Goodland, R. (eds) (1998) *Ecological Sustainability and Integrity: Concepts and Approaches*, Kluwer Press, Dordwech, the Netherlands.

Levitt, M. (2008) 'Al-Qa'ida's finances: evidence of organized decline?' *CTC Sentinel*, 1 (5).

Lewis, J. (2000) 'Manufacturing dissent: new democracy in the era of digital communication,' *International Journal of Cultural Studies*, 1, (1).

Lewis, J. (2002) 'Propagating Terror: 9/11 and the mediation of war', *Media International Australia*, 104, August.

Lewis, J. (2005) *Language Wars: The Role of Media and Culture in Global Terror and Political Violence*, Pluto Books, London.

—— (2006) 'Paradise defiled: the Bali bombings and the terror of national identity', *European Journal of Cultural Studies*, 16.

—— (2008) *Cultural Studies*, 2nd Edition, Sage, London.

Lewis, J. and Lewis, B. (2004) 'The crisis of contiguity: communities and contention in the wake of the Bali bombings', Conference proceedings, *Sources of Insecurity*, Melbourne, November. Accessed September 2010. www.informit.com.au/library/defaultasp?t=coverpage&r=L_SIC

—— (2006a) 'At the edge of the big wave: community recovery in a tsunami-affected area of Sri Lanka' in K. Cook and K. Gilbert, eds, *Life on the Margins: Implications for Health Research*, Pearson Educational, Melbourne.

—— (2006b) 'Trial by ordeal: Abu Ghraib in the global mediasphere', *Topia: The Canadian Journal of Cultural Studies*, Fall, 9 (2).

—— (2007) 'Taming the *Bhuta Kala*: the Bali bombings and Indonesian civil society' in D. Staines, ed., *Interrogating the War on Terror*, Cambridge Scholars Press, Cambridge.

—— (2009) *Bali's Silent Crisis: Desire, Tragedy and Transition*, Rowman and Littlefield, Lanham, MD.

—— (2011) 'Transactions in desire: media imaginings of narcotics and terrorism in Indonesia', *Cultural Studies Review*, forthcoming.

Lewis, J., Lewis, B. and Putra, D. (forthcoming) *Asian Studies Review*, 'The Bali bombings memorial: ceremonial cosmopolis'.

Love, D. (2008) *Unfinished Business: Paul Keating's Interrupted Revolution*, Scribe Publications, Sydney.

Lovelock, J. (1965) 'A physical basis for life detection experiments', *Nature*, 207.

Lyotard, J-F. (1984) *The Postmodern Condition*, Manchester University Press, Manchester.

—— (1991) *The Inhuman: Reflections on Time*, trans. G Bennington and R. Bowlby, Polity, Cambridge.

Maddison, A. (2003) *The World Economy: Historical Statistics*, Vol. 673, OECD Development Centre, Paris.

Mahoney, P. (2009) 'Revisiting symbolic exchange: Baudrillard's aristocratic critique', *International Journal of Baudrillard Studies*, 6 (1).

Mailer, N. (2003) *Why Are We at War?* Random House, New York.

Malthus, T. (2008, orig. 1823) *An Essay on the Principle of Population*, Oxford University Press, New York.

Manes, C. (1990) *Green Rage: Radical Environmentalism and the Unmaking of Civilization*, Little, Brown and Co., Boston, MA.

Maynard, W. B. (2004) *Walden Pond: A History*, Oxford University Press, New York.

McCall-Theal, G. (orig. 1886) *Kaffir Folklore*, S. Sonnenschein, Le Bas & Lowrey, London.

McCalman, I. (1984) 'Unrespectable radicalism: infidels and pornography in early nineteenth century London', *Past and Present Society*, 104 (1).

―――― (2009) *Darwin's Armada: How Four Voyagers to Australasia Won the Battle*, Penguin, Hammondsworth.

McChesney, R. (2008) *Rich Media, Poor Democracy: Communication Politics in Dubious Times*, University of Illinois Press, Champaign, IL.

McGuire, F. (2004) *A Guide to the End of the World: Everything You Never Wanted to Know*, Oxford University Press, New York.

McKelvey, T. (ed.) (2006) *One of the Guys: Women as Aggressors and Torturers*, Seal Press, New York.

McNair, B. (2006) *Cultural Chaos: Journalism and Power in a Globalised World*, Routledge, London.

McNeil, J. R. (2000) *Something New Under the Sun: An Environmental History of the Twentieth-century World*, Allen Lane, New York.

Micklethwait, J. and Wooldridge, A. (2009) *God Is Back: How the Global Rise of Faith is Changing the World*, Allen Lane, London.

Miller, A. (1995) *Acknowledging Consumption: A Review of New Studies*, Routledge, London.

Mir, A. (2008) 'Pakistan tops Iraq, Afghanistan in suicide bombing deaths', *The International*, 15 September.

Moore, J. (2007) *Swinging: Shared Pleasures Between the Covers*, Infinity Publishing, New York.

Mosher, W. D, Chandra, A. and Jones J. (2005) 'Sexual behavior and selected health measures: men and women 15–44 years of age, United States, 2002', *Advance ata from Vital and Health Statistics; no. 362*, National Center for Health Statistics, Hyattsville, MD.

Moynihan, R. (2005) *The Rise of Viagra: How the Little Blue Pill Changed Sex in America*, BMJ Publishing Group, New York.

Mulhall, J., King, R., Glina, S. and Hvidsten, K. (2008) 'Importance of and satisfaction with sex among men and women worldwide: results of the Global Better Sex Survey', *Journal of Sexual Medicine*, 5 (4).

Nacos, B. (2002) *Mass Mediated Terrorism: The Central Role of the Media in Terrorism and Counter Terrorism*, Rowman and Littlefield, London.

Nairn, T. (2002) 'Globalization and the unchosen', *Arena Journal*, 19.

Nairn, T. and James, P. (2005) *Global Matrix: Nationalism, Globalism and State-terrorism*, Pluto Books, London.

NASA (2009) *Extreme Space Weather: Understanding Societal and Economic Impacts*, NASA, Washington, DC.

―――― (2010) 'Beginning of the end: why the world won't end?'. Accessed May 2010, http://www.nasa.gov/topics/earth/features/2012.html.

National Geographic (2010) 'Polygamy in America', *National Geographic*, Single Issue, February.

NATO (2008) *Proceedings of the NATO Advanced Workshop on Suicide Bombers: Psychological, Religious and Other Imperatives*, 105 Press, Amsterdam.

NCFMR (2010) 'Divorce rates in the U.S., 2008', National Center for Family and Marriage Research. Accessed May 2010, http://ncfmr.bgsu.edu/family_%20marriage_lit/Family%20Profiles/Divorce%20in%20US_2008.pdf.

Nelson-Gammon, J. (2007) *'An Inconvenient Truth*: the scientific argument', *GeoJournal*, 79.

New York Times (2009) 'In rescue of captain, Navy kills 3 pirates', *New York Times*, April 12.

Nisbet, M. and Myers, T. (2007) 'The polls-trend: twenty years of public opinion about global warming', *Public Opinion Quarterly*, 72 (1).

Nitzsche, J. (1990) 'The structural unity of Beowulf: the problem of Grendel's mother' in H. Damico and A. Hennessey Olsen, eds, *New Readings on Women in Old English Literature*, Indiana University Press, Bloomington, IN.

Nobel, W. and Davidson, I. (1996) *Human Evolution, Language and Mind: A Psychological and Archaeological Inquiry*, Cambridge University Press, Cambridge.

Norris, F. (2009) 'The end of capitalism?', *New York Times*, 29 January. Accessed May 2010, http://norris.blogs.nytimes.com/2009/01/29/the-end-of-capitalism/.

Nygaard, J. (2009) 'Pirates, profits and propaganda', *Counterpunch*. Accessed May 2010, http://www.counterpunch.org/nygaard04282009.html.

Obama, B. (2009) 'Address to the Joint Sitting of Congress', US Government Press Office, 24 February. Accessed May 2010, http.www.whitehouse.gov/the_press_office/remarks-of-president-barack-obama.

OECD (2007) *The Social Expenditure Database: and Interpretative Guide*. Accessed May 2010, http://www.esds.ac.uk/international/support/user_guides/oecd/sed.asp#SED_Documentation).

———— (2008) 'OECD family database', OECD Social Policy Division. Accessed May 2010, http://www.oecd,org/els/social/family/database/.

———— (2009) *OECD Economic Survey and Surveillance*. Accessed May 2010, http://www.oecd.org/department/0,3355,en_2649_34111_1_1_1_1_1,00.html.

O'Grada, C. (2009) *Famine: A Short History*, Princeton University Press, Princeton, NJ.

Olfson, M. (2009) 'National patterns in antidepressant medication treatment,' *Archives of General Psychiatry*, 66 (8).

Ong, W. (2002) *Orality and Literacy: The Technologizing of the Word*, Routledge, London.

Osborne, D. (2005) *Suicide Tuesday: Gay Men and the Crystal Meth Scare*, Da Capo Press, New York.

Ostrom, E. (1990) *Governing the Commons: The Evolution of Institutions for Collective Action (Political Economy of Institutions and Decisions)*, Cambridge University Press, Cambridge.

———— (2006) *Understanding Knowledge as a Commons: From Theory to Practice*, MIT Press, Cambridge, MA.

Owusu, F. (2007) 'Post 9/11 U.S. foreign aid, the Millennium Challenge Account, and Africa: how many birds can one stone kill?', *Africa Today*, 54 (1).

Pallotta-Chiarolli, M. (2010) *Border Sexualities: Border Families*, Rowman and Littlefield, Lanham, MD.

Panter-Brick, C., Layton, R. and Rowley-Conwy, P. (eds) (2001) *Hunter-gatherers: An Interdisciplinary Perspective*, Cambridge University Press, Cambridge.

Pape, R. (2005) *Dying to Win: The Strategic Logic of Suicide Terrorism*, Random House, New York.

Parkin, K. (2007) *Food is Love: Advertising and Gender Roles in Modern America*, University of Pennsylvania Press, Philadelphia, PA.

Patomäki, H. (2008) *The Political Economy of Global Security: War, Future Crises and Changes in Global Governance*, Routledge, London.

Patton, C. and Sanchez-Eppler, B. (eds) (2000) *Queer Diaspora*, Duke University Press, Durham, NC.

Paul, J., Catania, J., Pollack, L. et al. (2002) 'Suicide attempts among gay and bisexual men: lifetime prevalence and antecedents', *American Journal of Public Health*, 92 (8).

Pawa, M. and Krass, B. (2006) 'Behind the curve: the national media's reporting on global warming', *Boston College Environmental Affairs Law Review*, 33 (3).

Perel, E. (2006) *Mating in Captivity: Reconciling the Erotic and the Domestic*, Harper Collins, New York.

Peters, G. (2009) *Seeds of Terror: How Heroin is Bankrolling the Taliban and al Qaeda*, Macmillan, New York.

Plato (1955, orig. 383 BC) *The Republic*, Penguin, Hammondsworth.

Plimer, I. (2009) *Heaven and Earth: Global Warming—The Missing Science*, Connor Court, Ballan, Australia.

Power, C. (2008) 'A one-woman war on injustice', *Glamour Magazine*, 1 July. Accessed May 2010, http://www.glamour.com/magazine/2006/10/mukhtar-mai-update.

Praver, F. (2006) *Daring Wives*, Greenwood Publishing, New York.

Ragland, E. (1995) *Essays on the Pleasures of Death: From Freud to Lacan*, Routledge, London.

Rao, P. (2007) 'Foreign aid, agricultural development and economic growth: an international perspective', PhD thesis, University of Queensland. Accessed May 2010, http://espace.library.uq.edu.au/view/UQ:131179.

Reed, C. (2009) 'Climate change and agriculture: agriculture's role in cap-and-trade', Conference paper delivered at the Feeding a Hot and Hungry World Conference, Princeton University, 1 May.

Reuters (2008) 'Somali pirates seize two more ships', *Reuters*, 14 April.

Ridley, N. (2008) 'Organized crime, money laundering, and terrorism', *Policing: A Journal of Policy and Practice*, 2 (1).

Ritzer, G. (2003) *The Globalization of Nothing*, Pine Forge Press, Los Angeles, CA.

Robertson, R. (1995) 'Glocalization: time-space and homogeneity-heterogeneity' in M. Featherstone, ed., *Global Modernities*, Sage, London.

—— (1997) 'Comments on the "global triad" and "glocalization"' in N. Inoue, ed., *Globalization and Indigenous Culture*, Institute for Japanese Culture and Classics, Kokugakuin University.

Rodrik, D. and Subramanian, A. (2006) 'Why India can grow at 7 percent a year or more: projections and reflections', IMF Working Paper, Updated version, February. Accessed May 2010, http://papers.ssrn.com/sol3/papers.cfm?abstract_id=878942 15.

Rojek, C. (2004) *Celebrity*, Reaktion, London.

—— (2009) *The Labour of Leisure: The Culture of Free Time*, Sage, London.

Rolins, J., Wyler, L. and Rosen, S. (2010) 'International terrorism and transnational crime: security threats, U.S. policy and considerations for Congress', Congressional Research Services. Accessed May 2010, http://www.scribd.com/doc/25018334/CRS-Report-International-Terrorism-and-Transnational-Crime-2010.

Roseman, J. (2003) *Distant Proximities: Dynamics Beyond Globalization*, Princeton University Press, Princeton, NJ.

Rosen, D. (2008) 'Viagra at 10: 1 billion pills later', *Counterpunch*, September. Accessed May 2010, http://www.counterpunch.org/rosen09202008.html.

Rossing, B. (2004) *The Rapture Exposed: The Message of Hope in the Book of Revelation*, Westview Press, Boulder, CO.

Rudd, K. (2009) *ABC News Online*, 24 October. Accessed May 2010, http://www.abc.net.au/news/stories/2009/10/16/2715667.htm.

Runsiman, W. G. (2010) *Great Books, Bad Arguments*, Princeton University Press, Princeton, NJ.

Said, E. W. (1993) *Culture and Imperialism*, Vintage Books, London.

Sameem, I. (2008) 'Suicide bomber kills 79 in Afghanistan', *GuardianOnline*, 18 February. Accessed May 2010, http://www.guardian.co.uk/world/2008/feb/18/afghanistan.

Sassatelli, R. (2007) *Consumer Culture: History, Theory and Politics*, Sage, London.

Scherrer, Christian P. (2002) *Genocide and Crisis in Central Africa: Conflict Roots, Mass Violence, and Regional War*, Preger, Westport, CT.

Schmid, A. P. (1983) *Political Terrorism: A Research Guide to Concepts, Theories, Data Bases and Literature*, Transaction Press, New Brunswick, NJ.

Sendel, M. (1998) *Liberalism and the Limits of Justice*, The Press Syndicate of the University of Cambridge, Cambridge.

―――― (2009a) *Justice: What's the Right Thing to Do?* Farrar, Allen Lane, New York.

―――― (2009b) 'A new citizenship', *The Reith Lecture Series*, BBC, Re-broadcast ABC Radio National, December.

Shaeffer, N. (2009) 'Deterring piracy at sea', *All Hands*, February.

Shaul, S. (2008) *Somalia: Between Jihad and Restoration*, Transaction Books, Edison, NJ.

Shipman, A. (2002) *The Globalization Myth*, Iron books, London.

Singer, P. (2010) *The Life You Can Save: Acting Now to End World Poverty*, Random House, New York.

Skaine, R. (2006) *Female Suicide Bombers*, McFarland, Jefferson, NC.

Smil, V. (1994) *Energy in World History*, Westview Press, Boulder, CO.

Smitha, F., Jankovićb, I. and Karavanićc, I. (2005) 'The assimilation model, modern human origins in Europe, and the extinction of Neandertals', *Quaternary International*, 137 (1).

Sontag, S. (2001) 'Letter' in the *New Yorker*, 24 September.

―――― (2004) *Regarding the Pain of Others*, Picador, New York.

Staun, J. (2009) 'A linguistic turn of terrorism studies', DIIS Working Papers, Issue 2, Danish Institute for International Studies (DIIS), Copenhagen.

Steger, M. (2005) *Globalism: Market Ideology meets Terrorism*, Rowman and Littlefield, Lanham, MD.

Steinem, G. (2006) 'Mukhtaran Bibi', *Time On*, 30 April. Accessed May 2010, http://www.time.com/time/magazine/article/0,9171,1187392,00.html, 30 April 2006.

Stern, J. (2003) *Terror in the Name of God: Why Religious Militants Kill*, Ecco, New York.

Taleb, Nassim Nicholas (2007). *The Black Swan: The Impact of the Highly Improbable*. Random House, New York.

Taylor, C. (2007) *A Secular Age*, Harvard University Press, Boston, MA.

Treas, J. and Giesen, D. (2000) 'Sexual infidelity among married and cohabitating Americans', *Journal of Marriage and Family*, 62, February.

Trosper, R. (2009) *Resilience, Reciprocity and Ecological Economics: Northwest Coast Sustainability*, T & F Books, London.

Turner, G. (2004) *Understanding Celebrity*, Sage, London.

UNAIDS (2009) *2009 Report: The Joint United Nations Programme on HIV/AIDS*. Accessed May 2010, http://www.unaids.org/en/default.asp.

UNIFEM (2009) *UNIFEM Annual Report 2009*, United Nations Development Fund for Women, New York.

United Nations Food and Agriculture Organization (2006) *Global Forests Assessment*, Forestry Paper, 47.

United Nations Population Fund (2000) *Honour Killings: A Human Rights and Human Health Priority*. Accessed Sepotember2010, http://www.unfpa.org/swp/2000/english/ch03.html.

United Nations Population Division (2010) 'Population facts No. 2010/5'. Accessed September 2010. http://www.un.org/esa/population/

UNTAD (2005) 'Economic development in Africa debt sustainability, oasis or mirage?' United Nations Trade and Development Conference Paper. Accessed September 2010. http://www.unctad.org/Templates/Webflyer.asp?intItemID=3246&lang=1

Updike, J. (2001) Untitled contribution to the *New Yorker*, 24 September, p. 28.

US Bureau of Economic Analysis (2010) *US Economic Accounts*. Accessed September 2010. http://www.bea.gov/

USC, 22-2656 [d]). US Code 22, Section d. Accessed May 2010, http://vlex.com/source/us-code-foreign-relations-intercous-1021.

Usdansky, M. (2009) 'Americans ambivalent about single parent families', *Journal of Marriage and the Family*, 71.

Vanderheiden, S. (2005) 'Eco-terrorism or justified resistance? Radical Environmentalism and the "war on terror" ', *Politics and Society*, 33 (3).

Wager, J. (2005) *Dames in the Driver's Seat: Rereading Film Noir*, University of Texas Press, Austin, TX.

Wall, D. (1999) *Earth First! and the Anti-Roads Movement: Radical Environmentalism*, Routledge, New York.

Ward, J. and March, M. (2006) 'Sexual violence and women and girls in war and its aftermath: realities, responses and required resources', *Symposium of Sexual Violence in conflict and Beyond*, Brussels, June.

Warraich, S. (2005) 'Honour killings and the law in Pakistan' in L. Welchman and S. Hossain, eds, *Honour: Crimes, Paradigms and Violence Against Women*, Zed Books, London.

Warriq, I. (2007) *Defending the West: A Critique of Edward Said's 'Orientalism'*, Prometheus Books, Amherst, NY.

Weber, M. (2002) *The Protestant Ethic and 'The Spirit of Capitalism'*, trans. G. Wells, Penguin, Hammondsworth.

Weeks, J. (1981) *Sex, Politics and Society: The Regulation of Sexuality Since 1800*, Longman, London.

White, G. (2006) *Jane Austen in the Context of Abolition*, Palgrave Macmillan, New York.

Whitehead, B. (2003) *Why There Are No Good Men Left: The Romantic Plight of the New Single Woman*, Broadway Books, New York.

Whitehead, B. and Popenoe, D. (2006) 'The state of our unions: marriage and family—what does the Scandanavian experience tell us?', National Marriage Project, Rutgers University, New Jersey, NJ.

——— (2009) 'The state of our unions, marriage in America: money and marriage', National Marriage Project, Rutgers University, New Jersey, NJ.

Wikan, U. (2008) *In Honor of Fadime: Murder and Shame*, University of Chicago Press, Chicago, IL.

Williams, E. (2009) 'Music teacher jailed for student sex', *Sydney Morning Herald*, 20 November.

Williams, J. (2008) 'The history of energy', The Franklin Institute. Accessed May 2010, http://www.fi.edu/learn/case-files/energy.html.

Willame, J-C. (1995) *Aux sources de l'hécatombe rwandaise* (Genesis of the Rwandan massacre), L'Harmattan, Brussels and Paris.

Williams, M. (2003) *Deforesting the Earth: From Prehistory to Global Crisis*, University of Chicago Press, Chicago, IL.

Williamson, J. (2000) 'What should the World Bank think about the Washington Consensus?', *World Bank Research Observer*, The International Bank for Reconstruction and Development, Washington, DC, 15 (2).

Williamson, J. (2002) 'Did the Washington Consensus fail?', *Outline of Remarks at CSIS*, Institute for International Economics, Washington, DC, 6 November.

Wilson, A. (1991) *The Culture of Nature: North American Landscape from Disney to Exon Valdiz*, Between the Lines Books, New York.

Wolf, N. (1991) *The Beauty Myth: How Images of Beauty are Used Against Women*, Vintage, London.

World Bank (2010) *World Development Report 2010: Development and Climate Change*, World Bank, Washington.

Wright, C. (2009) 'Resurrection and reaction in Alain Badiou: towards an evental historiography', *Culture, Theory and Critique*, 49 (1).

Wright, R. (2004). *A Short History of Progress*. Anansi, Toronto.

Žižek, S. (2006) *Interrogating the Real*, Continuum International Publishing, London.

Zolo, D. (1997) *Cosmopolis: Prospects for World Government*, Polity, Cambridge.

Zolo, C. (2010) 'What is globalization: some radical questions', Interview with Ulrich Beck. Accessed May 2010, http://www.cc.nctu.edu.tw/~cpsun/zolobeck.htm.

Index